CARS

OF THE SENSATIONAL

'70s

A DECADE OF CHANGING TASTES AND NEW DIRECTIONS

BY JAMES M. FLAMMANG
AND THE AUTO EDITORS OF CONSUMER GUIDE™

PUBLICATIONS INTERNATIONAL, LTD.

Louis Weber, CEO
Publications International, Ltd.
7373 North Cicero Avenue
Lincolnwood, Illinois 60712

Permission is never granted for commercial purposes.

Manufactured in China.

8 7 6 5 4 3 2 1

ISBN: 0-7853-2980-3

Acknowledgements

Chapter-Introduction Illustrations: Jairus Watson

PHOTOGRAPHY
The editors gratefully acknowledge the cooperation of the following people who supplied photography to help make this book possible.

Vince Manocchi; **American Motors Corporation Public Relations**; Nicky Wright; **Photofest**; Chan Bush; **Dodge Public Relations**; David Temple; **Chrysler-Plymouth Public Relations**; Doug Mitchel; Bob Bohovic; Bud Juneau; **Chicago Auto Trade Association; Ford Photographic**; Sam Griffith; Phil Toy; **Ford Parts and Service Division Public Relations; UPI/Corbis-Bettman; Lincoln-Mercury Public Relations; Buick Public Relations; GM Photographic; GM Media Archives**; Mike Mueller; W. C. Waymack; **Oldsmobile Public Relations, General Motors Corporation; Pontiac Public Relations**; Dan Lyons; **Porsche-Audi Public Relations; BMW of North America, Inc., Public Relations; Joseph H. Wherry Collection**; Milton Kieft; **Library of Congress; Mercedes-Benz of North America Public Relations; Opel Public Relations; Volkswagen of America**; Jeff Johnson; **Chrysler Photographic; R.C. Ellingsen Photography**; Joe Bohovic; **Petty Enterprises**; Steve Statham; Scott Baxter; **Ford Division Public Relations; Full Spectrum Photo**; William J. Schintz; Thomas Glatch; Terry Boyce; **Village Pontiac, Inc.**; Roger Imes; **Daytona International Speedway; Daimler-Chrysler Historical Collection; Chicago Historical Society;** *The Times,* Munster, Indiana; Nina Padgett; Robert H. Brown; **Toyota Motor Sales, U.S.A., Inc., Public Relations**; Jim Frenak; David Newhardt; John A. Conde; **Renault News Bureau; National Hot Rod Association Photographic Service; U.S. Automotive Sales & Service Public Relations;** *The Times* **Collection, The Calumet Room, Hammond Public Library,** Hammond, Indiana; Bob Garris; **Shooting Star; FPG International, Chevrolet Public Relations; Neville Public Museum of Brown County,** Green Bay, Wisconsin; *Press-Gazette* **Collection, Neville Public Museum of Brown County**; Jerry Heasley; Jim Thompson; Gregory Thomas; **Subaru of America, Inc.**; Debbie Anders-Bond; **Jimmy Carter Library;** *Azalea City News* **Collection, University of South Alabama Archives; William R. Eastabrook/Photography; American Automobile Manufacturers Association; Mazda Information Bureau; Stutz Motor Car of America, Inc.; Clenet Coachworks; San Remo Convertibles; American Honda Motor Company, Inc.; Chrysler Corporation, Fleet Public Relations**; Bob Tenney; Gary Smith; Helen Earley, **Oldsmobile History Center**; Rob Van Schaick; Richard Spiegelmen; **Nissan Motor Corporation in U.S.A. Public Relations.**

OWNERS
Special thanks to the owners of the cars featured in this book for their enthusiastic cooperation.

1970: Darryl A. Salisbury; Frank Kleptz; Larry Bell; Pete Haldiman; Stephen M. Witmer; Greg and Cecilia Carter; Tim Dusek; Wayne Hartye; Glen Stidger; Ronda Cunningham; David R. Mullett; Rick Cain; Kenneth Freeman; Leroy Lasiter; Dixen Polderman; Robert and Connie Barrett; Steve Potsek; Bill Draper; Jim Reilly; Brian Kwiatkoski; Jack Karleskind; Rick Shick; Richard P. Lambert; Barry Waddell; Charles A. Vance; Jim and Chris Ross; Dan Parrilli; Ben Barlage; Francis Dobson; Dave Cobble II; Marvin O. Smith; Bob Weggenmann; Patrick and Barbara Dugan; Show Cars of Fort Myers; Davin Stevens; Bill and Jan Everitt; Harvey L. North; Roger Vizard; Don and Rita Maxwell.

1971: Michael S. Gray; Milt Jenks; John Wells; Dave Lingle; David Arent; Yoshio and Eric Nakayama; Odus West; Stan Fritzinger; Dennis A. Barnes; Jay Dykes; Southwest Gallery of Cars; Charles and Mark Vandervelde; Thomas E. and Carol A. Podemski; Frank Frandsen; William Jenn; Dennis D. Rosenberry; Ron Walker; Ed Milas; Donald W. Glaeser; Ben Barlage; Neil Ehresman; Steven Jenear; Merle Preinflak; Tom Jervis; John Bentz; Ed McCoughlin; Joseph A. Fitzpatrick.

1972: John Gricki, Jr.; Clarence E. Ferguson; Frank Trummer; Ed Oberhaus; Ron Walker; Gordon Fenner; Rick Cybul; Kirk Alexander; Edward Baker; Gary Grillo; Donald P. Vrabec; Pauly Honda, Libertyville, Illinois.

1973: Gregg Gyurina; Brian Altizer; Sigfried Grunze; Gary M. Gumushian; Jim Hardy; Fernando F. Alvare; Carol Spangenberg; Leroy and Judy Williams; Dennis W. Riley; Fran Muckle; Larry Zidek; Charles M. Kerr; Virginia P. Burns; George Jarmusz; Joe Heine; Roger and Carol Erickson; David C. Newkirk.

1974: Sherman Lovegren; Bob Masi; Milt Jenks; Ernest R. Sutton, Jr.; Jeanine and Don Brink; Mark Alter; Brian Minton; James H. Carson; Richard Fluck; Don Cloarke; Norm Canfield; Duane Hedke; Jim Miller; Rebecca Munk.

1975: Milt Jenks; Berry Motor Cars; John Detente; Rob Bilott; Patricia A. Schelli; Larry Koetting; Keith W. Meiswinkel; Tony and Betty Fabiano; Ida Hammer.

1976: Bret M. Traywick; Joseph E. Pero; Ed Oberhaus; Rosanne Winny; James A. Ruby; Brad Young; Marty Young; David L. Hardgrove; Steve Rhodes; David L. Hucke; J. R. Betson, Jr.; Rob Bilott.

1977: Charles D. Barnette; Vince Manocchi; Harold S. Boershcinger; J. Glenn Dowd; Bob Reed; Stuart Popp; Richard Matzer; Dr. Milt McMillen; James A. Ruby; Dr. David D. Semrau; Ben Barlage; Brad Bishop.

1978: William Korbel; Phil Lagerquist; D. L. Bohart; Ed Oberhaus; Gordon and Dorothy Clemmer; Laura Martin; Harry Cornelius; Hilary Raab; Bob Briggs.

1979: Ron Kroell; Barton Butz; Harry Demenge; Berry Motor Cars, LLC; Michael Rooney; Jerry and Robin Driemeier; Jerry Capizzi; Cappy Collection; Larry Webb; Bob Lorenz, R+R Restoration.

Table of Contents

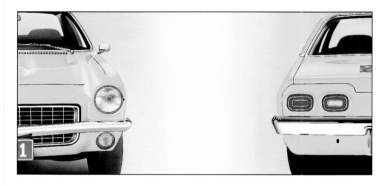

1975

The new reality sets in: Big-car loyalist Chrysler introduces the mid-sized personal-luxury Cordoba, Cadillac launches the trim Seville, and Toyota out-imports VW.

1976

A warmed-up national economy spurs a strong rebound in car sales. Large cars regain some of their lost popularity, but new smaller lines keep being added.

1977

General Motors rides the wave of the future when it introduces "downsized" versions of its full-size family cars. Noticeably smaller and lighter, they sell well.

1978

Management shakeups at Chrysler and Ford involve the same man—Lee Iacocca. Plymouth and Dodge trot out front-drive small cars; VW builds Rabbits in the U.S.

1979

A second oil crisis helps imports claim a record share of the American car market. Meanwhile, Chrysler tallies big losses and limping AMC leans on Renault of France.

Okay, so we're celebrating the Seventies here, man. It was bound to happen sooner or later. There's just one question, though: Which Seventies did you have in mind?

If your remember them as frivolous, fun years when couples thump, bump, thumped the night away under a mirrored ball to a disco dance beat, then you may have forgotten how deadly serious the decade was when it started. While U.S. troops were fighting in Vietnam, Americans back home were embroiled in their own divisive struggles over the war and other social issues. In May 1970, four college students were shot to death while protesting the war at Kent State University in Ohio. Two more were killed by police at Jackson State in Mississippi. Meanwhile, in New York, construction workers supportive of U.S. military policy marched on city hall and roughed up students. In 1971, a bomb went off in the U.S. Capitol building. Call it the ironic bomb; it was planted as an anti-war protest. Vietnam policy dominated the 1972 presidential campaign. In 1973, American Indians angered over the treatment of their people occupied buildings at a South Dakota reservation and traded shots with federal agents.

Should you be focused on the cynicism that sprang up in the wake of the Watergate political scandal that toppled a president, then you may be hazy on the details of a July day in 1976 when Americans caught their breath, puffed out their chests, and saluted 200 years of nationhood. Teenyboppers of 1971 who tolerated the cotton-candy pop of The Osmonds and the Jackson 5 were slam dancing to sneering punk-band rage by 1978. The tele-

vision network that dished out *The Brady Bunch*, *Three's Company*, and *Charlie's Angels* also saw fit to air the ambitious *Roots* miniseries.

And then there were the cars. Automotively, the Seventies picked up where the Sixties left off. The decade may have opened with the rise of a whole new class of American car—the subcompact—but for the most part, the names and fascias in the showrooms were familiar ones. For many youthful drivers, might still made right. Few may have realized it at the time, but 1970 would be the peak of the muscle-car era.

Then the tide shifted. Rising insurance rates were making it harder to afford a hot car, but Detroit was turning down the flame, anyway. That same federal government that was duking it out with its citizens in the street and on the reservation was also taking on the auto industry over emissions and vehicle safety. It was obvious new kinds of cars would have to be built. A few had air bags and anti-lock brakes. Many pretended to be luxurious. Landau roofs and opera windows replaced horsepower, and it seemed like everybody was making something called a "Brougham." Is it any wonder customized vans became the decade's biggest enthusiast trend?

Lest Washington get all the blame for breaking up the party, there was the Organization of Petroleum Exporting Countries to consider. Its two oil supply boycotts in response to unrest in the Middle East added fuel mileage to U.S. automakers' list of woes. Imported cars were best-suited to take quick advantage of the situation, and many Americans dumped their big domestic models in favor of foreign jobs. Volkswagen even began building cars in the U.S. But by decade's end, Detroit was staggering toward the future with downsized traditional cars and its first truly modern subcompacts.

It was the Seventies, man. Right on. Just one more question: How many times did you stand in line to see *Star Wars*?

U.S. car output for model-year 1970, at 6,550,077, was the lowest since 1961, and down sharply from the 9.4 million of 1969. Indeed, *Automotive News* dubbed 1970 a "miserable" year for the U.S. industry—and not simply because of droopy sales.

A UAW strike against General Motors shuttered the auto giant's operations in the United States for 67 days; in Canada for 95. The consequences were devastating: more than 1.5 million cars and trucks unbuilt, and better than $4.5 billion in lost sales.

Washington was giving Detroit a hard time too. Automakers, slow to come up with safety and emissions initiatives, had to be prodded by federal mandate. The considerable costs of these developments were borne by consumers in the form of increased sticker prices.

Well-made, affordable imports from Toyota, Datsun, and other Japanese firms widened their inroads into the U.S. market. Although Ford had a sales winner with the Maverick, and AMC (which bought Kaiser-Jeep Corp. this year) met success with the Hornet and Gremlin, demand for Japanese imports did not diminish, suggesting that the small-car market was no aberration.

An Oldsmobile 4-4-2 paced the Indianapolis 500; Al Unser won the race. In NASCAR, Bobby Isaac was the champion of the Grand National series (not yet known as Winston Cup racing).

1970

And in a fitting nod to carmaking's past, Fred Duesenberg was inducted into the Automotive Hall of Fame.

For seven days in April, the world was electrified by the plight of Apollo 13 astronauts Jim Lovell, Fred Haise, Jr., and John Swigert, Jr. Their moon mission had to be aborted following a fuel-cell failure and liquid-oxygen pressure loss. They splashed down safely on April 17.

President Richard Nixon ordered summertime bombing of Cambodia and a ground invasion as well. These initiatives signaled the beginning of the end of American ground action in the Vietnam War. Still, antiwar unrest swept American college campuses. On May 4, four students at Ohio's Kent State were shot to death by National Guardsmen.

Patton, Airport, Little Big Man, Myra Breckinridge, Five Easy Pieces, and *Joe* were among the top movies. The dominant television network was CBS with six shows in the top 10, but it was ABC that made a lasting impact on Americans' viewing habits when it brought professional football to Monday nights. On radio, we were listening to Stevie Wonder's "Signed, Sealed, Delivered I'm Yours," the Bee Gees's "Lonely Days," and Chicago's "Make Me Smile." In the World Series, the Baltimore Orioles defeated the Cincinnati Reds, four games to one, and in Super Bowl IV the Kansas City Chiefs defeated the Minnesota Vikings, 23-7.

AMC

American Motors buys Jeep from Kaiser Industries, a move that will prove crucial to AMC's ultimate future

Meanwhile, AMC gushes more red ink, losing $58.2 million on calendar-year sales of more than $1 billion and 276,000 passenger cars

A relic of the pre-AMC Nash era, the venerable Rambler name, is retired at last as the clean new Hornet, reviving a name from Hudson days, replaces the American as AMC's compact

Racing ace Mark Donohue pilots his AMC Javelin to the 1970 Sports Car Club of America's Trans-American championship in the most competitive season yet for the five-year-old "ponycar" series

The AMX follows its Javelin parent with a heavy restyle of its basic 1968 design; Sales of just 4116 make this the last year for AMC's performance two-seater

AMC offers a wild new red-white-and-blue muscle car to replace the '69 SC/Rambler; called "The Machine" and based on the mid-sized Rebel hardtop, it sees just 2326 copies

In April, AMC beats its Big Three rivals to the punch in getting on the burgeoning small-car bandwagon when it introduces the Gremlin, a truncated two-door Hornet that looks like nothing else

Rooflines are redesigned on Rebel and full-sized Ambassador two-door hardtops, which adopt thicker, slash-back sail panels

1

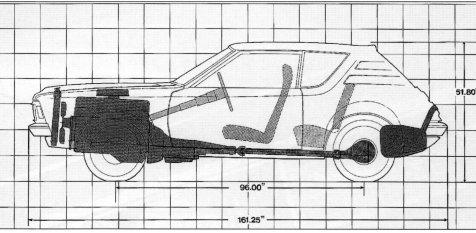

2

3

1. While Ford and Chevrolet were preparing to introduce totally new subcompacts as 1971 models, American Motors stole a march on the competition when it introduced the distinctively shaped Gremlin in April 1970. Based on the larger Hornet compact, another new AMC product, the Gremlin's wheelbase was shortened to 96 inches. Prices began at $1879 for a two-seat "commuter" version with a fixed backlight, and $1959 for a four-seat model with flip-up hatch glass in the rear. **2.** A superimposed outline drawing of the Gremlin shows that its overall dimensions compared favorably to those of the Volkswagen Beetle, then the standard by which small economy cars were measured. **3.** Despite its "out there" looks, the Gremlin's front-engine/rear-drive layout was quite conventional.

1

2

3

4

1. Though designed to provide basic, economical transportation, the Gremlin could be outfitted a bit more luxuriously with extras like full wheel covers, bumper guards, a roof rack, and broad bodyside stripes. There was a choice of two six-cylinder engines, as well. 2. The Gremlin's grille surround and domed hood helped mask the fact that it was essentially a Hornet from the doors forward. 3. Speaking of the Hornet, it was AMC's new compact entry and replacement for the venerable Rambler. The 108-inch-wheelbase car appeared in two- and four-door sedan styles in standard and glitzier SST trim levels. The price for the SST four-door sedan began at $2221. 4. Six-cylinder engines came standard in all Hornets, but the badge on the rear quarter panel of this SST two-door sedan indicates the presence of the optional 304-cid V-8. A vinyl top added $84 to the tab.

1

2

3

1. AMC still offered a full-sized car—the Ambassador—on a 122-inch wheelbase. This is the top-line SST four-door sedan. 2. Ambassador hardtops like this SST adopted a new roofline. 3. The intermediate Rebel line shared bodies with the Ambassador, but had a shorter chassis and different frontal styling. The SST two-door hardtop started at $2718. 4. The Rebel Machine carried the American Motors banner in the muscle-car market. It came with a 340-bhp 390-cube V-8 and drew 2326 orders. 5. The Rebel SST sedan had a six and manual transmission standard.

4

5

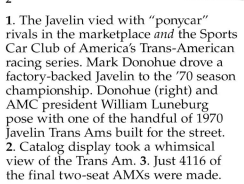

1. The Javelin vied with "ponycar" rivals in the marketplace *and* the Sports Car Club of America's Trans-American racing series. Mark Donohue drove a factory-backed Javelin to the '70 season championship. Donohue (right) and AMC president William Luneburg pose with one of the handful of 1970 Javelin Trans Ams built for the street. 2. Catalog display took a whimsical view of the Trans Am. 3. Just 4116 of the final two-seat AMXs were made.

CHRYSLER
CORPORATION

A national recession curtails new-car sales

Chrysler releases its last full-size convertibles

A Hurst-modified Chrysler 300-H reminds fans of the old "Letter-Series" models

Dodge responds to Ford and General Motors "ponycars" with the Challenger; the redesigned Barracuda is similar

This is the final year for high-performance Dodge Coronets

The last Imperial Crown models go on sale; the LeBaron series continues

Plymouth adds a Duster coupe and Superbird "Winged Warrior"

Chrysler vehicles take 38 NASCAR Grand National stock-car race wins

A headlight-delay system is optional on Chryslers

Chrysler begins to import the British-made Plymouth Cricket late in the year as a 1971 model

Dodge's Super-Lite road light option is dropped after only two years

New show cars include the Concept 70-X and Cordoba d'Oro

Chrysler fields two teams in Trans-American Challenge racing in which Barracudas and Challengers compete

Engineers continue work on the sixth-generation turbine engine

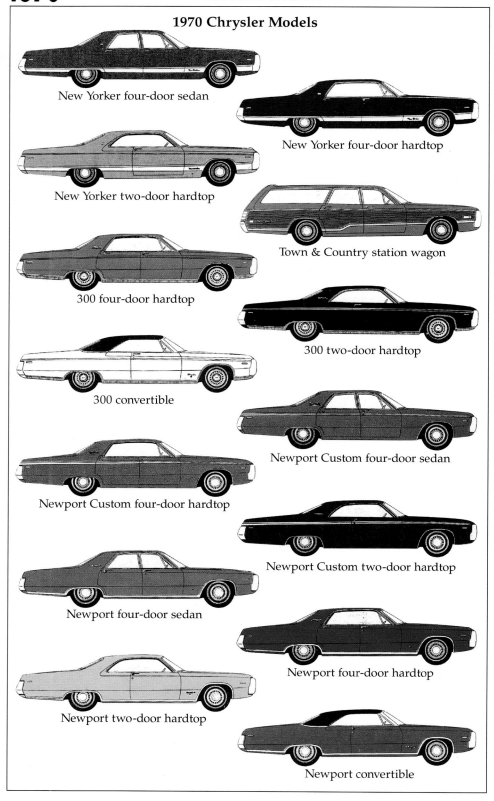

1970 Chrysler Models

New Yorker four-door sedan

New Yorker four-door hardtop

New Yorker two-door hardtop

Town & Country station wagon

300 four-door hardtop

300 two-door hardtop

300 convertible

Newport Custom four-door sedan

Newport Custom four-door hardtop

Newport Custom two-door hardtop

Newport four-door sedan

Newport four-door hardtop

Newport two-door hardtop

Newport convertible

In the early Sixties, when its competitors in the medium-price field were beginning to diversify their product lines with compact models, Chrysler defiantly advertised "Positively No Jr. Editions." That decision was still in force in 1970, when Chrysler issued nothing but full-sized cars in four trim levels on a 124-inch-wheelbase chassis, and Town & Country station wagons on a 122-inch stretch. Base prices ranged from $3514 for the Newport four-door sedan to $4824 for the nine-passenger version of the Town & Country. Newports and Customs shared grille and wheel cover designs, T & Cs and New Yorkers displayed another combination, and 300s wore a third. Standard power for the Newport/Custom and wagons came from a 290-bhp 383-cid V-8. New Yorkers and 300s were granted a 350-horse version of the corporate 440-cid engine, with 375 ponies available.

1

1. The 300 convertible was the rarest 1970 Chrysler with just 1077 assemblies. Bucket seats were standard, but a cloth-and-vinyl bench seat was available. Notable options included a floor console for the TorqeFlite automatic transmission shifter, power front disc brakes, and a heavy-duty suspension.
2. Hurst Performance Products teamed up with Chrysler for the 300-H, recalling the "letter series" 300s of yore. Chrysler threw in all the best performance parts available for the 300 (including the 375-bhp engine), while Hurst provided a modified hood and decklid made of fiberglass, as well as its famed shifter. The upholstery was in brown leather. Production came to 501 two-door hardtops, one sunroof hardtop, and two or three convertibles.

2

1970 CHRYSLER CORP.　　　　　*DODGE*

1

2

Full-size Dodges shared the corporate "fuselage styling," but adopted a new loop-type front bumper. The optional Super-Lite in the grille was dropped at the end of the year. 1. The most popular top-line Monaco was the four-door hardtop. 2. Polara two-door hardtop prices started at $3224.

Dodge entered the "ponycar" field in 1970 with the Challenger. **1**. The T/A was a street version of Trans-Am racing Challengers. **2-3**. R/Ts had big-block engines. Special Edition trim added a vinyl roof and small window. **4**. World Series MVP Donn Clendenon won a Challenger from *Sport* magazine. **5**. A Challenger had a central role in the film *Vanishing Point*. **6**. Sam Posey raced a Dodge in Trans-Am competition.

1

2

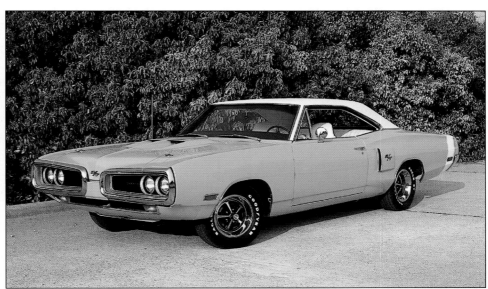

3

1. The brawny Charger hardtop took on a new full-circle front bumper for 1970, but otherwise was little changed visually from the 1969 model. The R/T was the top performer and could be outfitted wth a 425-bhp Hemi V-8 and SE decor, as seen on this example. 2. Joan Parker's face was familiar to car buffs who took note of Dodge advertising. 3. A twin-venturi frontal design distinguished the 1970 Coronet intermediates, headed by the R/T series. 4. This catalog touted the suitability of Dodges as police vehicles. 5. Hardtop fanciers on a budget could select a Coronet 440.

1970 **Dodge** POLICE FLEET

4

5

17

1

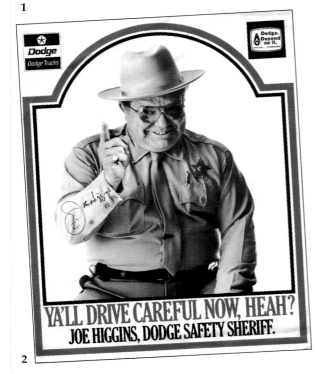

2

3

1. The Dart Swinger 340 took over from the discontinued GTS as the top-performing Dodge compact. Equipped with a 340-cid V-8 that developed 275 bhp, it drew 13,785 orders. 2. A humorous presence from Dodge ads in the Sixties, "Southern Sheriff" Joe Higgins was still a part of the division's promotional efforts as the Seventies began. 3. The more enthusiastic patrons of "Mr. Norm's" Grand-Spaulding Dodge in Chicago would have done well to heed Higgins. Some of the fastest Dodges in the country came from the dealership.

Imperial, Chrysler Corporation's luxury marque, had rarely been a sales threat to its rivals from Ford and General Motors, but it still had a place in the corporate marketing plan in 1970. Wheelbase of its unit-body platform stayed 127 inches, and a 350-bhp 440-cid V-8 returned under the hood. Compared to the previous year's car, the '70 had revisions to the grille, side-marker lights, and wheel covers. For a final time, buyers could choose from two trim levels: Crown and costlier LeBaron. The fading Crown series included this two-door hardtop, which, at $5779 and 254 made, was the year's cheapest and rarest Imperial.

1. One of the more curious hybrids ever offered by Plymouth in its full-size line was the '70 Fury Gran Coupe. Based on the Fury II pillared coupe, it featured a paisley pattern on its vinyl roof and cloth-and-vinyl upholstery. A host of comfort and convenience goodies came standard, as did deluxe wheel covers and hidden headlamps. 2. More in the mainstream was the Fury III four-door hardtop. With 47,879 built, only the Fury III four-door sedan exceeded it in popularity with Plymouth customers. 3. Furys could still change their stripes, going from family car to muscle machine via the Sport Fury GT. At 3925 pounds, a GT truly needed its standard 440-cube V-8 to move with authority. 4. Plymouth planners went out on a limb to create a new kind of compact for 1970: the Valiant Duster. Instead of facelifting the dowdy Valiant, they quietly spent their development money to style and engineer a fastback coupe based on Valiant mechanicals. The gamble paid off in big sales increases for Plymouth's compact line. Here, plant manager E. C. Shawe and executive secretary Patrina Palazzola hail the first Duster built on the Los Angeles assembly line. 5-6. Most Dusters had sixes, but 24,817 more raucous V-8 Duster 340s were built.

1

2

3

1. The Barracuda, Plymouth's sports compact since 1964, finally stepped away from its Valiant roots in 1970. Its broad-shouldered long hood/short deck "E-body" platform was shared with the new Dodge Challenger. Engines ranged from a 145-bhp "Slant Six" up to a thumping 425-horse Hemi V-8. Hardtop coupes and convertibles were available in base, plush Gran Coupe, and racy 'Cuda series. **2**. The starting point for the 'Cuda, which took its name from enthusiasts' slang for Barracudas, was a 383-cid V-8 rated at 335 bhp and hooked to a three-speed manual transmission. Options included 340- and 440-cid V-8s and a choice of four-speed or TorqueFlite automatic transmissions. **3-4**. The Barracuda with the biggest teeth was the Hemi 'Cuda. Stuffed with 426 cubic inches of twin-carb V-8 breathing through a "shaker" hood scoop, it could snap off quarter-mile runs in less than 13.5 seconds. Of all the fish in the pond, this was the big one that had no trouble getting away. **4**

1

2

1-2. Like Dodge, Plymouth needed an homologation special to be able to run in the Trans-American series. The AAR 'Cuda did the trick. Central to the package was a beefed-up 340-cid V-8 with triple two-barrel carburetion and side-exit exhausts, a setup that generated 290 bhp. Other specific touches included a fiberglass hood with functional scoop, a ducktail spoiler on the decklid, and a jacked-up rear-end to accommodate large rear tires. The AAR (initials that came from honored driver Dan Gurney's All-American Racers team) was priced at $3966 basic and accounted for 2724 assemblies in its only year on the market. **3**. Sox & Martin Plymouths began cutting a swath through the drag-racing world in the Sixties. In 1970, the Hemi-powered Super Stock Barracuda campaigned by Ronnie Sox (left) and Buddy Martin went through the traps first in the finals of 17 major drag meets. **4**. A sales catalog illustration used a Barracuda "funny car" to show the 25 color choices available for Plymouths in 1970. A few, the so-called High Impact colors, had funky names like In-Violet, Tor-Red, Lemon Twist, and Moulin Rouge.

3

4

Almost from the day it was introduced in 1968, the low-buck, big-go Road Runner connected with fans of high-performance cars. Having an unflappable ground-pounding cartoon character for a mascot didn't hurt. **1.** In 1970, Plymouth used its goggle-eyed spokes'toon to show off the new Air Grabber power-operated scoop. **2.** As Plymouth's all-business mid-sized muscle car, the 'Runner was at the heart of the "Rapid Transit System" collection of performance machines. **3.** A hungry snarl decorated the sides of the Air Grabber, available only with 440 or Hemi engines. **4-5.** The GTX was still around for those who wanted a hot car with creature comforts, but now only as a hardtop. Just 7748 were made.

1

2

3

4

5

At the end of the Sixties, Ford and Chrysler began trying a number of aerodynamic tricks to make their cars faster in stock-car racing. Chrysler's solution for superspeedway cars was an extended shovel-nose and a tall rear stabilizer. But to win NASCAR's acceptance, the aero specials had to be at least nominally available in showrooms. The Dodge Charger Daytona got the call in 1969, but for '70, the focus was shifted to Plymouth. **1.** The speedway package was applied to a Road Runner newly dubbed the Superbird. At $4298, its price was as lofty as its 24-inch-high stabilizer; a regular 'Runner hardtop cost $1264 less. **2.** Superbirds of a feather flocked together to await shipment in Detroit. Just 1920 were made. **3-4.** One side effect of building the Superbird was that it lured driver Richard Petty back to Plymouth following a one-year abdication by stock-car racing's "king" over to the Ford camp. Superbirds accounted for eight big-track victories in 1970; Petty was at the wheel for five of them. **5.** Petty (right) accepts the congratulations of Chrysler-Plymouth Division General Manager Glenn White for one of his triumphs in a "winged warrior," as the cars came to be called.

FORD
MOTOR CO.

After a brief fling with a presidential "troika," Lee Iacocca, "father of the Mustang" is named company president on December 19th

Dearborn thinks globally, buying Italian coachbuilders Ghia and Vignale, plus specialist builder deTomaso Automobili

Ford's low-cost Maverick two-door is unchanged from its mid-'69 debut but keeps piling on sales; meantime, Ford's original compact, the Falcon, is transformed at midyear into a cut-price version of the mid-sized Torino/Fairlane 500

All mid-size Fords are now "shaped by the wind," but the new styling actually proves less slippery on NASCAR super-tracks; the Torino wins *Motor Trend* Car of the Year honors.

Mustang returns from its '69 redesign with racy styling options reflecting the influence of recently hired ex-Corvette designer Larry Shinoda

Thunderbird gets a pointy-nose face accompanied by exposed headlamps

Lincoln Continental is redesigned, gaining a "coffin nose" hood and, for the first time in 13 years, body-on-frame construction

The mid-sized Mercury Montego and Cyclone get a swoopy restyle announced by a protruding nose; the Cyclone Spoiler is now a regular-production muscle machine

In November, Ford withdraws from all forms of racing activity, thus ending the "Total Performance" era

1

2

3

1-2. High-performance cars were at their peak in 1970, but by then it had largely been forgotten that the muscle-car era got its start with big-engined "buckets and console" full-size jobs. Ford made its last foray into the field with the '70 XL SportsRoof hardtop and convertible. A 351-cid V-8 was standard; options ran up to a 360-bhp 429-cube mill. **3**. Buyers were beginning to demand more sophisticated car audio systems and Ford was happy to oblige with stereos, tape players, and even citizen's band radios. **4**. The Berline was Ford's full-size show car.

4

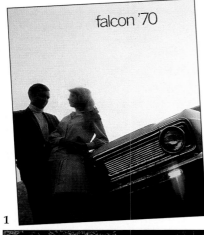

It's not
a superbomb,
it's more of a
jazzy firecracker.

NEW
MAVERICK GRABBER

MAVERICK

1-3. A virtually unchanged Falcon compact arrived for 1970, albeit briefly. At mid-model year, it was axed and the name transferred to a stripped down Torino. Two- and four-door sedans and a station wagon were offered to the end. 4-5. One reason the Falcon wasn't needed was the slightly smaller Maverick. Offered only as a six-cylinder coupe, Ford dubbed it the "first car of the '70s at 1960 prices" when it came out in April 1969. Advertising played up its $1995 base price. 6. As the long first model year wore on, a Grabber option was introduced. Key features included a 200-cid six, a black-out grille, hood and bodyside striping, and wheel trim rings. 7. Thunderbird eschewed its "electric razor" grille and hidden headlights for a bold beak and exposed lamps. Two-door hardtop rooflines were lower and sleeker, too.

25

mustang '70

BOSS 429

Mustangs were unique among the now-crowded "ponycar" field in that they continued to come in three body styles. **1.** The convertible generated 7673 orders. Buyers could select one of two six-cylinder engines or V-8s of 302 and 351 cid. **2.** The price leader in the Mustang corral was the two-door hardtop, a $2721 vehicle without options. A flossier Grandé version cost $155 more. **3.** The cover of the '70 Mustang catalog emphasized the car's new grille design. **4.** Though it too had a 302-cube engine under the hood, the road-racing-inspired Boss 302 fastback's powerplant was rated at 290 bhp. **5-7.** The rarest (498 units) and costliest ($4798) Mustang of the year was the Boss 429. Its 375-bhp hemispherical-head engine was actually developed for stock-car racing.

1. New to the Ford engine family was the "Cleveland" version of the 351-cid V-8. It became a performance mainstay. **2.** Passing from the Mustang scene was the 428-cube Cobra Jet engine, an option for the popular Mach I fastback. The extra-cost "shaker" scoop drew more air into the 335-bhp mill's four-barrel carb. **3.** The hatchback roof on this low, lean Mustang Milano show car foreshadowed the vastly different Mustangs that would arrive in a few years. **4-5.** At the height of the muscle-car era, Ford issued this catalog to highlight its hottest cars. One of the booklet's inside spreads was devoted to the Torino Cobra, Ford Division's most muscular intermediate. **6.** The Cobra's ID badge was designed to stir up some hiss-teria.

1

Ford completely restyled its extensive line of intermediates, from the pointed fender caps up front to the horizontal taillamps in back and from the roofs to the rocker panels. Overall length and tread width increased. Wheelbases grew an inch, too, going to 114 inches on wagons and 117 inches on all others. **1.** A broad array of models ranged from the stripper Falcon (added mid-year) up to the plushly appointed Torino Brougham. For those whose tastes ran to something hotter, there was the Torino Cobra. Built only as a SportsRoof hardtop, it tallied 7675 assemblies. **2.** The $3270 base price included a 429-cid V-8, but the 370-bhp Cobra Jet Ram-Air variant, with a shaker scoop and 11.3:1 compression ratio, cost extra. **3.** Torino also served as the basis for the half-car/half-truck Ranchero, seen here in Squire trim.

2

3

1

2

3

4

1. An altogether new Continental issued from Lincoln in 1970. Styling was more imposing and the rear "suicide doors" of 1961-69 were exchanged for the front-hinged type. More importantly, the standard Lincoln line returned to body-on-frame construction for the first time since 1957. **2.** The White House used Lincoln limousines extensively. President Richard Nixon basks in the cheers of a crowd in Savannah, Georgia, from the hood of one in October 1970. **3.** Most buyers of two-door Lincolns—21,432 of them—opted for the Continental Mark III. The personal coupe was little changed from 1968-69, but a power sunroof was added to its list of options. **4.** A Continental hardtop was still available to those who sought something bigger.

1

2

3

4

Having gotten a thorough redesign and a slight wheelbase stretch in 1969, the big Mercurys made do with a mild facelift for 1970. And big they were, with a majority of models weighing in at more than two tons. **1-2.** A step above the bottom-rung Monterey range was the Monterey Custom. The four-door sedan and two-door hardtop seen here were joined in the series by a four-door hardtop. **3.** At the top of the heap was the Marquis series, including Brougham models. The Marquis Brougham four-door hardtop stickered for $4500 sans options and filled 11,623 orders. **4.** Mercury claimed six- and 10-passenger seating capacities for its 1970 station wagons, headed by the Marquis Colony Park. Wagons rode a 121-inch wheelbase three inches shorter than that used on most other big Mercs. **5-6.** Never a consistent player in the sporty big-car field, Mercury made one final stab in 1969-70 with the Marauder and Marauder X-100. The more powerful X-100 came with a standard bucket-seat interior and a 429-cid V-8. **7.** The X-100 took on a more purposeful look with optional styled wheels and matte decklid paint.

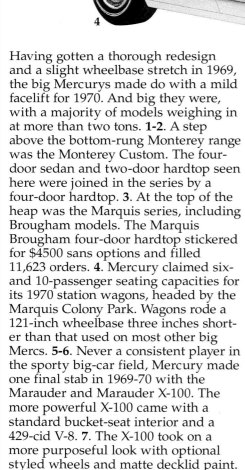

5

6

7

1

2

3

4

5

Like its Ford Torino cousin, the Mercury Montego/Cyclone family was redone for '70. The mid-size Mercs were 3.7 inches longer and about 100 pounds heavier than their Ford counterparts, and two-doors had slightly different roof styling. Convertibles disappeared from Mercury's intermediate lineup. **1.** Despite having just a 250-bhp two-barrel 351-cid V-8 for standard power, the GT's sporty looks and bucket-seat style made it the most popular member of the Cyclone line with 10,170 produced. **2.** Though cheaper, yet cushier and more family friendly, the Montego MX Brougham four-door hardtop did about a third as much business as the Cyclone GT. **3.** Rarer still—and rarin' to go—the Cyclone Spoiler packed FoMoCo's 370-horse ram-air 429 V-8, a four-speed transmission with Hurst shifter, sports suspension, gauge package, and front and rear spoilers into its $3759 base price. **4.** Mercury's "ponycar" was a cat: the Cougar. For 1970, it prowled with a new vertical central grille and revised taillamps. Just $3114 would put a driver behind the wheel of a Cougar two-door hardtop; 49,479 leapt at the chance. **5.** The Eliminator option package allowed Cougar enthusiasts to select one of three hot V-8s: the Boss 302, 300-bhp four-barrel 351, or CJ 428.

GENERAL
MOTORS CORP.

GM loses some $5 billion from a 67-day UAW strike, the longest and costliest action against GM since 1946

Buick drops the Special name, meaning all mid-size models are now Skylarks; also available are new GS455 and bespoilered GS-X models with big-block 455 V-8 power

Cadillac Eldorado gets a massive new 500-cid V-8, the world's largest production passenger-car engine

Chevrolet introduces Monte Carlo, a posh "personal-luxury" hardtop coupe in the Pontiac Grand Prix mold; a storming SS 454 version contributes to strong first-year sales

After an interim run of carryover '69s, a striking new second-generation Chevy Camaro bows with sleek, tasteful styling but no convertible; RS, SS, and Z-28 options remain

"America's Sports Car" powers up: Chevy's Corvette big-block V-8 swells to 454 cubic inches

Oldsmobile turns up the heat with a standard 455 V-8 for the hot 4-4-2, plus more sizzling "W" options for other mid-size models; a 4-4-2 paces this year's Indy 500

A new face with first-time exposed headlamps freshens Olds's big front-drive Toronado

Like Camaro, Pontiac's Firebird is reborn with slick Euro-inspired coupe styling; Ram Air V-8s, including the first of the soon-to-be-legendary "Super Duty" engines, make the racing-inspired Trans Am the hottest of the lot

1. Forty-seven years and about 14 million cars separate these two vehicles. The 1970 Skylark Custom hardtop coupe in the background was the 15 millionth Buick produced when it came off the line in October '69. The accompanying touring car dates from 1923, the year in which Buick built its 1 millionth auto. 2-3. The Wildcat had been Buick's "banker's hot rod" since '62, but with performance buffs looking to smaller cars for their kicks, the 'Cat was on its ninth—and final—life come 1970. The three body types offered came with Custom-level equipment and a 370-bhp version of Buick's new 455-cid V-8 standard. The two-door hardtop was the least expensive, but the four-door hardtop accounted for more than half of the year's total 23,615 Wildcats. There was a convertible, too.

1. For the first time since 1964, there was a full-size station wagon on the Buick roster. The Estate Wagon was on a 124-inch wheelbase. 2. Even the entry-level LeSabre had a convertible. Custom ragtop prices began at $3700. 3. Limited trim was a $318 decor option for Electra 225 Customs like the two-door hardtop. 4. LeSabre four-door hardtops saw 65,221 sales in '70.

33

1

2

3

1. Buick advertised its 1970s as cars that would "light your fire," a task best left up to Gran Sports like the GS455 Stage I. Its conservatively rated 360-bhp V-8 generated a mighty 510 pound-feet of torque at just 2800 rpm. **2-3.** The wildest GSs were the 687 GSX hardtops painted Apollo White or Saturn Yellow. **4-5.** A heavily facelifted Riviera returned to fixed headlamps. Skirted rear wheels gave the flanks a massive look, but an optional bodyside molding tended to put some swoop back in the design. **6.** A vinyl top and more open rear-wheel look were available. **7.** The Silver Arrow II was one of a series of Riviera-based show cars.

4

5

6

7

1

2

3

4

5

Though just freshened versions of their immediate predecessors, the 1970 Cadillacs scored a model-year production record of 238,745 units. **1.** The De Ville convertible accounted for 15,172 of those assemblies in this, the model's final year. **2.** Four Dumbarton cloth-and-leather upholstery combinations were among 15 interior choices for the premium Fleetwood Brougham sedan. Fleetwoods utilized a stately 133-inch wheelbase. **3-4.** The most popular Caddys were the Coupe de Ville and Sedan de Ville hardtops. They were powered by a 472-cid V-8; wheelbase was 129.5-inches. **5.** Demand for the front-wheel-drive Eldorado personal coupe was on the rise. Underhood was a new 500-cid V-8 of 400 bhp. A power sunroof joined the options list.

1

3

2

4

5

Full-size Chevrolets entered 1970 with carryover bodies, but wore a new grille and a stout front bumper. Vertical taillights replaced horizontal lamps seen on '69s. **1-2.** Two styles of two-door hardtop were offered in the Impala series, but the top-line Caprice used only the more formal of the two designs. Caprices came with color-keyed wheel covers and could be had with or without fender skirts. **3.** Four-door choices abounded, with the $3527 Caprice hardtop atop the list. **4.** At the other end of the spectrum was the Biscayne sedan. It sold for as little as $2787 with a six-cylinder engine. **5.** The sole convertible in the big-car line was an Impala. It drew 9562 customers. **6.** Chevy's familiar 327-cid V-8 was dropped after '69, but a new small-block engine displacing 400 cubic inches took its place. A 265-bhp version went into full-size cars. **7.** The 1969-style Camaro spilled over into '70 when production problems delayed a new-generation "ponycar."

6

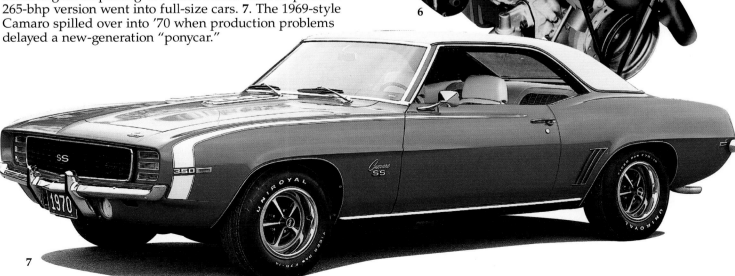

7

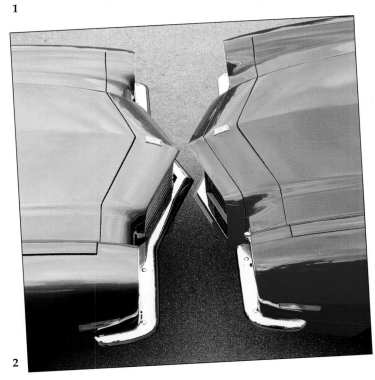

1

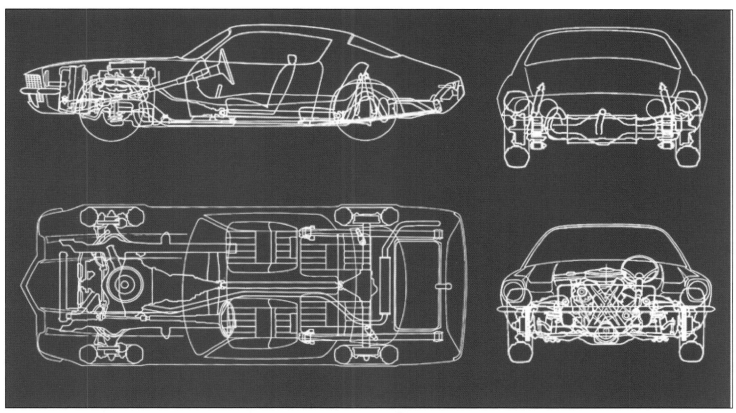

2

3

4

1. When it finally arrived in late February 1970, the new Camaro came only as a coupe with a sloping roofline. Like prior Camaros, wheelbase was 108 inches. Overall length grew a couple inches, though. **2**. The 1970 Camaro showed two faces to the world: the standard full-blade bumper style and the Rally Sport package's Endura grille surround, inboard parking lights, and twin bumperettes. **3**. Ad copy put a positive spin on the new Camaro's late arrival. **4**. The $169 Rally Sport option was added to 27,136 of the '70 cars.

1

2

3

4

1-3. The ultimate Camaro continued to be the Z28, Chevy's body double for its SCCA Trans-American racers. New Trans-Am rules for the 1970 season made it possible for Chevrolet to drop the special 302-cid V-8 used in previous Zs and replace it with a 360-bhp version of the solid-lifter LT1 350-cube engine newly available for the Corvette. **4**. When applied to specially marked Corvettes, the LT1 made 370 horsepower. The grille and side vents were revised from the '69s.

1

A group picture of all the cars in Monte Carlo's field.

2

3

4

5

1. The Corvette coupe had a convertible companion that accounted for 6648 of the total 17,316 fiberglass-bodied two-seaters built for the year. The top engine option was a 390-bhp big-block mill newly grown to 454 cid. 2. The Monte Carlo debuted for 1970 with the longest hood in Chevy's history, as the division was fond of pointing out. Built on a 116-inch wheelbase borrowed from General Motors's four-door intermediates, the Monte Carlo put buyers in a personal-luxury coupe for just $3123 to start. 3. Assembly lines churned out 130,657 of the new models. 4. A discreet Super Sport package built around a 360-bhp 454 V-8 (but available only with automatic transmission) cost $420. It found favor with 3823 buyers. 5. Another option was an instrument group that added a tachometer, ammeter, and temperature gauge to the wood-toned dashboard.

1

Chevelle SS. A winner in the 1970 *Car and Drivers'* Poll.

2

3

1-2. The muscle-car era at Chevrolet reached its zenith in 1970 with the mid-sized Chevelle SS. The starting point was the SS396 (though its engine really displaced 402 cubic inches); the step up was the SS454 with 360 or a tire-frying 450 bhp on tap. Either SS could be ordered with the cowl-induction hood to gulp in more air for better performance. 3. More common—and more practical—were Malibus like this four-door hardtop with the humble 307-cid engine standard in V-8 Chevelles. 4. Six-cylinder economy was still a hallmark of the compact Nova, but a racy Super Sport package put a hot 350 or 396 V-8 underhood. 5. A vinyl top and custom exterior package were available to spruce up Novas.

4

5

1

Full-size Oldsmobiles entered 1970 with slightly revised looks. Wheelbase lengths were set at 127 inches for the senior Ninety-Eights and 124 inches for the Delta 88 family. **1**. The Ninety-Eight Holiday two-door hardtop's $4582 base price included a 365-bhp 455-cid Rocket V-8 and power front disc brakes. **2**. The Ninety-Eight's two four-door bodystyles were available in base or upgraded Luxury Sedan trim. This Luxury Sedan Holiday hardtop was one of 19,377 built, but the companion four-door sedan was more popular by about 10,000 units. **3**. A step up from the basic Delta 88 was the Delta 88 Custom. It came as a four-door sedan, hardtop coupe, and this hardtop sedan. **4**. The top-line Delta 88 was the Royale, a two-door hardtop with a halo vinyl roof and a 310-horse 455 V-8 among its standard equipment.

2

3

4

1

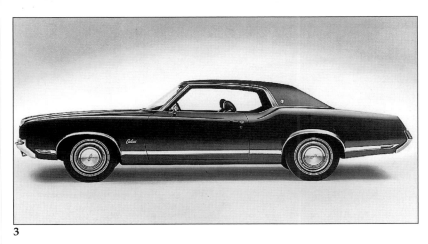

2

1. General Motors began switching most of its many cars with concealed headlights back to fixed lamps in 1969. The Toronado's turn came in '70. 2. If you can't stand the heat, get off the highway: Motorists on New York's Long Island Expressway feel the effects of a traffic jam at the start of the Labor Day holiday weekend in 1970. 3. The Cutlass Supreme coupe adopted a hardtop roofline unique among GM intermediates. Sales blossomed. 4. Olds concocted the wacky Dr. Oldsmobile to hawk high-performance cars. Here, "Doc" and assistant Rose Lewis set their sights on the Detroit Auto Show. 5. In print, Dr. Oldsmobile had a *Yellow Submarine* aura about him.

4

3

5

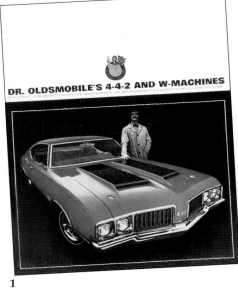

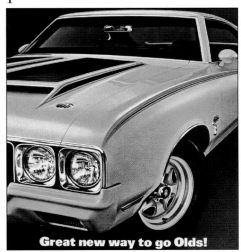

1. The 4-4-2 was Oldsmobile's top entry in the muscle-car field. It and other Olds mid-sizers were enhanced via options coded by the letter W. 2. The W-30 put a 370-bhp 455-cid V-8 in a 4-4-2 lightened by such tricks as a twin-scoop fiberglass hood; quarter-mile times were in the low 14s. 3. F-85 and Cutlass two-doors could be ordered with option W-45, which turned them into a Rallye 350. 4. The year's rarest 4-4-2 (1688 built) was the sport coupe. 5. Cutlass four-door sedans came with six- or eight-cylinder engines. 6. The 4-4-2 convertible cost $3567.

43

1

2

3

5

4

1. Pontiac had become a sales force to be reckoned with during the Sixties with bold, exciting cars. By 1970, that boldness was exemplified in its large cars such as (from left) the personal-luxury Grand Prix, the Catalina four-door sedan and two-door hardtop, the Bonneville convertible, and the Executive Safari wagon. Unfortunately for Pontiac, big and brawny was beginning to fall out of favor, and sales would suffer. 2. The face of '70 full-sized Pontiacs harked back to the classic era with a narrow vertical grille and a biplane-style bumper. Bonnevilles like this two-door hardtop had a distinct grille texture and the series name in block letters on the hood. 3. Pontiac's former 428-cid V-8 was bored and stroked into a 455-cube, 360-bhp power plant for 1970. It came standard in Bonnevilles. 4. The Executive Safari came in six- and nine-passenger versions. Faux wood trim was included; a roof rack was an $84 accessory. 5. At $3538, the Executive four-door sedan was its series's cheapest car. It shared the Bonneville's 125-inch wheelbase.

1

2

3

4

5

6

1-2. The glitziest low-line Catalinas were the two-door hardtop and convertible. Catalinas (and all wagons) had a 122-inch wheelbase. **3.** Like the Camaro, the Firebird was all new—and late arriving. The base car's standard engine was a 250-cid six. **4.** The Trans Am sat atop the line. Ram Air 400-cid V-8s of 345 or 370 bhp provided go. **5.** In between was the Formula 400. A Hurst shifter came with its standard three-speed trans. **6.** GM tested two steam cars in 1970, including one made from a '69 Grand Prix.

45

1

2

3

1. The Pontiac GTO was credited with starting the mid-size muscle-car trend in 1964 and it was still going strong six years later. This convertible, one of 3615 made in basic form, sports an accessory hood-mounted tachometer. The redesigned Endura nosepiece gave the "Goat" something of a monochromatic look. 2. Though it never quite got the hang of being a Road Runner–like budget bomb (as was intended), The Judge injected some new life into the GTO concept with its decklid airfoil and wild striping. Power offerings began with a 366-bhp Ram Air engine of 400 cid. Production of '70 Judges came to 3629 two-door hardtops and 168 convertibles. 3. Pontiac sold about 10 times more regular GTO hardtops than Judge coupes. Late in the year the 360-horse 455-cube mill became available. 4. Just below the GTO in the intermediate ranks was the LeMans Sport; hardtop coupes started at $2953.

4

IMPORTS

Audi goes upscale in America with the larger new 100LS front-wheel-drive sedan

BMW sales continue growing due to the now-legendary 2002, a more potent 2.0-liter version of the 1600 two-door sedan

British Motor Corporation ends U.S. sales of the Austin-Healey Sprite; near-identical MG Midget continues

Datsun of Japan shakes up the sports-car world with the 240Z, a slick two-seat coupe offering European performance and American-style amenities for just $3500

Ford's successful "Euro Mustang," the Capri, comes to Lincoln-Mercury dealers in April

Honda, another rising Japanese sun, expands from motorcycles to cars in the U.S. with a boxy micro hatchback, the two-cylinder front-wheel-drive N600

Mazda opens for U.S. business with the unique Wankel rotary-powered R100 coupe

A much-awaited "People's Porsche" bows with a new lower-cost model, the mid-engine two-seat 914 with lift-off hardtop

Toyota, "Japan's General Motors," introduces the subcompact Corolla, plus a new-generation Corona compact

Volkswagen's ageless Beetle gets more go from a new 1.6-liter engine; prices reach a new high at $1874 to start

Volvo's 1800 coupe becomes the speedier 1800S via a new fuel-injected 2.0-liter engine

1

3

1. The 100 LS was the larger and more powerful of two models Audi began importing to the U.S. in 1970. **2**. The 2.0-liter four-cylinder BMW 2002 excited the press and owners alike. **3**. Citroën combined front-wheel drive, interior opulence, and impossible-to-ignore styling in the DS21 *Pallas*. **4**. Datsun introduced the six-cylinder 240Z in 1970 and struck a resonant chord with U.S. enthusiasts. **5**. Even Datsun's family cars had some life in them. The 510's overhead-camshaft four and independent rear suspension made it a hit with road racers. **6**. U.S. prices for a four-place dohc six-cylinder Jaguar XKE 2+2 began just under $6000.

4

5

6

1

2

3

4

5

6

7

1. Japanese automakers were on the verge of a breakthrough in the American market, but to many of their prospective customers circa 1970, a foreign car usually meant something European. Here, two MGB convertibles are virtually surrounded by Volkswagens and a few other cars from the continent. 2. Mercedes-Benz touted the sensible packaging and four-wheel disc brakes of its 250 sedan. 3. Buick dealers sold the GM-owned, German-built Opel in the U.S. Power for the Kadett Sport Sedan, one of five Kadett models, came from a 63-bhp four with twin single-throat carburetors. 4. The Opel GT had the looks of a mini-Corvette, right down to its two-seat cabin and hideaway headlights. Prices began at $3328. 5. The 914/6 was the six-cylinder variant of Porsche's new-for-'70 joint venture with Volkswagen. It arrived several months after the four-cylinder 914/4. Only the Porsche name appeared on U.S. versions. 6-7. Toyota's 1970 offerings included the Crown station wagon and Hi-Lux mini-pickup.

1

2

3

4

5

1. Triumph's TR-6 was in its second year. **2**. The TR was accompanied from Britain by the GT6 Mk II, a six-cylinder coupe version of the four-cylinder Triumph Spitfire roadster. **3**. The king of them all in the import world, the Volkswagen Beetle, saw displacement and power gains in its air-cooled flat-four engine. **4**. The VW 1600 series, which tallied a best-ever 99,012 U.S. sales in calendar-year 1970, grew four inches in length and added 25 percent more front cargo space. **5**. The Beetle-based Karmann-Ghia also hit its peak in the States; 38,825 of the '70s were snapped up. **6**. VW's Campmobile was a home away from home.

6

ETC.

Production of the Corvette-powered Avanti II, a continuation of Studebaker's Avanti sports coupe, comes to 111 units; prices for the largely hand-built cars start at $7500

Excalibur issues a new Series II version of its classically inspired roadster and phaeton; changes include a longer wheelbase and adoption of Corvette's 350 V-8

Nearly identical to the 1960 model that marked the beginning of Checker sales to the general public, the 1970 Marathon sedan rode a 120-inch wheelbase. Power choices were a 230-cid six or 350-cube V-8, both Chevy designs. A station wagon and long-wheelbase sedan and limo were available, too. Taxi sales stayed strong, but passenger-car output slumped. Checker founder Morris Markin died in 1970.

49

1971

The year's most important automotive development was driven by politics and the economy. In order to combat a deepening recession, President Nixon instituted a wage and price freeze—a *de facto* devaluation of currency—a temporary increase in import duties, and the repeal of the excise tax. These initiatives, while hard for many to swallow, also gave encouragement to car shoppers. Sales of domestic automobiles jumped to nearly 8.7 million for the model year—a dramatic increase from the disappointing 6.5 million for 1970.

The auto industry had plenty of critics, however. Some regarded the motorcar as a dangerous nuisance, and even as an irredeemable agent of apocalypse, as witnessed by Kenneth Schneider's 1971 book, *Autokind vs. Mankind*. Of greater significance was that despite concessions made by General Motors to end the debilitating UAW strike of 1970, worker dissatisfaction at GM and the other automakers remained a very real problem. A 1971 *Newsweek* ad focusing on the American worker spoke of "discontent rooted in monotony, boredom and loss of job pride . . . an overt discontent many fear may turn 'Made in U.S.A.' into a sign of shoddy workmanship."

Newsweek knew that a little melodrama in the quest for readers and ad revenue goes a long way. Still, there is no denying that Detroit was sliding into real trouble. Take the good-looking subcompact Chevrolet Vega, one of the most significant debuts of the '71 model year, and a car with inexcusably leaky cylinder-head gaskets and bodywork that quickly succumbed to rust.

Imports helped to spur Ford's Pinto, which bowed to good press reaction and tremendous consumer acceptance: 353,000 of the functional subcompacts found homes in '71. Later, of course, came the stories of deadly fires, which suggests that *Newsweek* may have been on to something.

Chrysler Corp. was still missing the boat, small-car-wise: The company's shortest wheelbase was 108 inches (Valiant and Barracuda), as contrasted with the 94.2-inch Pinto; 97-inch Vega; and 96-inch, chopped-tail AMC Gremlin.

At Indy, Al Unser and Colt-Ford made it two wins in a row. The year's pace car was a Hemi Orange, stock-engine Dodge Challenger rated at 300 gross horsepower. The dominant driver on the NASCAR circuit was Richard Petty, 1971 Winston Cup champion. The ultimate in far-out motoring, though, had to be the battery-powered lunar rover operated on the moon that summer by the crew of Apollo 15.

K. T. Keller, onetime president of Chrysler Corporation and lover of bulbous cars tall enough to accommodate his hats, was inducted into the Automotive Hall of Fame.

Passage of the 26th Amendment lowered the voting age of U.S. citizens to 18. In Washington, D.C., on May 3, at least 10,000 anti-war demonstrators were arrested. The U.S. Supreme Court ruled unanimously that school districts may utilize busing in order to achieve racial desegregation. The year's most important international development was Red China's admission into the United Nations.

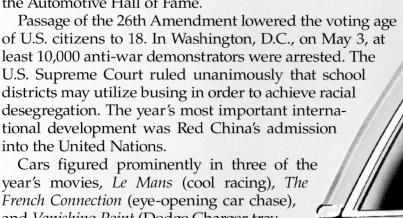

Cars figured prominently in three of the year's movies, *Le Mans* (cool racing), *The French Connection* (eye-opening car chase), and *Vanishing Point* (Dodge Charger travels from Denver to San Francisco, flat out). Other big movies: *Carnal Knowledge, The Last Picture Show, Shaft, Diamonds Are Forever, Play Misty for Me, Straw Dogs, Klute, A Clockwork Orange, Dirty Harry,* and *The Andromeda Strain.*

Americans tuned their groove tubes to *The Flip Wilson Show, Marcus Welby, M.D., The Mod Squad, Adam-12,* and *Hawaii Five-0.*

FM radio was coming on strong by this time and AM Top 40 was fading; "45s" still got plenty of airplay, though. Top hits were "Me and Bobby McGee" by Janis Joplin, "Want Ads" by the Honey Cone, "Maggie May" by Rod Stewart, "Family Affair" by Sly & the Family Stone, "Brand New Key" by Melanie, and—saints preserve us—"One Bad Apple" by the

AMC

Gremlin scores more than 73,000 sales despite new Big Three competition, helped by a low $1899 base price and a sporty new "X" option package

The formerly extra-cost 232-cid six becomes the Gremlin's new standard power plant, with a 258-cube six added to the options list

The Sportabout station wagon, equipped with a hatch-type tailgate, joins the Hornet family

Hornet also serves as the basis for the latest of AMC's high-performance specials, the SC/360 two-door sedan; it comes with a standard 360-cubic-inch V-8 good for 245 horsepower, or 285 ponies when ordered with the ram-air hood

Javelin gets a swoopy new look via reshaped outer sheetmetal characterized by distinctive humps over the front wheel openings

Though no longer a two-seater, the AMX lives on as a new top-line version of AMC's Mustang-fighting Javelin

Mark Donohue hustles his Javelin to a second straight Sports Car Club of America Trans-Am crown

The mid-sized Rebel is facelifted and renamed Matador

The big Ambassador puts on a new face and gains standard air conditioning, an industry first

Jeep's pioneering Wagoneer sport-utility wagon switches to AMC powerplants

AMC's market share continues shrinking, slipping to just under three percent of the domestic industry

1

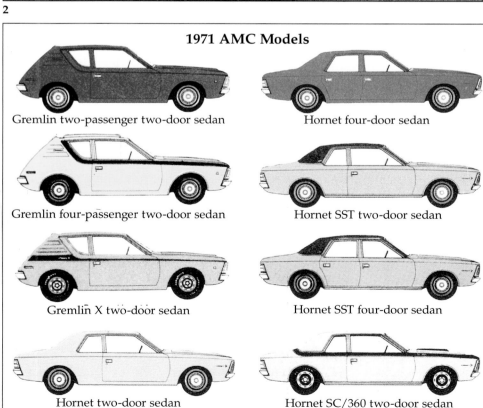

2

1971 AMC Models

Gremlin two-passenger two-door sedan

Hornet four-door sedan

Gremlin four-passenger two-door sedan

Hornet SST two-door sedan

Gremlin X two-door sedan

Hornet SST four-door sedan

Hornet two-door sedan

Hornet SC/360 two-door sedan

3

4

5

6

1. Full-size AMC cars weren't exactly leaping off dealer lots. The design of the Ambassador, which dated back to 1967, simply failed to lure buyers. Despite being the highest-priced model, the Ambassador Brougham—in hardtop, sedan, and station wagon form—was the top seller. 2. The mid-range Ambassador SST also came in three body styles, including this sedan. A DPL sedan was the cheapest model. 3. AMC gamely tried to match its larger domestic competitors with a roster of five car types. 4. Javelins got swoopier sheetmetal, with crisper lines highlighted by bulges over the front wheels. Most popular by far was the SST. 5-6. The slow-selling two-seat AMX disappeared, but AMC tacked that badge onto its top-of-the-line Javelin. 7. Mark Donohue piloted this earlier-model Javelin to his second straight crown in the '71 SCCA Trans-American Challenge.

7

Hornet Sportabout station wagon

Matador station wagon

Ambassador DPL four-door sedan

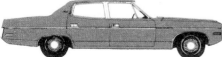

Hornet Sportabout D/L station wagon

Javelin two-door hardtop

Ambassador SST four-door sedan

Matador four-door sedan

Javelin SST two-door hardtop

Ambassador SST two-door hardtop

Matador two-door hardtop

Javelin AMX two-door hardtop

Ambassador SST station wagon

1

2

3

1. Gremlin's unconventional shape attracted younger buyers. **2.** AMC chairman Roy D. Chapin poses with his company's pioneering subcompact. **3.** H.L. Shahan tuned Gremlins and Hornets for drag racing; his wife, Shirley, drove them. **4-5.** The hot new Hornet SC/360 held a potent 360-cid V-8 and four-speed trans with a Hurst shifter. Only 784 were made. **6.** New for '71 was the Hornet Sportabout wagon.

4

5

6

CHRYSLER CORPORATION

Plymouth and Dodge mid-size models are completely restyled; Dodge Coronets come only as four-door sedans and wagons, with a line of new-look Chargers to tempt customers who favor two-doors; two- and four-door Plymouth Satellites also get separate grille and rear bumper designs

Plymouth returns to third place in sales as Pontiac drops to fourth

Dodge's version of the Duster, called the Demon, joins the Dart line at midyear; protests later lead to a name change

Plymouth adds a Scamp two-door hardtop to the Valiant line

Imperial—now in a single LeBaron series—employs the first four-wheel anti-skid braking system

The Plymouth GTX makes its final outing

The Hemi engine option and convertibles both take their final bows; the hot Plymouth 'Cuda and base Dodge Challenger are the last ragtops

Chrysler buys a share of Mitsubishi Motors; Dodge dealers begin marketing the Japanese-built Colt as the "captive-import" business grows

While Chevrolet and Ford introduce domestically built subcompacts, Plymouth tries to establish a toehold in the mini-car market with the Cricket, which is based on the British Hillman Avenger sedan

French-built Simcas bid U.S. Chrysler dealerships adieu at the end of the sales year

1

2

3

Full-size Chryslers had a sizable flock of loyal customers. **1.** A lower-priced Royal sub-series joined the Chrysler Newport lineup this year, carrying a new 255-bhp, 360-cid V-8 engine—an enlargment of the small-block V-8 that debuted in the late Sixties. Newports could be equipped with V-8s up to 440 cubic inches and 370 horsepower, and sold rather well. **2.** A $5041 sticker didn't scare buyers away from the Chrysler New Yorker hardtop sedan. Its 440-cid V-8 helped make it one of the year's most-popular Chryslers. **3.** Town & Country station wagons rode a shorter wheelbase than other full-sized Chrysler models. Priced at around $5000 and equipped with either two or three seats and a choice of 383- or 440-cid V-8s, they tipped the scales at greater than 4500 pounds. More than 16,000 were sold.

1

2

3

4

5

1. Though just in its second year on the market, the high-performance R/T version of Dodge's Challenger "pony-car" made its final appearance. **2.** A Challenger convertible—last of the Dodge ragtops—paced the Indianapolis 500. **3.** No more brawny Charger R/T hardtops would be seen after '71. **4.** A Ramcharger hood scoop was optional on Charger R/Ts and Super Bees, helping to shove gobs of air into the hungry V-8. **5.** The Charger R/T packed a 370-bhp, 440-cid V-8 as standard. **6.** SE was one of six Charger models. **7.** Buddy Baker, driving for Petty Enterprises, won the Rebel 400 NASCAR race at Darlington in this Dodge—his only victory of 1971.

6

7

1

2

3

4

5

6

7

8

9

10

1-3. Dodge turned to "captive" imports in an attempt to capture buyers seeking small cars. Built in Japan by Mitsubishi, which was partly owned by Chrysler Corporation, Colts came in four body styles and with a 100-bhp four-cylinder engine. **4.** Practical-minded families leaned toward the Coronet—shown in upscale Brougham trim—with its new "fuselage" shape. **5.** A three-seat Coronet Crestwood station wagon set customers back $3687 to start. **6.** Chargers could get an optional headlight washer, an accessory uncommon even years later. **7.** Dart Swinger hardtops could be plain or fancy, with a 318-cid V-8 available. **8.** Compared to a Swinger or Demon coupe, the Dart Custom sedan was straightforward transportation with a bit of extra trim. **9.** An optional sport-style steering wheel added panache to the interior of a Dodge Demon—a Dart-based fastback whose devilish name spurred protests. Three engines were available. **10.** Aside from its 275-bhp V-8, the Demon 340 coupe had a beefed-up chassis, tape stripes, and dummy hood scoops.

1

2

3

1. Dodge promoted its "Scat Pack" cars at the 1971 Chicago Auto Show. In the foreground is a Dart Demon 340. **2.** A 383-cid V-8 was standard in the line-topping full-sized Dodge Monaco two-door hardtop, but a 440-cid engine might take its place. **3.** Polaras came in base, Custom, and Brougham trim. Barely more than 2500 Brougham hardtop sedans were built. Engine choices ranged from the modest Slant Six to a 335-horse, 440-cube V-8. **4.** The only Polara station wagon was this Custom four-door with either two or three seats.

4

1971 CHRYSLER *IMPERIAL*

5. Chrysler's posh 1971 Imperial line was reduced to a pair of LeBarons, this four-door hardtop and a two-door companion. Imperials featured the same rounded, low-roofed "fuselage" shape as in 1969-70, again with concealed headlights. The standard 440-cid V-8 engine dropped to 335 horsepower, as a result of emissions tuning—a phenomenon that would soon dominate the industry. Bendix anti-lock braking was a new $250 option. More than 10,000 four-door Imperial LeBarons were built, but only 1442 two-doors. Prices started at $6632 for the coupe.

5

Mildly facelifted, Barracudas gained quad headlights for 1971. **1.** With hood tie-downs and a "shaker" hood scoop, the Plymouth 'Cuda 340 looked the part of a muscle car. **2.** Central to the 'Cuda 340 was its 340-cid V-8 that produced 275 bhp. **3.** If you're going to go 'Cuda at all, why not drive one home with a hotter V-8? This one has a 383, but everything up to the legendary Hemi could be installed. **4.** Big rubber and back-end rollers let everyone know this 'Cuda show car was ready for the strip. **5.** Don "The Snake" Prudhomme drag raced this 'Cuda "funny car." **6.** The Gran Coupe hardtop tempered the Barracuda's sportiness with luxury.

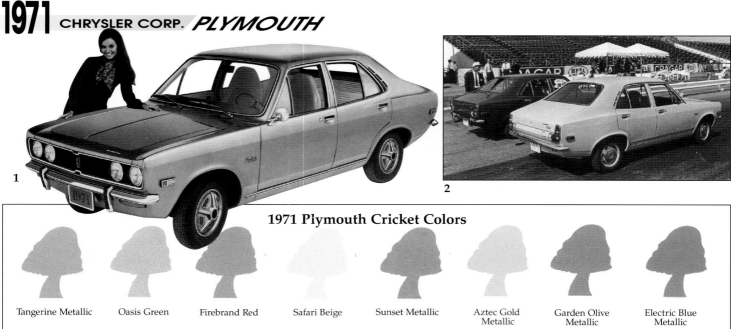

1

2

1971 Plymouth Cricket Colors

Tangerine Metallic	Oasis Green	Firebrand Red	Safari Beige	Sunset Metallic	Aztec Gold Metallic	Garden Olive Metallic	Electric Blue Metallic

3

4

5

6

7

1-3. Plymouth dealers began to market the British-built Cricket in 1971. The mini-sized four-door sedan was similar to the Hillman Avenger. 4-5. Plymouth's counterpart to the Dodge Demon 340 was named Duster 340. This performance-oriented member of the Valiant line held a 275-horsepower V-8, as well as a floor gearshift, special instrument panel, and heavy-duty suspension components. Stepping down a peg, Dusters could have a new "Twister" option that included a matte-black hood, 340-type black grille, tape stripes, and Rallye wheels. 6. New to the Valiant line this year was the Scamp hardtop coupe. Scamps were built on the Dodge Dart Swinger platform. 7. "Akron Arlen" Vanke campaigned this Duster in drag racing's pro-stock class. 8. A full-sized Sport Fury Brougham four-door hardtop fronts the Plymouth display at the Chicago Auto Show in February 1971.

8

1

2

Restyling of Plymouth's Fury amounted to an update of the corporate "fuselage" design first seen on '69 models. Sport Fury topped the lineup, while the three other Fury models were simply called I, II, and III. **1.** Detroit's last bastion of big-car muscle was the Sport Fury GT hardtop (foreground). Priced at $4111, only 375 were made. A 440-cid V-8, heavy-duty suspension, and long axle ratios were standard. At the rear is a Sport Fury Brougham hardtop. **2.** Four-door hardtops continued to attract customers who considered regular sedans dowdy. Plymouth's Fury III cost $3612 and sold more than 55,000 copies. **3.** All Sport Furys, like this hardtop coupe, had V-8s, ranging from 318 to 440 cid.

3

2

3

1

4

5

6

7

All mid-size Plymouths now fell under the Satellite banner. Radically sculpted metal replaced the squarish look of 1968-70. **1.** Road Runners got a 383-cid V-8 with 275 or 300 bhp. **2.** NASCAR fans could easily spot Richard Petty on the track, with the familiar "43" gracing his blue Road Runner. **3.** Petty (right) brought his Plymouth to a White House reception to meet President Richard Nixon in '71, the year he won his third NASCAR championship. **4.** The top-of-the-line GTX hardtop was in its last year as a stand-alone model. **5.** A Sport Satellite station wagon could be just the thing for a big family. **6.** The plushest Satellite sedan was the $3189 Brougham. **7.** Satellite and Fury buyers could get a sunroof for the first time in '71.

FORD
MOTOR CO.

Ford gets small with the Pinto, a subcompact four-cylinder two-door sedan sized and priced like economy imports; a hatchback "Runabout" version arrives at midyear

Maverick goes the other way, adding a longer four-door sedan body style

Mustang gets really big, adding inches, pounds, and more heroic styling; rarest of the breed is the Boss 351 fastback, dropped midyear after some 1800 units

Full-size Fords go formal with a heavy facelift and a prominent vertical-theme grille

Mercury gets a new compact by reviving the Comet name on slightly upscale two- and four-door Mavericks

Like Mustang, Mercury's Cougar is greatly enlarged, but adopts a much more formal look; the hot Eliminator is eliminated and other performance options are de-emphasized

Big Mercurys follow big Fords with newly styled outer sheetmetal, but unlike Ford, convertibles are absent from the lineup

Lincoln celebrates its 50th year by offering a limited-edition Golden Anniversary Town Car

Lincoln-Mercury begins regular sale of the DeTomaso Pantera, an Italian "exoticar" with a Ford 351-cid V-8 and a bargain price of around $10,000

Dearborn's market share declines nearly four points to 27.4 percent, thanks partly to aggressive new product moves by General Motors

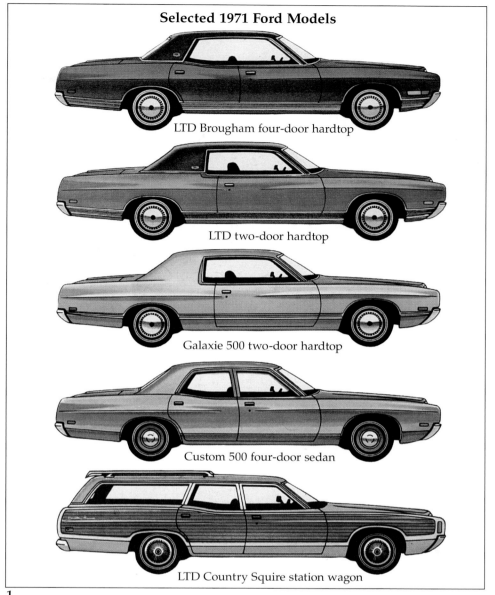

Selected 1971 Ford Models

LTD Brougham four-door hardtop

LTD two-door hardtop

Galaxie 500 two-door hardtop

Custom 500 four-door sedan

LTD Country Squire station wagon

1

2

1. A major facelift gave big Fords a more formal look for 1971, led by a prominent vertical grille. Body styles included two- and four-door hardtops, four-door sedans, station wagons, and a convertible newly upgraded to LTD series status. **2.** The Galaxie 500 four-door hardtop, with its full bench seat in front, promised stylish accommodations for six passengers. A 351-cid V-8 came standard, but buyers could select a 400- or 429-cid V-8 instead. With 46,595 assemblies, the four-door hardtop was only half as popular as the Galaxie 500 four-door sedan.

1. The LTD Brougham topped Ford's full-size line-up. The $4097 hardtop coupe was its best-selling version. **2.** Country Squire wagons, sporting customary fake wood side trim, could be had with a new option this year: a wiper/washer for the back window. **3.** Ford's lowest-priced full-sized model was the $3288 Custom four-door sedan. **4.** A four-door Maverick sedan arrived in 1971 with a wheelbase 6.9 inches longer than that of the two-door model. Four-doors did not sell as well, even with the newly optional V-8 engine. **5.** In an attempt to spark sales to youthful customers, Ford launched the Maverick Grabber, a sportier-looking two-door. **6.** Bold striping and wheel trim rings were standard on the Grabber, but a 302-cid V-8 engine that made 210 bhp cost extra.

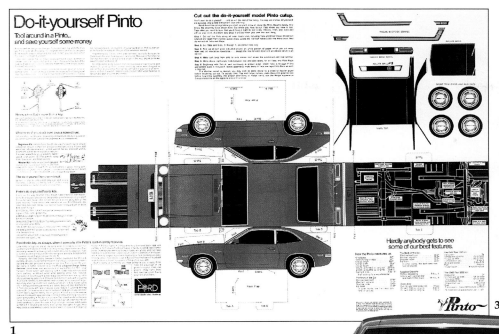

Do-it-yourself Pinto

Tool around in a Pinto...
and save yourself some money.

1. Ford joined the subcompact revolution in 1971 with the Pinto, targeting import buyers and challenging Chevy's new Vega. The Pinto catalog included this cutout paper model of the new car. Sales were brisk from the start until lawsuits stemming from incidences of exploding fuel tanks did harm to the company's image. **2.** CEOs weren't ordinarily seen in subcompacts, but Henry Ford II, chairman of Ford Motor Company, got to drive this particular Pinto. **3.** With its handy roof rack, the hatchback Pinto Runabout promised plenty of utility; still, the regular two-door fastback sold better. **4.** With a 429 Cobra Jet V-8 and automatic, the Mach 1 Mustang could dash to 60 mph in 6.5 seconds. **5.** The new third-generation Mustangs were eight inches longer, six inches wider, and 600 pounds heavier than the original '65 ponycar.

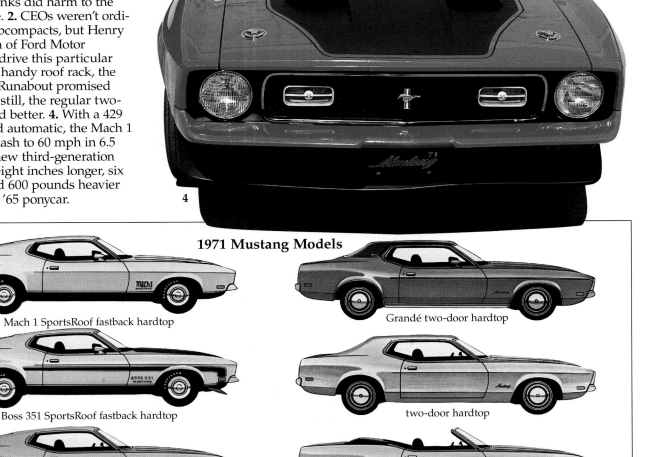

1971 Mustang Models

Mach 1 SportsRoof fastback hardtop

Boss 351 SportsRoof fastback hardtop

SportsRoof fastback hardtop

Grandé two-door hardtop

two-door hardtop

convertible

1

1. A new Mustang Boss 351 replaced both prior Boss models in 1971. Only 1800 copies of the Boss 351 rolled off the assembly line, packing an efficient, highly-tuned small-block V-8 that whipped up an appealing 330 horses. A hefty selling price of $4124 (nearly $1000 more than a Mach 1) helped keep sales down and limited the Boss 351 to its single season in the Mustang stable. **2-3.** Nearing the end of its fifth generation, the little-changed Thunderbird again came in three models: hardtop coupe, Landau formal coupe, and Landau four-door sedan. Buyers of the Landau coupe, the most popular T-Bird model, could now omit the dummy S-bars, if desired. A 360-bhp, 429-cid V-8 was standard. Total sales dipped near 36,000 units.

2

3

1

2

3

1. The Torino GT was the modestly sporty member of Ford's intermediate clan. 2. The Torino Cobra hardtop continued as Ford's no-nonsense muscle car. It featured a distinctive concave back window and came equipped with a 285-bhp, 351-cid V-8 engine, Hurst-shifted four-speed transmission, and a heavy-duty suspension. It was quite a package for $3295, but only 3054 were built this year, another sign of the waning market for hot cars. 3. Simulated wood adorned the bodysides of the Torino Squire station wagon. The mid-sized Torino had a 14-model lineup and proved highly popular, helping Ford beat Chevrolet in the annual sales race. 4. This Torino 500 wears a "formal" roof, but hardtop coupes were also available in a SportsRoof fastback style.

4

1. Ford Motor Company issued this "family reunion" photo to mark the 50th anniversary of the Lincoln nameplate. In the foreground is a 1971 Continental four-door sedan. **2.** Lincoln's Continental Mark III personal coupe was a lot smaller than the regular Continental, with a wheelbase almost 10 inches shorter. However, the Mark III cost considerably more. **3.** Apollo 15 astronauts (from left) Alfred Worden, David R. Scott, and James Irwin encountered a hail of confetti as they rode down lower Broadway in New York City on August 24, 1971—in an open Continental. The trio received the New York City Gold Medal. **4.** The 100,000th Lincoln "Mark," a redesigned '72 Mark IV, left the assembly line in 1971. **5.** Except for a slight grille revision, the Continental coupe looked the same as in 1970.

1

2

3

4

5

1

2

3

Markedly bigger than before, the Mercury Cougar adopted a bulkier, more formal appearance, significantly different from the original design—and further removed from Mustang. **1-2.** In addition to chrome rocker panels and special wheel covers, the Cougar XR-7 got a half-vinyl roof. Inside, its high-back bucket seats had leather seating surfaces. A convertible XR-7 also was available, but sold far fewer copies than the hardtop. A 240-bhp, 351-cid V-8 was standard, but the top choice was a 429-cid V-8 that cranked out 370 horses. Performance options were starting to fade, and the Cougar Eliminator was, well, eliminated. **3.** Stylists extended the hardtop's quarter panels above the trunklid and enclosed the taillights in the rear bumper.

1

2

3

4

5

6

1. Full-size Mercury models came with a new look for 1971.
Topping the big Merc line, with a price in the $5000 neigh-
borhood, was this Marquis Brougham, offered in three body
styles, including this two-door hardtop. **2.** The base-model
Marquis came in four body styles: four-door hardtop
(shown), two-door hardtop, four-door sedan, and station
wagon with a choice of two or three rows of seats. **3.** Marquis
Brougham hardtop sedans sold only half as well as the equivalent plainer, pillared four-door sedans. **4.** Mercury's
Monterey series delivered the presumed benefits of a full-
size model at a price a good $600 lower than that of the
Marquis. The Monterey came in hardtop coupe, hardtop
sedan, pillared four-door sedan, and wagon variants. Better-
trimmed Monterey Customs served as a half-step up toward
Marquis territory. **5.** Options like a vinyl roof and fender
skirts gave even the basic Monterey hardtop coupe a lavish
appearance. **6.** Mercury's top-of-the-line station wagon was
the Colony Park, shown complete with roof rack and air
deflector. **7.** Montego was Mercury's mid-size series. This MX
hardtop coupe might have a 250-cid six-cylinder engine or a
302-cid V-8. **8.** Even in the Montego family, the Brougham tag
signified the most luxurious rendition. Offered in four body
styles, including a station wagon, the Montego MX
Brougham was a feeble seller. Only 1156 four-door hardtops
were built for 1971.

7

8

1

1. The name might have tempted performance-car fans, but few buyers fell for the Mercury Cyclone Spoiler. Shrinkage of the car's standard V-8 to 351 cubic inches helped account for the lack of interest; a mere 353 were made. Even the cheaper Cyclone GT sold only in modest numbers. 2. In 1972, NASCAR ace David Pearson (seen here racing at Darlington) was hired to drive the Wood Brothers' 1971 Cyclone. 3. Mercury revived the old Comet name for a new compact, which was little more than than a restyled Ford Maverick with a Montego-style nose. 4. Two-door Comets (shown here in GT trim with a big hood scoop) sold nearly twice as well as four-doors.

2

3

4

GENERAL MOTORS CORP.

The General strikes back after strike-plagued 1970, adding more than nine points in market share to claim 53.4 percent in a record Detroit year

GM begins quoting more realistic SAE net horsepower and torque figures instead of traditional gross ratings—and detuning engines to run on unleaded fuel, a response to the Clean Air Act of 1970

A complete redesign with a smooth "fuselage" theme is featured on all full-size GM cars from Chevy Impala to Cadillac Fleetwood

Buick launches a new third-generation Riviera with controversial "boattail" styling

Cadillac's Eldorado follows Riviera with a full redesign and heroic new proportions, but retains front-wheel drive; Eldo also gets a convertible at the expense of the drop-top De Ville

Chevy parries Ford's new Pinto with the all-new subcompact Vega 2300, offering two-door sedan, hatchback coupe, and "Kammback" wagon models, plus a "sedan delivery" wagon; the innovative (but ultimately flawed) aluminum-block four-cylinder engine helps Vega win *Motor Trend* "Car of the Year" honors

A full redesign makes Oldsmobile's Toronado bigger and blockier; predicting a future safety requirement is a second set of taillights, mounted at eye level just below the rear window

Pontiac gets back to compacts with the Ventura II, a Chevy Nova in Pontiac warpaint

2

1

3

4

5

6

1. Like other full-size GM models, the Buick Electra 225 earned a total redesign for 1971, featuring a smoothly curved "fuselage" shape and a massive hood. Broadened glass area made the car look even larger. All told, this new C-body made the term "big Buick" more accurate than ever before. Not only was the '71 "Deuce-and-a-quarter" the largest and heaviest model to date, but this would be as big as any Buick would get. A hardtop coupe and hardtop sedan came in base or Custom guise. Priced in the $5000 vicinity and run by a 455-cid V-8, big Buicks continued to sell well. **2.** The replacement for the Wildcat was the new Centurion, which took its name from a Fifties show car. Centurion rode the same B-body platform as the LeSabre, but came with a standard 455-cid V-8. **3.** In these pre-minivan days, Americans still needed big, boatlike station wagons. Buick again answered the call with its Estate Wagon, now on the Electra's 127-inch wheelbase and with a 315-bhp V-8. **4-6.** All Estate Wagons were fitted with a Glide-Away "clamshell" tailgate. The back window slid upward, allowing the tailgate door to open. Buick's Full-Flo ventilation system included louvers in the tailgate.

1

2

3

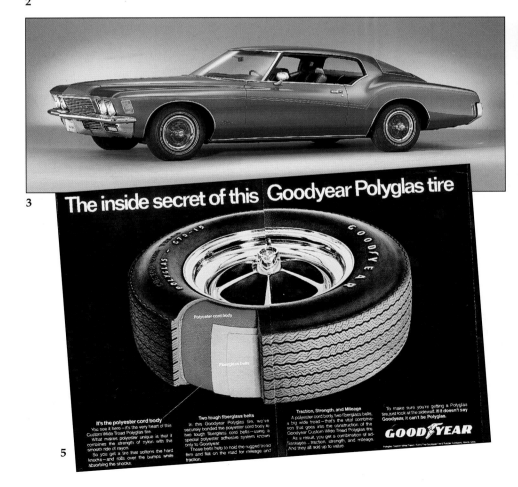

4

5

1. Buick bulked up the Riviera personal-luxury coupe for 1971, the start of the car's third generation. Wheelbase grew by three inches to 122. A sporty GS option was offered, too. 2-3. The most distinctive feature of the Riviera was its controversial "boattail" rear end. William Mitchell, GM's design chief, had ordained the first Riviera in '63 and kept encouraging daring styling for the car. 4. The flow-through ventilation system on General Motors's all-new large cars was in evidence on the Riviera, as well. 5. Manufacturers sought improvements that enhanced tire life as well as ride and handling qualities, including Goodyear's Polyglas belt construction.

1

2

1. Buick Skylark buyers could drive home a hot number in 1971: the GS Stage I hardtop. Considered more driveable than the earlier 400-cid version, the 455 Stage I was dubbed "Buick's crowning glory in street engines" by performance expert Roger Huntington. **2.** Except for a truly small car, the Buick catalog contained something to suit almost any motorist in 1971. **3.** The intermediate Skylark was the smallest Buick, shown here as a Custom four-door sedan.

3

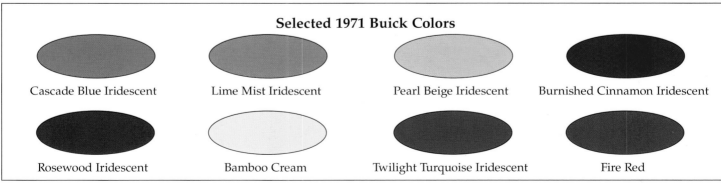

Selected 1971 Buick Colors

Cascade Blue Iridescent	Lime Mist Iridescent	Pearl Beige Iridescent	Burnished Cinnamon Iridescent
Rosewood Iridescent	Bamboo Cream	Twilight Turquoise Iridescent	Fire Red

1

2

3

4

5

1. As big as cars were in the Sixties, shoppers had some surprises in store at the dealerships as the Seventies got under way. Reworking of GM's C-body gave the Cadillac Sedan de Ville a smoother but still-larger appearance, highlighted by "fuselage" flanks and softer contours. An extensive lineup included Calais and De Ville on a 130-inch wheelbase, the Eldorado coupe on a 120-inch span, Fleetwood Sixty Special at 133 inches, and the massive Seventy-Five series on a 151.5-inch platform. The Sedan de Ville stickered for $6498, and more than 69,000 were produced. Americans still aspired to own a Cadillac whenever their fortunes rose. **2.** Cadillac's 472-cid V-8 engine, installed in all models but the Eldorado, was one of the biggest on the market, making 345 bhp. **3-5.** Interior upholstery could complement the body color of a Cadillac Coupe de Ville, which cost $234 less than a Sedan de Ville and sold nearly as well.

1

1. Known as the "Standard of the World" since its early years, Cadillac continued to stand for prestige and success. Owning a big automobile—better yet, a big luxury model—still conveyed a certain stature in the early Seventies, before two fuel crises began to change the way Americans looked at cars. Cadillac's advertising expertly got the message across to upwardly mobile strivers, as well as to those who had already "arrived." **2.** Still driven through the front wheels, the Cadillac Eldorado grew bigger and bulkier. For the first time, Cadillac offered a front-drive Eldorado convertible—in place of the soft-top De Ville. Eldorados carried a monstrous 500-cid V-8 (the biggest engine ever in a production automobile) that produced 365 bhp. The Eldo convertible sold for $7751 to start.

2

1

2

3

4

Chevrolet Caprice. Looks and rides like twice the price.

5

6

Full-size Chevrolets wore bodies in the new GM big-car mold. **1.** Impala remained the high-volume line. Shown is a Custom hardtop coupe. **2.** The same body style was offered in the plush Caprice line. **3.** Kingswood Estate led the station wagon family. **4-5.** Caprice also came as a hardtop sedan packing plenty of luxury for the money. **6.** Biscaynes were price-leaders. A six-cylinder sedan started at $3096.

1.

2.

3.

1. Malibu was the upscale edition of the mid-sized Chevelle line. Wheelbases were 112 inches for two-door cars, 116 for four-doors and wagons. Engines ranged from a 250-cid six to a 454-cube V-8. 2. Allstate Insurance ads promised rate cuts when the auto industry started producing 5-mph bumpers. Readers were urged to send in a coupon in support of this standard. 3. A midyear option for V-8 Chevelles, the "Heavy Chevy" cost less than a Super Sport. 4. A scant dozen Corvettes came with the LS6 big-block mill and ZR2 suspension combo.

4.

1. In its second season on the market, Chevrolet's Monte Carlo "personal" hardtop, kin to the Pontiac Grand Prix, gained a fresh grille and raised hood ornament. This would be the final outing for the Monte Carlo SS454, of which 1919 were produced. The standard engine was a 245-bhp, 350-cid V-8. 2. Ads for the Nova coupe promised a "change in attitude" for the buyer. Four-cylinder and big-block models were gone, giving buyers the choice of a 250-cid six, or 307- and 350-cid V-8s. 3. Strong sellers in the early Seventies, Novas came in just two body styles: coupe (shown) and four-door sedan. Chevrolet promoted the little-changed Nova as "America's not-too-small, not-too-big car." Many coupes were ordered with the smaller of the two available V-8s. 4. With the 270-bhp, 350-cid V-8 engine included in the SS package, a Nova could be transformed from tame family carrier to relatively fast-moving machine. The Super Sport package cost just $328. It included a sport suspension with E70×14 tires, dummy hood louvers, and black body accents. 5. Chevrolet added the "Rally Nova" coupe option at mid-season.

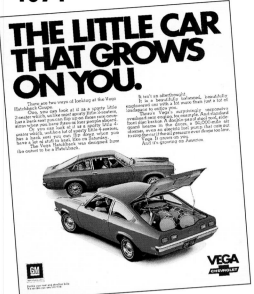

1-2. Billed as "The Little Car That Grows on You," the new subcompact Vega quickly won honors as *Motor Trend* Car of the Year. Despite great early interest, popularity of Chevrolet's rival to the new Ford Pinto soon waned, due in part to well-publicized flaws, including serious body rusting, engine oil leaks, and cylinder-head warpage. **3.** A Camaro-like front end decorated the Vega hatchback coupe, the best-selling of the four body styles. Heavily promoted and expensively designed, the Vega was built in a special factory. An all-new, all-aluminum alloy four-cylinder engine made either 90 or 110 horsepower. Vegas could get a new, short-lived Torque Drive semi-automatic transmission, with a torque converter that replaced the clutch. **4.** The highest-priced Vega in 1971 was the Kammback wagon that stickered for $2328. **5.** Vega sedans looked a bit less dashing than the hatchback, but they also cost less, starting at $2090. At 97 inches, the Vega's wheelbase was the shortest of any Chevrolet. **6.** Vega was available as a wagon-based sedan delivery to attract commercial users who might like the frugal engine. **7.** Chevrolet announced the name of its new subcompact—Vega 2300—by having a helicopter tow a banner over Detroit's skyline in 1970. Vega came from the name of one of the brightest stars in the sky; 2300 indicated engine size in cubic centimeters.

1

2

3

1. Oldsmobile marketed three convertibles in 1971, including this mid-sized Cutlass Supreme, which listed for $3507. Other ragtops included the the performance-focused 4-4-2 intermediate and the full-sized Delta 88 Royale. Mid-size coupes and convertibles had a 112-inch wheelbase; sedans rode a 116-inch span. **2.** "S" was the step-up Cutlass model, offered as a pillared sport coupe or Holiday hardtop coupe. A six-cylinder engine was available, but rarely ordered. **3.** The Vista Cruiser (foreground) was the most popular Oldsmobile station wagon, with more than 26,000 produced in 1971. Its 121-inch wheelbase was five inches longer than that of the Cutlass wagon (background). **4.** Not many customers gravitated toward the Oldsmobile F-85 four-door Town sedan, despite its compelling price. Only 4419 went on sale this season. Engine choices ran up to a 340-bhp 455-cube V-8. **5.** In the full-size range, the Royale topped the Delta 88 line, which used a 124-inch wheelbase. The Holiday hardtop coupe sold for $4549. Base and Custom Delta 88s were also cataloged.

4

5

1-2. Oldsmobile had a simple, but highly effective, word to describe the Ninety-Eight hardtops in these magazine ads: "beautiful." The redesigning of GM's C-body made this Ninety-Eight the biggest Olds ever, with its 127-inch wheelbase. Hardtop coupes and sedans came in two states of trim. The Luxury models were more popular, despite their higher prices. **3.** The 455-cid V-8 engine in a Ninety-Eight hardtop coupe delivered 320 bhp. Big-block engines would be needed a while longer to move these 4400-pound cars, but performance was starting to fade. **4-5.** The Custom Cruiser was Oldsmobile's first full-sized station wagon since 1964. It could be equipped with two or three bench seats. **6-7.** Like many other GM models, the Toronado hardtop coupe got a full-bore restyle for 1971, making it bigger and blockier than ever. At $5457, it was the most expensive Olds around. Built on a new 123-inch wheelbase, the front-drive Toronado now oozed opulence rather than sportiness.

1

2

3

4

5

1. Grand Ville was Pontiac's new top model for 1971, edging past the Bonneville in plushness. The Grand Ville convertible stickered for $4706, and only 1789 were produced. The two- and four-door hardtops in the series sold considerably better. All Grand Villes were equipped with a 455-cid V-8 engine that produced 325 horsepower. 2. Like other GM models, the full-size Pontiacs coming off the assembly lines were bigger than before. The division expanded production and testing facilities in '71. 3. Pontiac promoted its 15 millionth car—a black Grand Ville hardtop sedan produced in July—by photographing it in the "cold room," where carburetor and heater tests were performed with the thermometer hovering near zero. 4. Catalinas trailed Bonnevilles and Grand Villes in dimensions, but not by much. The priciest Catalinas were the Broughams, sold in a hardtop sedan (shown), hardtop coupe, and four-door sedan styles. 5. In base trim, the Catalina hardtop proved to be a good seller: 46,257 were built. Catalinas could have a 350-, 400-, or 455-cid V-8 engine.

1

2

'71 Firebird

3

4

5

6

7

8

1. Pontiac's Firebird Trans Am continued to dominate the performace end of the spectrum, though its 455-cid V-8 engine dipped to 335 bhp. 2. A 455-cube V-8 could be installed in the Firebird Formula coupe, which looked the part of a performance machine with its huge hood scoops. 3. Buyers of the basic Firebird coupe could choose either a 250-cid inline six or, as in this car, a 350 V-8 for power. 4-7. Firebirds roll off the assembly line at Norwood, Ohio: (4) A body is taken from a conveyor line and positioned on the chassis; (5) the front end is fitted with a rubber like Endura bumper; (6) a car in need of paint repair goes through a drying oven; and (7) a Trans Am heads toward the final assembly area. Firebirds were also built in Van Nuys, California. 8. The standard V-8 in a Firebird Formula 400 coupe (shown) was rated at 300 bhp. The same mill was available at extra cost in the luxury-oriented Esprit model. 9-10. A basic Grand Prix Model J two-door hardtop started at $4557, with standard 400-cid V-8 or optional 455. Grand Prix adopted single headlamps this year, mounted in square housings. An automatic transmission became standard during the 1971 model year, so only a handful had manual shift. An SJ option was available for the Grand Prix, as was a limited-edition Hurst SSJ with a sunroof and gold-tone sports wheels.

9

10

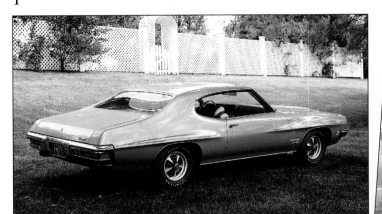

1

3

2

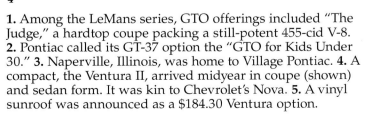

4

1. Among the LeMans series, GTO offerings included "The Judge," a hardtop coupe packing a still-potent 455-cid V-8. **2.** Pontiac called its GT-37 option the "GTO for Kids Under 30." **3.** Naperville, Illinois, was home to Village Pontiac. **4.** A compact, the Ventura II, arrived midyear in coupe (shown) and sedan form. It was kin to Chevrolet's Nova. **5.** A vinyl sunroof was announced as a $184.30 Ventura option.

5

IMPORTS

BMW's swank 2800 sedan becomes the Bavaria, offering more features for less money

Buick dealers begin selling larger new Opel "1900" models from GM's German subsidiary; their 1.9-liter engine becomes a new option for the "mini-Corvette" Opel GT coupe

More looming federal regulations prompt Citroën of France to end U.S. sale of the futuristic ID/DS sedan

Italy's Fiat has Europe's Car of the Year in its front-drive 128, a two-door sedan that arrives Stateside in summertime

Jaguar's sexy six-cylinder E-Type sports car gives way to a restyled Series III coupe and roadster with V-12 power

Mercedes-Benz starts a new era with a new two-seat SL, offering V-8 power for the first time

Rover of England abandons the U.S. market after continuing slow sales; it won't try again until 1980

Saab hopes its lucky number is 99, the designation of a larger front-drive sedan new to America this year

Subaru hitches its star to the FF-1 Star, a larger but more conventional sedan with front drive; despite its air-cooled flat-four, ads proclaim "The Subaru is not a Japanese Beetle"

Toyota joins the mini-ponycar ranks with the Celica, and adds a hardtop companion for its Corona sedan

VW's Beetle gains a big-nose Super Beetle version; also new is the 411, the biggest Vee-Dub yet produced

1. A 192-bhp inline six-cylinder engine with twin Zenith carburetors powered the BMW 2800 CS coupe, which seated four. 2. Baur did the bodywork for this BMW 1600 cabriolet (convertible). Marketed as a two-door sedan, cabriolet, and Touring hatchback, the 1600 series was facelifted during the 1971 model year. The Touring was new—slightly lower and shorter, with a concave hatchback. 3. Datsun's 240Z quickly established legions of diehard fans for the Japanese-built sports car. Priced at $3596, the coupe used a 2.4-liter six-cylinder engine that made 151 bhp. 4. The French-built Citroën DS was finally nearing the end of its long run in the U.S. market. Stunningly futuristic when introduced in the mid-Fifties, the DS21 came in four editions, plus a less-costly D Special with a smaller engine. 5. Officially called the 365 GTS/4, the Ferrari Daytona convertible was propelled by a 4.4-liter V-12 engine of 352 bhp. 6. A conventional Mercedes-Benz 250 sedan (top) is pictured with the Daimler-Benz ESV13 (Experimental Safety Vehicle).

1

2

3

4

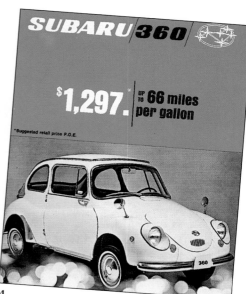

5

1. Saab continued to sell the 96 sedan (shown) and wagon with V-4 engine, but a new upscale 99 series headed for the U.S. market. 2. Opel took the engine from its GT sports car and dropped it into the new 1900 series to create the Rallye coupe, with foglights, striping, and a stiffer suspension than its mates. 3. By 1971, the Subaru 360 was about to depart from the U.S. market, replaced by a more conventional FF-1 Star with front-wheel drive. 4. Subaru promoted the 360's price ($1297) and frugality (66 mpg). The tiny car had a two-cylinder, air-cooled, two-stroke engine mounted in the rear. Subaru sold 1675 cars in the U.S. in '71. 5. Toyota launched the Celica in mid-1971. Shown in ST trim, the stylish coupe had an appealing dashboard and sports-style steering wheel. 6. Toyota's Corolla now came in two versions: budget-priced 1200 series and a new 1600 with a larger engine.

6

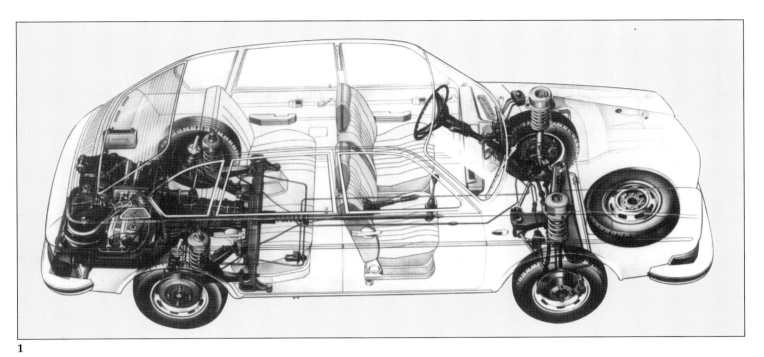

1

2

3

1. Volkswagen's biggest-ever model was the new 411 four-door sedan. The rear-mounted 1.7-liter engine produced 85 horsepower. 2. The 411 sedan also came in this two-door style. Each body style was priced at $2999. Sales proved disappointing, though. 3. On the U.S. market for more than two decades now, Beetles continued to attract a loyal and enthusiastic following—though demand had begun to soften somewhat in the early Seventies. Nevertheless, there was still plenty of call for the "Bug" to keep the German assembly lines busy. A new Super Beetle debuted in 1971, equipped with a coil-spring front suspension and a prominent nose. Purists decried the altered shape, preferring the regular model. The flat-four engine grew in size and strength, now developing 60 bhp.

Domestic auto sales posted a gain for the second straight year, with 9,326,776 cars sold. The year also saw production of the 250 millionth American automobile. Never mind that automotive critic Ronald Buel published a book called *Dead End*—Detroit was pretty darned confident.

Chrysler Corporation continued to resist the subcompact idea. The oversight may have been excusable, for even that august journal of American business, *The Wall Street Journal,* completely ignored buyers of subcompacts in an ad trumpeting demographic profiles of its readers.

Japan's Toyo Kogyo, the parent company of Mazda, achieved significant refinement of Wankel rotary-piston-engine technology, which Toyo had acquired years before from Germany's NSU. GM hinted at offering a Wankel-powered Vega by 1975.

Racing fans cheered on Mark Donohue, who ran a Sunoco McLaren-Offenhauser to victory at the Indianapolis 500. The event's pace car was a 300-net-horsepower Hurst/Olds. On the stock-car circuit, Richard Petty repeated as NASCAR Winston Cup champion.

The newest inductee into the Automotive Hall of Fame was Roy Chapin, founder of the Hudson Motor Car Company.

The year's most significant news stories were international: President Nixon—heretofore a dedicated anti-Communist—paid an unprecedented eight-day visit to Red China. At the Summer Olympics in Munich, Germany, 11 Israeli athletes were seized and murdered by eight Arab terrorists.

It was a presidential election year, and at a rally in Laurel, Maryland, Democratic candidate George Wallace, governor of Alabama, was shot and seriously wounded by Arthur Bremer. In November, President Nixon won re-election by trouncing

1972

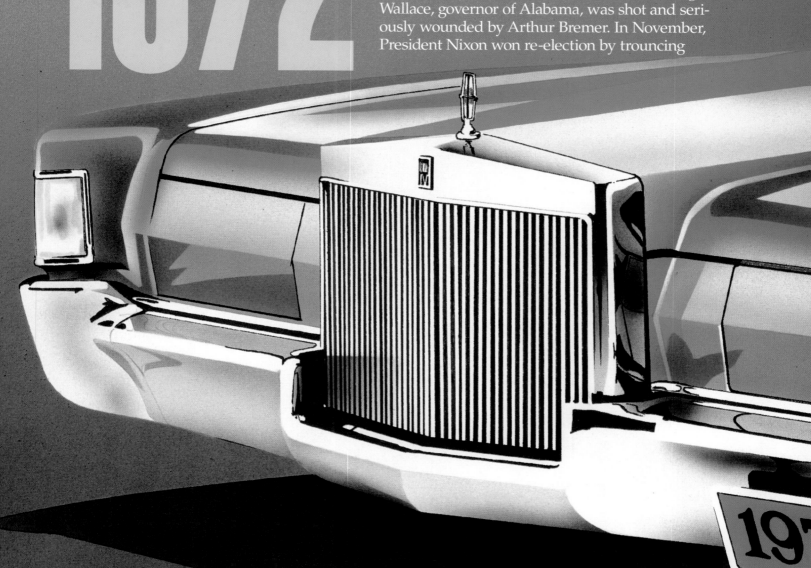

Senator George McGovern, despite the beginnings of public unease about an apparently politically motivated June burglary of Democratic headquarters at a Washington office-and-apartment building called the Watergate.

Movie box offices were dominated by *The Getaway* (in which Steve McQueen uses a pump shotgun to annihilate a police cruiser), *Deliverance, The Candidate, Frenzy, Cabaret,* and a majestic crime epic, *The Godfather.*

All in the Family was a television sensation; hardly less popular were *Gunsmoke, Sanford and Son, Mannix, Ironside, Medical Center,* and *The Partridge Family.*

The best-selling pop tune of 1972 was Roberta Flack's "The First Time Ever I Saw Your Face," while the most intriguing was Don McLean's historical outline of rock 'n' roll, "American Pie." Other big singles were Al Green's "Let's Stay Together," Neil Young's "Heart of Gold," and Michael Jackson's ode to a rodent, "Ben."

U.S. runner Frank Shorter won the Olympic marathon. The real golden boy of American Olympians was swimmer Mark Spitz, who claimed seven top awards.

Super Bowl VI went to the Dallas Cowboys, who battered the Miami Dolphins, 24-3. In the World Series, the Oakland A's squeaked by the Cincinnati Reds, four games to three.

AMC

Accountants again reach for the black ink as AMC earns $30.2 million on record sales of $1.4 billion

AMC's market share inches up to 3.35 percent of the U.S. industry on calendar-year production of more than 279,000 cars

Helping its cause, AMC introduces the Buyer Protection Plan, offering free parts replacement and other owner benefits over the basic 12-month/12,000-mile warranty

The compact Hornet loses its sporty SC/360 model; all AMC products receive only minor cosmetic and mechanical updates

Hornet goes *haute couture*, as Sportabout wagons offer a new trim option created with famed fashion designer Aldo Gucci

1. In 1972, underfunded American Motors, a small-car specialist, persisted in its attempt to match the Big Three, segment for segment, with the full-sized Ambassador and mid-sized Matador. 2. This Ambassador Brougham hardtop coupe ran with the optional 401-cid V-8 rated at 225 bhp. 3. With the budget DPL dropped from the line, the SST four-door sedan was the cheapest Ambassador at $3537. 4. An Ambassador Brougham wagon is put through its paces.

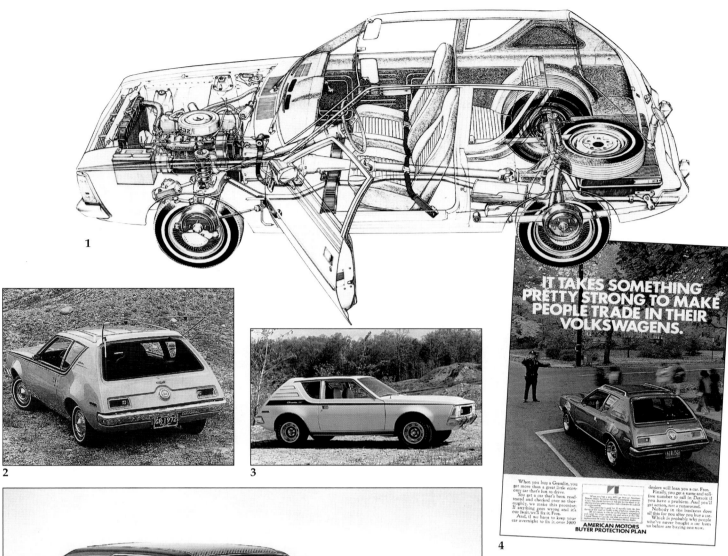

1

2

3

4

5

1-2, 4. Besides offering appealingly economical transportation, the Gremlin made clever use of its interior space. The car was backed by AMC's 12/12 Buyer Protection Plan. **3.** The "X" package was the most popular of numerous Gremlin options offered throughout the Seventies. This was primarily tape stripes and wider tires on slotted wheels, but they added a sporty touch. **5-8.** Aldo Gucci personalized a one-of-a-kind Hornet Sportabout, adding designer upholstery, Gucci bags, and fold-down snack trays.

6

7

8

1

2

3

4

1. The '72 "Gucci" Hornet Sportabout was a real-world offshoot of the one-off Sportabout customized by Aldo Gucci—he of overpriced accessories fame. Considerably less flashy than its inspiration, the Gucci Hornet had pleasing custom vinyl upholstery (red, green, and buff) and a nifty Gucci badge. Only 2584 of the special models were produced this year. **2.** The D/L, like all Sportabouts, had a single-piece hatch. Every Hornet picked up the "SST" designation for the model year. **3.** A 360-cid, 175-horse V-8 was optional; the standard Hornet eight was a 304 rated at 150 bhp. **4.** The Javelin AMX was a strong performer with its top engine, a 225-horse 401 V-8. **5.** A cross-hatch grille was new for the "standard" Javelin.

5

1

2

3

1-3. Nearly 55,000 Matadors were built during the 1972 model year; sober good looks and a range of inline sixes and V-8s encouraged buyers. Seen here, in sequence, are a four-door sedan, hardtop coupe, and wagon. Matador prices ranged between $2784 and $3239. **4.** Police departments liked the Matador's size and relative economy. **5.** Mark Donohue's racing Matador ran with a non-standard 366 V-8.

4

5

CHRYSLER
CORPORATION

Plymouth drops to fourth place in production, behind Oldsmobile

Gran Fury Coupe and Gran Sedan replace Sport Fury as the top of the full-size Plymouth lineup

Plymouth's "little car that can" gets extra sales chirp as a four-door wagon joins the Cricket sedan

A heavy restyling of the corporate "fuselage" body touches all big-car lines, from Plymouth Fury to Imperial LeBaron

Chrysler offers solid-state ignition systems

A 400-cid V-8 replaces the 383

The New Yorker Brougham joins the Chrysler lineup; the 300 disappears

Dodge deletes the Charger R/T and Super Bee performance models; a tamer Rallye version becomes the new "hot" Charger

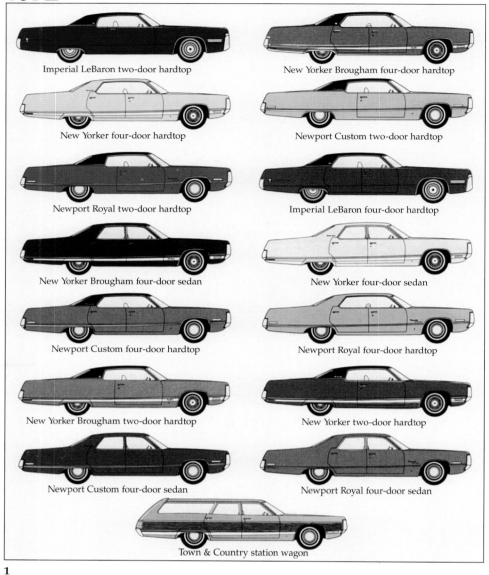

Imperial LeBaron two-door hardtop

New Yorker Brougham four-door hardtop

New Yorker four-door hardtop

Newport Custom two-door hardtop

Newport Royal two-door hardtop

Imperial LeBaron four-door hardtop

New Yorker Brougham four-door sedan

New Yorker four-door sedan

Newport Custom four-door hardtop

Newport Royal four-door hardtop

New Yorker Brougham two-door hardtop

New Yorker two-door hardtop

Newport Custom four-door sedan

Newport Royal four-door sedan

Town & Country station wagon

1

2

1. "A commitment to quality" was the corporate slogan for the 1972 line of Chrysler cars. Despite increasing public interest in small cars—even imports— Chrysler stayed true to its course of big, imposing automobiles. The catalog from which this illustration is taken boasts that Chrysler is "coming through with luxury that lasts," adding that a luxury car "should give you more room than lesser cars." Catalog pages devoted to Newport note that "Big is a byword for '72." 2. This ad carries the tag line "Coming through with the kind of car America wants," and features Chrysler spokesman Arthur Godfrey, who touts Chrysler's engineering and manufacturing quality.

1

2

3

4

1-2. All '72 New Yorkers came standard with Chrysler's 440-cid V-8, rated now at 225 *net* horsepower rather than the 335/370 gross figure cited for '71. Though the drop was due more to the new measuring system than any real loss of power, it was an omen of things to come. Regardless, more than 50,000 New Yorkers and New Yorker Broughams were sold this year. The top model, the Brougham hardtop sedan, was priced at $5350. **3-4.** Newport was Chrysler's entry-level model, with prices ranging from $4051 to $4435. Newport four-doors handily outsold coupes this year, approximately 97,000 to 33,000. This would be the final year for the 360-cid, 175-horse V-8 that was the base Newport engine.

1

2

3

4

5

1. The Dodge Charger was by now metamorphosing from a gritty performance machine into a sporty luxury car that happened to go pretty fast. But the R/T and Super Bee performance models were deleted. The Special Edition (S.E.) coupe cost a hefty $3249. 2. By contrast, the base coupe started at $2652. 3. The flashy Rallye package with a 330-horse 440 Magnum V-8 was more in keeping with the Charger's previous character. 4. Charger brochures hinted at luxury. 5. Challenger, never a real rival to Ford's Mustang, moved about 26,600 units. A 240-bhp 340 V-8 was the top engine.

1

2

3

4

5

1. Coronet was Dodge's mid-priced car, ranging from $2721 for the base four-door sedan to $3683 for the top Crestwood wagon. **2-3.** Concern about gas mileage and alternate fuels prompted this experimental gas-turbine Coronet. Chrysler had touted turbine-engine technology in the Sixties; now, the idea was funded by the EPA. **4.** The fastback Demon added some sportiness to the Dart lineup. **5.** The reliable Dart was Dodge's bread-and-butter car; the Swinger coupe alone accounted for nearly 120,000 sales.

1

2

1-3. For the time being, the big Polara continued to prosper, finding nearly 109,000 buyers for its full range of sedans, coupes, and wagons. Prices began at $3618 for a base four-door sedan and progressed upward to $4371 for the top three-seat Custom wagon. A small-block 318-cid V-8 rated at 150 horsepower was the base Polara engine; top choice was a 285-bhp 440. None of the Dodge inline sixes were available with a Polara. **4.** A sampling of Dodge station wagons suggests the choices available to families on the go. The Coronet, of course, was Dodge's entry-level wagon, and rode the standard 118-inch wheelbase. Polara and the uplevel Monaco wagons had 122-inch wheelbases, and offered additional amenities and considerably more interior room. Combined Monaco, Polara, and Coronet wagon sales were unarguably niche-level: about 31,750.

3

Monaco station wagon

Coronet Crestwood station wagon

Polara Custom station wagon

Coronet Custom station wagon

Polara station wagon

Coronet station wagon

4

1

1972 CHRYSLER *IMPERIAL*

2

3

1. Monaco was the top-level Dodge in 1972. Hidden headlights and a full vinyl roof highlight this $4153 hardtop coupe. 2-3. Imperial entered its eighteenth model year as a separate marque, carrying on a hopeless battle against Cadillac and Lincoln; the Imperial coupe and sedan—both dubbed "LeBaron"—found just 9100 buyers. Note the chic "loop" bumper.

1

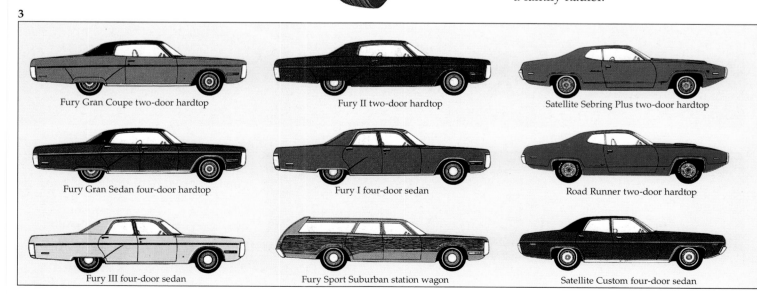

2

3

1-2. Barracuda dropped its ragtop, and sold only about 20,000 units this year. **3.** Some of the '72 Plymouths; note the British-made Cricket, a "captive import." **4-6.** The biggest '72 Plymouth was the Fury, which could be fitted with a 318-, 340-, 400-, or 440-cid V-8, with up to 285 horsepower. With its smartly sculpted bodysides and distinctive dual grille, Fury was a do-it-all full-sized car, marketed in some iterations as a luxury cruiser and in others as a big sportster. **7.** The Satellite Sebring combined sportiness with creature comforts. **8.** The Satellite Custom was a family hauler.

Fury Gran Coupe two-door hardtop

Fury II two-door hardtop

Satellite Sebring Plus two-door hardtop

Fury Gran Sedan four-door hardtop

Fury I four-door sedan

Road Runner two-door hardtop

Fury III four-door sedan

Fury Sport Suburban station wagon

Satellite Custom four-door sedan

4

5

6

8

7

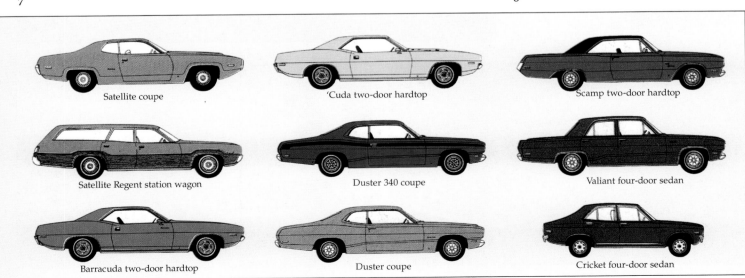

Satellite coupe

'Cuda two-door hardtop

Scamp two-door hardtop

Satellite Regent station wagon

Duster 340 coupe

Valiant four-door sedan

Barracuda two-door hardtop

Duster coupe

Cricket four-door sedan

103

1-2. Road Runner, a separate model as late as 1970, was by now a trim level of the Satellite. Top power output, 240 bhp, was courtesy of a 340-cid V-8. Striping and other cosmetics were presumed by Plymouth to suffice as replacements for what had been. Just 7628 were produced for the year.
3. The Duster was Valiant's sporting iteration—and a credible one at that, with up to 240 bhp available in the Duster 340. **4.** The workaday Valiant sedan found nearly 53,000 buyers.
5. The Valiant Scamp did nearly as well, with 49,000 sold.

FORD
MOTOR CO.

Ford adds three-door Pinto wagons in April, including a woody-look Squire version

Dearborn's venerable 302 V-8 becomes optional for the compact Ford Maverick and Mercury Comet; Maverick also adds a plush new Luxury Decor Option (LDO)

Ford Mustangs get colorful "Sprint" exterior trim packages at midyear

The mid-size Ford Torino and Mercury Montego are all-new for '72 and near full-size; convertibles vanish, while other two-doors ride a shorter wheelbase than four-doors per GM practice

Torino loses its hot Cobra, while Merc's companion Cyclone gives way to a single Montego GT fastback

Ford's Thunderbird is redesigned and enlarged; the slow-selling sedan and blind-quarter hardtop are dropped

Lincoln-Mercury's Capri becomes a more serious sporty coupe, thanks to a new 2.6-liter V-6 option

Lincoln introduces a redesigned Continental Mark IV built on the same platform as the new T-Bird

All these new models help Dearborn's market share recover to 28.6 percent, up 1.2 points

1

2

3

1. The truck-based Bronco wagon picked up standard bucket seats for 1972. The Sport edition seen here runs with Ford's marvelous, small-block 302 V-8. A midyear addition was a deluxe "Ranger" option, which included special paint with white accents and a swingaway outside spare tire. **2.** The LTD Country Squire wagon rode a 121-inch wheelbase and had more than 96 cubic feet of cargo space. A lockable storage compartment in the left quarter panel was an intriguing option. Standard powerplant was a 351-cid V-8 rated at 153 bhp. Six or eight-passenger seating was available. **3.** LTD prices ranged from $3882 to $4430.

1

2

3

1-2. Nearly 255,000 Mavericks were sold this year—less than half the figure for debut-year 1970, but enough to qualify Maverick as a notable Ford success. Available engines encompassed a trio of inline sixes (82, 91, and 98 horsepower) and a 143-horse 302 V-8. The four-door sedan model seen in these photos was described by Ford as "a true family car." **3.** The Grabber was the "performance" Maverick, and was distinguished from standard models mainly by its tape stripes and hood scoops. At just $2309, the Grabber wasn't a bad deal, costing some $400 less than a base Mustang. **4.** Though not the sexiest horse in the corral, the base Mustang proved the most popular with over 57,000 sales. **5.** Mustang's big-block V-8s were history; trim options, like the lively Sprint package on this SportsRoof, took up the slack.

4

5

1

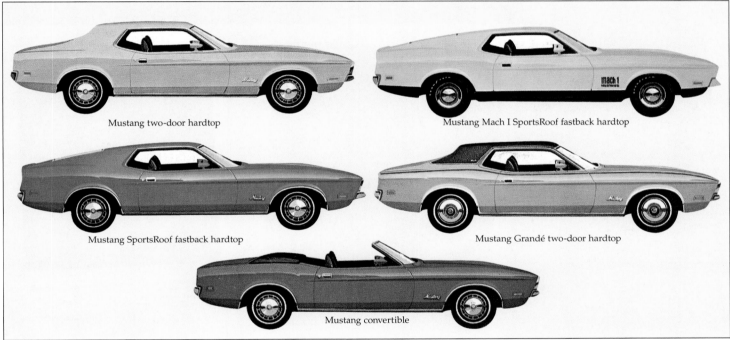

Mustang two-door hardtop

Mustang Mach I SportsRoof fastback hardtop

Mustang SportsRoof fastback hardtop

Mustang Grandé two-door hardtop

Mustang convertible

2

3

1. The USA emblem and body colors of the Mustang Sprint package were visual reminders of an Olympic year. Although the general public could purchase Sprint Mustangs in hardtop or fastback body styles only, Ford built 50 Sprint ragtops for the 1972 Cherry Day Parade held in Washington, D.C. **2.** Mustang's catalog illustrated the entire line for 1972. Prices ranged from $2729 for the base hardtop to $3053 for the Mach I **3.** Base-priced at just $1960, Pinto found nearly 480,000 buyers.

1

2

3

4

1-2. Torino was all-new for 1972. In two-door guise, as here, the car rode a 114-inch wheelbase; four-door wheelbase was 118 inches. Although the smallest available engine was a 250-cid, 95-bhp inline six, shoppers found that a V-8 was a more satisfying choice; five were available for Torino, ranging from 302 to 429 cubic inches. The red car is Torino's GT Sport variant. 3-5. An electronically controlled suspension gave the neo-Classic Thunderbird a composed ride.

5

1

2

1. Sales rose smartly for the Continental, despite a hefty sticker. Riding a 127-inch wheelbase, the $7068 hardtop coupe carried a 460-cid V-8 that developed 224 horsepower. 2. More than 36,500 Continental four-door sedans went to dealerships in 1972, priced at $7302. 3-4. New for 1972, the Continental Mark IV hardtop coupe was less agile than its predecessor, with less passenger space and a greater thirst for fuel. Even at $8640, it sold far better than the Mark III.

3

4

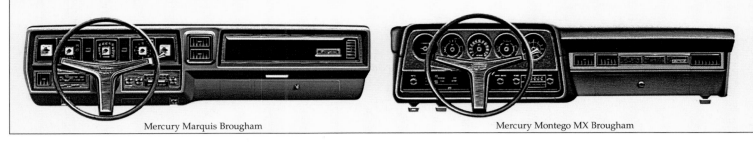

Mercury Marquis Brougham   Mercury Montego MX Brougham

1

2

3

1. Marketed by Lincoln-Mercury dealers, the European-built Capri coupe came in three series: 1600, 2000, and 2600—the latter with a new German-made V-6 engine that made 107 horsepower. Dual exhaust pipes helped identify the 2600, which sold for $2821. **2.** The compact Comet was the only other smaller-size car at L-M dealerships. This coupe has the GT option. **3.** A Custom decor option became available for four-door Comets at midyear. **4.** In basic trim, a fastback two-door Comet stickered for $2342 and handily outsold the four-door.

4

Mercury Cougar XR-7

Mercury Comet

1. Sport-minded mid-size fans could get a Cougar in base or XR-7 form, as a coupe or convertible. 2. A Monterey wagon could have two or three seats. 3. Strong sales of the Marquis Brougham suggested that shoppers favored top-of-the-line models. 4. Plenty of customers went all the way to a posh Colony Park wagon. 5. A 351-cid V-8 was standard in the Monterey Custom hardtop.

1

2

1. Top mid-sized Mercury wagon was the Montego MX Villager, with a $3438 sticker. **2.** The Montego MX Brougham four-door sedan listed for $3127. **3.** Related to the Ford Torino, Mercury's Montego enjoyed fair sales. Pictured is an MX hardtop coupe. **4.** Lincoln-Mercury dealers also could sell a European sports car: the DeTomaso Pantera coupe. Styled by Tom Tjaarda at the Ghia studios in Italy, the mid-engined machine carried a 351-cid V-8 that made an impressive 266 horsepower.

3

4

GENERAL
MOTORS CORP.

It's a largely stand-pat year for all divisions as "The General's" U.S. market share slips to 51.8 percent

However, GM's worldwide calendar-year output exceeds 7.7 million vehicles for the second straight year

Chevrolet alone now accounts for more than 3 million units of GM's world production tally; for the model-year, Chevy ends Ford's two-year reign as "USA-1" in cars

Richard C. Gerstenberg replaces James M. Roche as GM chairman on January 1st. Edward N. Cole remains company president

GM's "split-wheelbase" intermediate lines are in the final year of their basic 1968 design

With convertible sales waning, some GM models offer optional sliding cloth sunroofs for a semblance of "wind in the hair" fun

Oldsmobile observes its 75th anniversary while demoting the 4-4-2 to option status a sign of the times, but there's a hot new limited-edition Hurst/Olds, and it's named pace car for the 1972 Indianapolis 500

1

2

3

4

5

1. Biggest of the Buicks—and a strong seller—was the Electra 225, shown in posh Limited trim. Full-size models had been restyled in '71. **2.** Buick's Centurion rode a 124-inch wheelbase. Only 2396 Centurion convertibles were built, with a $4616 sticker. **3.** Centurions held Buick's 455-cid V-8, yielding 225 or 250 horsepower. **4.** Little-changed this season, the family-focused LeSabre came in base or Custom form (shown), packing a 350- or 455-cid V-8. **5.** Like other full-size Buicks in '72, the 5000-pound Estate Wagon needed to make plenty of stops at the gas pump.

113

1

2

1-2. A dramatic "boattail" rear end again made Buick's Riviera easy to spot on the street. Riviera was the most costly Buick, and a GS option could be ordered for $200. **3.** "Extraordinary" was Buick's description of the personal-luxury Riviera, slightly restyled for '72. **4.** This Buick GS hardtop with "Stage I" tuned engine had the new Sun Coupe option—a sliding vinyl sunroof. **5-6.** This year's Skylarks, pictured in Custom trim, would be the last of the design that had arrived in '68.

Extraordinary car.

We purposely designed an extraordinary car for people who don't want a car like everybody else's.

The 1972 Buick Riviera. With extraordinary features. Extraordinary comfort. Like AccuDrive, our unique suspension system. It has forward steering stability that helps you ride smoothly

and securely even when the road is rugged or crosswinds are heavy.

Along with the front power disc brakes a special valve in Riviera's braking system adds even more smoothness by proportioning the braking force evenly from front to rear.

To help keep the air clean, we've added an air injection reactor which burns pollutants in the engine rather than emitting them to the outside air. This also gives us

smooth engine operation.

Test drive a new Riviera soon. Compare it to your present car. In ride. In handling. In braking. In everything. We think you'll find that there isn't any comparison.

And when you get behind the wheel, be assured of this: you're not driving a copy of anything.

1972 Buick Riviera. Something to believe in.

3

4

5

6

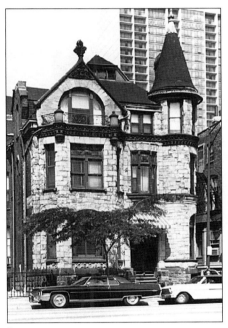

1

2

3

4

1. More than 95,000 Cadillac fans drove home a Coupe de Ville, one of the best-known model names. 2. Formal in form, the Fleetwood Sixty Special Brougham rode a unique 133-inch wheelbase. 3. The classic stance of a Cadillac coupe looked just right, parked in front of this elegant home on Chicago's LaSalle Street. (Chicago Historical Society) 4. Beneath an Eldorado hardtop's hood sat the biggest engine on the market: a 500-cid V-8, generating 235 horsepower. 5. A front-drive Eldorado convertible cost $7546.

5

Chevrolet. Building a better way to see the U.S.A.

Your new Impala. Starts you relaxing long before you get where you're going.

1. Only V-8 engines went into the Impala, which was the only full-size Chevrolet convertible in '72. Ragtop fans could drive one home for $3979. Buyers could choose from four sizes of V-8s up to 454 cubic inches. Impalas grew slightly this year, after a major redesign for 1971. 2. Chevrolet ads in '72 featured locales all over the country, building upon the "See the U.S.A." theme. This promotional piece featured an Impala Custom hardtop coupe. 3. Impala four-door sedans might not have looked glamorous, but they attracted plenty of customers—helping Chevrolet return to the top spot in annual sales, ahead of Ford. 4. About 180,000 Impala Custom hardtop coupes went to dealerships in 1972.

1

2

3

4

5

6

1. Topping the full-size station wagon line was this Kingswood Estate, with two or three seats and a 400-cid V-8 engine. **2.** Shoppers who sought all the elegance Chevrolet could offer usually wound up with a Caprice. **3.** In mid-size wagons, the Chevelle Concours Estate led the pack, which also included a Nomad and Greenbrier. **4-6.** Malibu hardtops sold far better than their base-Chevelle mates. A Maine lighthouse served as backdrop for one Malibu ad.

117

1

2

3

1. "Muscle cars" continued to attract young folks—but not for long. Close to 25,000 Chevelle hardtops came with Super Sport (SS) equipment—a $350 option. 2. Older Chevrolets can be spotted in this scene of the Lake County Courthouse in Crown Point, Indiana, shot in May 1972. 3. Chevelles were aimed at families on a budget. 4. Personal-luxury Monte Carlo coupes earned a fresh grille, which now held parking lights. A 350-cid V-8 was standard, but lots of Monte owners preferred the big-block 454.

4

1

2

3

4

1. Camaro buyers didn't always want their "ponycars" plain. More than 11,300 of the '72 models were Rally Sports (shown), and 6562 had Super Sport (SS) fittings. **2.** This '72 model would be the last Camaro SS coupe until the 1990s. **3.** Distinctive literature failed to help keep Corvette sales at prior levels. **4.** The $483 LT-1 option gave Corvette a small-block, solid-lifter 350-cid V-8, with 255 horsepower.

1

1. Compact Nova coupes outsold the sedans. Both were quite popular, with a six-cylinder engine or choice of V-8s. **2.** Best-selling sub-compact Vega was the hatchback coupe, with 262,682 going to dealers. **3.** Models in the Vega catalog included the Kammback wagon and the sedan delivery. **4.** A Vega Kammback cost $2285. Despite the Vega's mechanical woes, total sales topped 390,000.

2

OUR WAGON. **OUR TRUCK.**

"A car for all occasions."
CAR & DRIVER MAG.

"The roadability and handling of the Vegas was excellent, quick and sure."
MECHANIX ILLUSTRATED

3

4

1

2

3

4

5

1. Oldsmobile's 4-4-2 was reduced to a Cutlass appearance/handling option package in 1972. This 4-4-2 ragtop packs W-30 equipment—a $648 option that included a 300-horse, 455-cid V-8 with air induction. 2. The Cutlass Cruiser (left) was Oldsmobile's smallest wagon, while the Vista Cruiser, which rode a longer wheelbase, ranked as mid-size. 3. Suburbanites carried on their love affair with station wagons, like the Vista Cruiser. 4. Heading the mid-size line: the Cutlass Supreme two-door hardtop. This would be the last year for a Cutlass Supreme convertible. 5. Oldsmobile issued its final F-85 four-door sedan in 1972.

1

The Limited-Edition Regency.
A very special Ninety-Eight with the Tiffany touch to mark Oldsmobile's 75th Anniversary.

Today you rarely have the opportunity to buy a true limited-edition luxury car. This year provides you such an opportunity. Oldsmobile's 75th Anniversary.

To celebrate being the first American auto manufacturer to reach this milestone, Olds is building a very special luxury car in limited quantity—the Ninety-Eight Regency.

The specially-styled custom interior with its "pillow effect" and

velour upholstery is an example of its distinction and is available in black or covert.

And there are three very special Tiffany touches. The exterior is painted in Tiffany Gold, an exclusive custom metallic color created especially for this fine motor car. Even the face of the electric timepiece has been styled especially for this fine car. Even the face of the electric timepiece has been cloth styled by Tiffany's, and

bears the famous Tiffany name. Each Ninety-Eight Regency is registered at Tiffany's, and each Regency owner will receive a distinctive sterling silver key ring as a gift. If ever lost, the keys can be dropped in a mail box, and Tiffany's will return them to the owner.

Finally, underneath all the things that make the Regency extraordinary, are all the other solid values you've come to expect from Oldsmobile.

The limited-edition Ninety-Eight Regency. At your Olds dealer's now.

OLDSMOBILE NINETY-EIGHT. QUITE A SUBSTANTIAL CAR.

2   3

Some down-to-earth reasons for buying an Olds Ninety-Eight:

1 Many of the "extras" you want are standard on Ninety-Eight. Automatic transmission, for example. Power steering. And power front disc brakes. On Ninety-Eight Luxury models, six-way power front seat is standard. And power side windows.

2 The Ninety-Eight is a big car. And that's a very practical consideration if you happen to have a big family. Or if you like to take driving vacations. Or week-end trips to the lake. The Ninety-Eight turns size—not affluence alone—but comfortably, with room to stretch out. And you can pack your golf clubs, outboard motor, lunch gear and luggage into the generous 20.6 cubic-foot trunk.

3 Ninety-Eight's got a superb road car. Olds' exclusive ride system incorporates a combination of engineering advances in chassis, suspension and steering. You ne-

gotiate scrub-board roads, chuck-holes, hairpin curves and smooth American highways with ease.

4 Ninety-Eight's front bumper is exactly what the name implies, a bumper, it's built of heavy-gauge plated steel—and mounted on a new spring-and-support that flex to help absorb minor impacts, then return to position.

5 The Ninety-Eight engine is a 455-cubic-inch Rocket V-8. While it's so well-spoken you hardly know it's there, you have all the reserve you could ever want. And it uses just fine on unleaded, low-lead or regular gas.

6 Surely security is an important reason for considering an Olds Ninety-Eight. The very fact that makes you feel secure, that there's metal in the doors beside you that tough-to-ground beam. Over you the reinforced double-steel roof.

in front of you is an energy-absorbing steering column. And all around you are other GM safety features.

7 Ninety-Eight is loaded with little niceties that make traveling by auto more than just transportation. Extra-nicely-efficient sound-proofing helps keep outside noise out. The front seats are six inches of solid foam—not a thin layer of padding on ordinary-car springs. Fine fabrics and plush carpeting surround you. The outside mirror is remote-controlled. Luxury models have front and rear cigarette lighters, an antenna in the center of the rear seat, even a clock exclusively for the convenience of rear-seat passengers.

If you spend a lot of time in your car, and think you should spend that time in as much comfort and luxury as possible, consider a Ninety-Eight.

OLDSMOBILE NINETY-EIGHT. QUITE A SUBSTANTIAL CAR.

4   5

6

1. This special Ninety-Eight Regency marked Oldsmobile's 75th anniversary. 2. Added at midyear to herald the company's birthday, Regency was a variant of the Ninety-Eight Luxury sedan.
3. How much luxury could $5098 buy? Try a Ninety-Eight Luxury hardtop sedan. 4. The Ninety-Eight came in base form as well as Luxury guise. 5. Few would have called Oldsmobile's Custom Cruiser wagon anything but huge—even in 1972. Part of the Delta 88 lineup, it could have two or three seats.
6-7. Royale was the upscale rendition of the Delta 88 series. 8. Front-drive Toronados carried a special 455-cid V-8, whipping up 250 eager horses.

7

8

1

2

3

1. On a sizable 126-inch wheelbase, full-sized Grand Ville Pontiacs got new slotted taillights and a Bonneville-type grille for '72. Three body styles went on sale, including a convertible. The Grand Ville's 455-cid V-8 engine made 185 horsepower, but a 220-horse edition could be specified instead. **2.** Pontiac Catalinas wore new energy-absorbing bumpers—a portent of things to come as government regulations took hold. Hardtop coupes came in basic or Brougham form, with a $188 price differential between the two. Basic Catalinas had a standard 350-cid V-8; Broughams, a 400-cid engine. Either could get an optional 455-cid V-8. **3.** A 400-cid V-8 powered the Catalina Safari wagon—necessary to propel so much automobile. Like most large wagons, the Catalina could be equipped with either two or three seats, to hold as many as nine passengers. **4.** The Grand Ville could get this optional cloth/vinyl interior. Americans still liked to load up their automobiles with extra-cost items.

4

1

2

3

4

1. Performance-car fans continued to pay homage to the Trans Am. This example packs the 455 H.O. V-8 engine good for 300 horsepower. Only 1286 T/As were built in '72. **2.** A fiberglass hood with dual air scoops helped identify the Formula coupe, one of a four-model Firebird lineup. **3.** Formula interiors featured cloth and Morrokide vinyl upholstery. A long strike led to speculation that Firebirds might disappear. **4-5.** This limited-edition Hurst SSJ Grand Prix hardtop even sported a sunroof.

5

1

2

3

4

5

1. Twin hood scoops helped shoot air into the carb of this GTO hardtop with the 455 H.O. V-8 engine. GTO was now a $344 option for Pontiac's LeMans. 2. Fake wood trim cost an extra $154 on a LeMans wagon, which was not a big seller. 3. Pontiac interiors used cloth and Morrokide vinyl, or the vinyl alone. 4. The Luxury LeMans two-door hardtop wore a distinctive twin-cavity grille. 5. A sliding fabric sunroof was something special on a Ventura II Sprint coupe. Related to Chevy's Nova, compact Venturas debuted in March of '71. The Sprint option included a three-speed floor shift and blacked-out grille.

IMPORTS

BMW adds a more potent 2002 tii with fuel injection

Citroën's SM coupe arrives in the U.S., melding way-out French styling with twincam V-6 power from Italy's Maserati

Fiat drops its rear-engine 850 line save the cute little Spider convertible; the 128 series expands to include a four-door sedan and two-door wagon; a 128 SL fastback coupe arrives late in the year

Jaguar brings V-12 power to its respected XJ sedan

Jensen of England brings out a new Healey sports car, a modern-traditional roadster with four-cylinder Lotus/Vauxhall power

Mazda's "rotary club" expands for '72 with addition of the new Wankel-powered RX-2 coupe and sedan

The legendary Porsche 911 gets a slightly larger engine, and all models now have fuel injection

Renault adopts orthodox styling for the 12 sedan and wagon, along with sporty coupe off-shoots called 15 and 17

Saab's rare Sonnett III gains a larger engine and a neater face; midyear brings a sportier 99 two-door called EMS

Subaru 1100 models graduate to a 1300cc engine; a low-roof GL coupe joins the family

Toyota adds a new in-between subcompact two-door called Carina

VW's Beetle gets a larger rear window and an electronic in-car diagnostic system

1

2

3

4

1. Bigger than the Super 90, the Audi 100LS adopted a 1.9-liter four-cylinder engine, to replace the former 1.8-liter. Front-drive Audis came to the U.S. in 1970. 2. In addition to the mini-sized 1200 series (shown), Datsun marketed a larger PL510 and 610, as well as the popular 240Z sports car. 3-4. Far different from Hondas of the future, the little 600 coupe held a two-cylinder air-cooled engine. Note the upswept, swing-open rear quarter windows. "Every outing is an adventure," said *Road & Track* of the Honda 600.

Mazda RX-2
The car with the rotary engine.

1

2

3

4

6

5

7   8

1. Mazda tucked a Wankel rotary engine into the RX-2 coupe and sedan. 2. Opel's selection included (clockwise from front) a stylish GT mini-sports car, 1900 Rallye coupe, 1900 sedan, and 1900 wagon. 3. Buick dealers marketed the Opel 1900 Sport Coupe as well as a racier Rallye edition, with stiffer suspension. 4. Bizarrely shaped when introduced to the U.S., Subarus soon adopted a conventional look. 5. Porsche's engine grew a bit, to 2341 cc, for the basic 911T coupe. 6. Toyota's Corona Mark II hardtop replaced the Crown as its top-of-the-line model. 7-8. Introduced to the U.S. in 1967, basic Toyota Coronas came in sedan and hardtop form.

1. In 1972, total Volkswagen Beetle sales passed the mark set long before by the Model T Ford. 2. A station wagon joined the VW 411 line. 3. Still based on the Beetle, VW station wagons could seat up to nine. 4. Style leader was the Karmann-Ghia convertible, with 60 horsepower. 5-6. Super Beetles added an energy-absorbing steering wheel this year.

129

The first unraveling of the American auto industry, as well as the beginning of a long and painful rebirth, can be traced to October 6, 1973, when Egyptian and Syrian forces attacked Israel. By the time a cease-fire took effect two weeks later, Israel had reversed initial Arab gains. The Arab states, once again coming out on the short end of yet another Arab-Israeli war (the fourth), and acting under the aegis of the Organization of Petroleum Exporting Countries (OPEC), voted to halt oil exports to the United States and other pro-Israel nations.

American oil companies, eager to cash in on the crisis, raised pump prices—and consumer anxiety—as well. Motorists gathered in serpentine lines at gas stations, and were often frustrated when pumps ran dry. Speed limits were lowered in some states, and Washington even made noise about gasoline rationing.

In the midst of all this uncertainty, Datsun marketing department types came up with the "Datsun Saves" slogan, complete with a cutesy and hard-to-miss drawing of a gas can. Significantly, though, most Americans continued to favor large American cars with V-8s, and thus encouraged Detroit to continue in that direction, oil scare be damned.

The federal government was by this time quite concerned about automobile safety, and ordered that all 1973 American cars have five-mph front "crash" bumpers—hence the proliferation of clunky, protruding slabs that looked like soft-serve I-beams. (A pleasing exception was the "squeezeable" plastic nose of the '73 Pontiac Grand Am, which had a front bumper that managed to look integrated with the rest of the front end.)

The Indianapolis 500 was postponed for two days because of rain, and was called after 332.5 miles on May 30 because of more rain. Gordon Johncock, driving an STP Eagle-Offenhauser, was the winner. This year's pace car was

1973

a Cadillac Eldorado convertible modifed to wring 500 gross horsepower from its 500-cid V-8. The NASCAR Winston Cup champion was longshot Benny Parsons.

Pioneer aviator and auto racer Eddie Rickenbacker was the year's Automotive Hall of Fame inductee.

A peace settlement signed in Paris on January 27 put a formal end to American involvement in Vietnam, and effectively ceded South Vietnam to communist North Vietnam. President Nixon, meanwhile, accepted responsibility, but no blame, for the unfolding Watergate scandal. Vice President Spiro Agnew resigned from office and subsequently pled no contest to charges of income tax evasion.

Top movies included *The Sting*, *Paper Moon*, *Papillon*, *Live and Let Die* (Roger Moore's first turn as James Bond), *The Last Detail*, and *The Last American Hero*, the true story of moonshine-runner and stock-car legend Junior Johnson. *All in the Family*, *The Mary Tyler Moore Show*, *Sanford and Son*, *Cannon*, and *Bridget Loves Bernie* were some of the year's most popular TV shows. Pop music fans were digging Carly Simon's "You're So Vain," Stevie Wonder's "Superstition," The O'Jays's "Love Train," and that celebration of mawkish sentiment, Tony Orlando & Dawn's "Tie A Yellow Ribbon Round the Ole Oak Tree." Miami edged Washington, 14-7, to win Super Bowl VII and go undefeated in the bargain. The World Series was won by the Oakland Athletics, four games to three, over the New York Mets. "Super horse" Secretariat became the first Triple Crown winner in 25 years.

AMC

Stockholders beam as AMC earns $44.5 million on record sales of $1.7 billion

AMC's market share swells to just over four percent, the highest in years

Gremlin studies its jeans and offers a new Levi's trim option with denim-like interior fabric

Hornet adds a smart hatchback coupe body style

AMC's Jeep division introduces full-time Quadra-Trac four-wheel drive as an option for its Wagoneer sport-utility vehicle

Mark Donohue drives a Matador to win the Winston 500 at Riverside, California, the first victory for AMC's fledgling NASCAR effort

1

2

3

1. The upscale Brougham edition of the Ambassador was the only full-size car AMC offered for 1973. The two-door hardtop Brougham might have a 304-, 360-, or 401-cid V-8. **2.** A $4861 station wagon remained in the Ambassador Brougham line-up. Already well-equipped, Ambassadors added seven new standard items, including power steering and an AM radio. **3.** Both a regular Javelin hardtop coupe and a Javelin AMX (shown) continued to attract sport-minded AMC buyers, helped by their highly sculpted shape with its long hood, rakish windshield, and snipped-off rear deck. New steel-reinforced rubber bumper guards were installed. Close to 5000 AMX coupes went on sale, at $3191. Either a six-cylinder engine or a V-8 might go under the Javelin's hood.

1

2

AMC's compact Hornet earned some noticeable appearance changes for 1973, especially from the windshield forward. All Hornets were 6.5 inches longer this year, though on the same 108-inch wheelbase as before. That difference was a result of the new recoverable bumper system—AMC's way to meet the federal regulation, which required front bumpers to withstand a 5-mph impact. Hornets came in four body styles, with any of four engines: a 232- or 258-cid inline six-cylinder, or a 304- or 360-cid V-8. The biggest V-8 produced 175 horsepower. **1.** Star of the 1973 Hornet pack was the new hatchback coupe, shown with the sporty "X" option package. Handsome in appearance, with its own distinct roofline, the hatchback also offered vast load space. A hinged floor panel option made it even more useful. **2.** Pictured here in DL trim, the Sportabout wagon was one of the four Hornet body types, offering an extra helping of versatility. **3.** Just $2343 bought a four-door Hornet, but a V-8 engine added $138 to the tariff. **4.** Least-expensive, at $2298, was the six-cylinder, two-door Hornet sedan.

3

4

1

2

3

4

1. Young folks continued to fall for AMC's little Gremlin, even if their elders considered it—and them—rather weird. Gremlins grew five inches longer thanks to protruding bumpers. Either of two six-cylinder engines, or a 304-cid V-8, might go under the hood. This year's "Levi's" edition, with upholstery like the famed blue jeans, was created with the cooperation of the Levi-Strauss firm. **2.** An AMC official called the sporty Gremlin "X" edition "a gold mine" for the company. This one has the 304-cid V-8. **3-5.** Offered in three body styles, the '73 Matador got a new grille, and could have any of six engines.

5

CHRYSLER
CORPORATION

On July 26, Chrysler Corporation builds its one-millionth '73 model, a Chrysler Newport sedan

Subcompact and compact models enjoy record industry sales

Electronic ignition is now standard on all Chrysler engines

Anti-theft devices operate the horn and lights

Dodge's Demon is renamed the Dart Sport

Plymouth sags to a fifth-place production ranking, behind Oldsmobile and Pontiac

Plymouth's "Space Duster," like Dodge's "Convertriple," blends a fold-down rear seat with a sliding steel sunroof

1

2

3

1. All Chryslers, including the Newport, wore blockier lower-body sheetmetal this year, with bigger bumpers in a more conventional-looking, rectangular-themed front end. Newports came in three body styles, in base or Custom guise, with a 400- or 440-cid V-8 engine. In a sign of the times, the biggest V-8 dropped to 215 horsepower. **2.** The millionth car produced by Chrysler-Plymouth division in 1973 was this Newport four-door sedan, which left the Jefferson Avenue assembly plant in Detroit on July 26, 1973. Francis Hazelroth (left), the division's general sales manager, held the sign along with plant manager Richard Cummins. **3.** Only 8541 buyers chose to pay $5364 for the New Yorker Brougham four-door sedan, one of three body styles and two trim levels. Chrysler sales topped 234,000 in 1973.

1

2

3

1-3. Note the tiny portholes in the rear pillar of this special-edition Chrysler "Mariner." The interior built upon an aquatic theme, with blue/white upholstery. Special editions helped draw attention at dealerships. **4.** Chrysler-Plymouth dealers got a broad lineup, including, left to right: (front row) Chrysler New Yorker Brougham and Imperial; (middle) Plymouth Satellite Sebring Plus, Duster, and Fury Gran Coupe; (back) Plymouth Cricket, and 'Cuda.

4

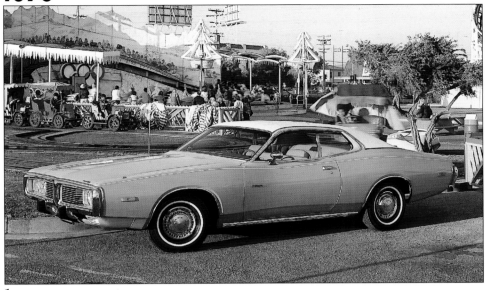

1. An all-new front suspension went into the mid-sized Dodge Charger and Coronet. This Charger hardtop has a "halo" vinyl top. Dodge also offered a Landau-style roof with only the forward section in vinyl. Chargers could have a six-cylinder engine or any of four V-8s. **2.** A vinyl Landau roof was standard on the new Charger SE (Special Edition). Extra sound insulation was supposed to refine Charger's performance image, to blend "exuberance with restraint." **3.** Still aiming at the youth market, the Challenger Rallye hardtop featured a heavy-duty suspension, tachometer—and power bulge hood. **4.** A regular Challenger hardtop could be driven home for $3011 with the standard 318-cid V-8, or for a few dollars more, a 340-cid V-8 pumping out 240 horses.

1

2

3

1. Wearing a new vee-shaped grille and restyled taillights, the mid-sized Coronet Custom sedan cost $3017.
2. Note the distinctive two-toning on this Dart Sport 340 coupe—previously known as the Demon. More than 11,300 folks drove one home. 3. Mitsubishi, in Japan, produced the Dodge Colt station wagon (top) and GT two-door hardtop.

4. A lot more people liked the $2617 Dart Swinger hardtop coupe than its cheaper Swinger Special mate. 5. Concealed headlights were installed on the Monaco Brougham hardtop.
6. Plenty of Polara four-door sedans saw police service, when packing a 440-cid V-8. 7. Polaras came in either base or Custom trim (shown), in four body styles.

4

5

6

7

1

2

1-2. Changed only moderately since its 1969 debut in this form, the Imperial LeBaron four-door hardtop was now in its final season for that basic body. All Imperials carried a 440-cid V-8 engine, though its output diminished to 215 horsepower this year. **3.** Ads promoted the Imperial's lush comforts. Even though the gasoline crunch was about to begin, and full-size gas-guzzling automobiles would be dealt a crushing blow, Americans continued to strive for roadgoing luxury. Prosperity was still the rule, and plenty of successful people were eager to pay the $7000 or so for an Imperial or its Cadillac or Lincoln competitor—if not one of the German rivals that vied for high-end dollars. **4.** Imperial remained a separate make from Chrysler. Despite a higher price, the LeBaron hardtop sedan handily outsold its hardtop coupe counterpart. **5.** Thanks in part to its bigger bumpers, a '73 LeBaron hardtop sedan tipped the scales at over 5000 pounds.

3

4

5

1

2

3

4

5

1-2. Now in its final season of the "fuselage" shape, the full-sized Plymouth Fury Gran Sedan was again a pillarless four-door hardtop, sporting a fresh hood and grille. Standard fare was a modest 318-cid V-8, but buyers could opt for a 360-, 400-, or 440-cid engine instead. Four-doors could be equipped with front vent windows. **3.** GM abandoned the two-door pillarless body style, but Plymouth's Fury Gran Coupe stuck with that styling. **4.** Anyone who didn't love the color blue might have steered clear of the interior in this Fury Gran Coupe. **5.** Big station wagons, like this top-of-the-line Fury Sport Suburban, continued to appeal to families.

1   2

3

1. A mongrel of sorts in the early Seventies, Plymouth's Barracuda shared its two-door hardtop body with the Dodge Challenger, and its running gear with the Plymouth Road Runner. Engine choices included a 225-cid six, along with 318- and 340-cid V-8s, the last rated at 240 horsepower. **2.** The roof rack on a Satellite Custom station wagon added to its already-ample storage capacity. **3.** A still-sporty member of the Satellite series, the Road Runner hardtop coupe stickered for $3115 and found more than 19,000 buyers. **4.** Plymouth claimed that the '73 Satellite was the quietest intermediate Plymouth ever, thanks to a newly isolated suspension. A sporty Satellite coupe could be taken home for as little as $2755.

4

1. Most luxurious—and most expensive—Satellite two-door hardtop was the Sebring Plus at $3258. **2.** Plymouth display narrator Eleanor Glass (left) chats with Chrysler president John Riccardo and *Ward's Auto World* editor David Smith during the charity preview for the 1973 Detroit Auto Show. **3.** Profit margins were nothing to shout about, but the Valiant compact was Chrysler Corportation's top-selling line. **4.** A Duster coupe could be equipped with a "Twister" option, or as a new "Space Duster" with fold-down rear seatback.

FORD

Performance is out, plush is in: Ford's Torino line drops its GT fastback for a milder Gran Torino Sport while adding a luxury Brougham hardtop and sedan

Thunderbird starts another fashion trend with newly optional rear-roof "opera" windows

Big Fords and Mercurys show more slab-sided lower bodies, plus reworked rooflines on sedans and wagons

Ford's F-Series pickups get new cab styling that will last through 1979

Mustang convertible sales nearly double after Ford announces the end of its factory ragtops after '73; Mercury's Cougar convertibles sell nowhere near as well

Lincoln retails close to 70,000 Continental Mark IVs; it will be the high-water mark for the model's five-year run

Lincoln-Mercury's Capri receives style updates to meet Washington's newest safety mandates, plus larger standard and optional engines

Dearborn recovers a bit of market share, ending at 27.6 percent of the U.S. industry

President Nixon presents Soviet premier Leonid Brezhnev with a new Lincoln Continental sedan

1973 Ford Station Wagon Models

Custom 500 Ranch Wagon, 6 pass.

Custom 500 Ranch Wagon, 10 pass.

Galaxie 500 Country Sedan, 6 pass.

Galaxie 500 Country Sedan, 10 pass.

LTD Country Squire, 6 pass.

LTD Country Squire, 10 pass.

1. Ford launched the Bronco in 1966, in roadster as well as wagon form—long before the term "sport-utility vehicle" was coined, but after Jeep and International had paved the way. Refinements arrived in '73, along with a new Ranger luxury trim option. A 200-cid six-cylinder engine was now standard, with 302-cid V-8 optional. Ford's SelectShift Cruise-O-Matic transmission was available for the first time in Broncos. **2-3.** Chicago Bears football coach Abe Gibron promoted Fords on TV during the early Seventies in the Chicago market. So did Melody Rogers, who later became a local TV weatherperson. Both made personal appearances for Ford at the Chicago Auto Show. **4.** Ford offered full-size wagons in three trim levels, the top-line Country Squires being decorated with simulated wood. All came in six- and ten-passenger versions, the latter courtesy of dual center-facing rear seats. Best seller by far was the Country Squire, with 142,983 rolling off the assembly line.

2. LTD Country Squire ads emphasized comfort/convenience features as well as the wagon's spacious rear cargo area. **3.** Offered in Custom 500, Galaxie 500, and LTD renditions, full-size Ford sedans and hardtops rode a 121-inch wheelbase and held a standard 351-cid V-8. **4.** Easily outselling Chevrolet's subcompact Vega, the Ford Pinto ambled into 1973 with new front/rear bumper guards and a new suspension option. **5.** A 2.3-liter (122-cid) overhead-cam four had been optional in the Pinto since its 1971 debut. By '73, it was rated at 83 horsepower, versus 54 for the standard 1.6-liter (98-cid) four.

1

2

1973 Ford Models

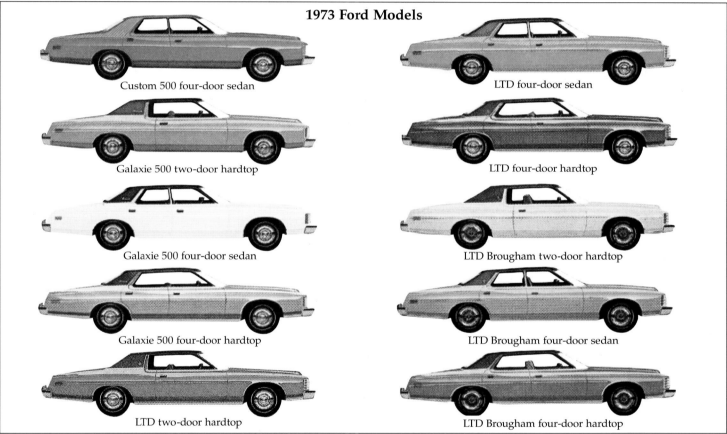

Custom 500 four-door sedan

LTD four-door sedan

Galaxie 500 two-door hardtop

LTD four-door hardtop

Galaxie 500 four-door sedan

LTD Brougham two-door hardtop

Galaxie 500 four-door hardtop

LTD Brougham four-door sedan

LTD two-door hardtop

LTD Brougham four-door hardtop

3

4

5

1

2

3

1. For the last time, Ford's Mustang was a biggie. "We started out with a secretary's car," said design chief Eugene Bordinat, "and all of a sudden we had a behemoth." Four engines were available. Front ends got a fresh look, led by federally mandated bumpers. Sales rose to nearly 135,000. 2. Unlike most upscale editions, the $2946 Mustang Grande sold more slowly than its base-model companion. New color-keyed molded front bumpers went on base and Grande models. 3. A black honeycomb grille for the Mustang Mach 1 SportsRoof fastback had new turn/park lights at its outboard edges. More than 35,000 folks put one in the garage.
4. Who wouldn't have liked to be seen in a '73 Mustang convertible? It represented Ford's last ragtop of the decade, as well as the last of the "big" Mustangs.

4

1973 Torino Models

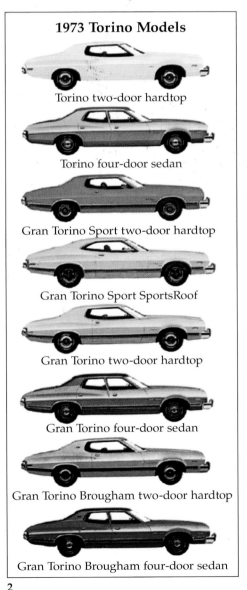

Torino two-door hardtop

Torino four-door sedan

Gran Torino Sport two-door hardtop

Gran Torino Sport SportsRoof

Gran Torino two-door hardtop

Gran Torino four-door sedan

Gran Torino Brougham two-door hardtop

Gran Torino Brougham four-door sedan

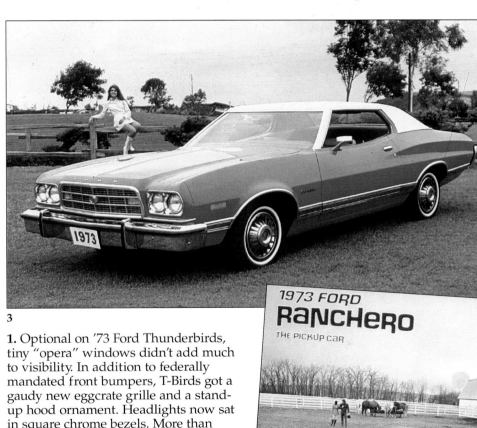

1973 FORD
RANCHERO
THE PICKUP CAR

1. Optional on '73 Ford Thunderbirds, tiny "opera" windows didn't add much to visibility. In addition to federally mandated front bumpers, T-Birds got a gaudy new eggcrate grille and a stand-up hood ornament. Headlights now sat in square chrome bezels. More than 87,000 were sold, starting at $6437. **2.** Restyled a year earlier, the mid-sized Torino lineup consisted of four series and four body styles: two-door hardtop, SportsRoof hardtop, four-door hardtop, and station wagon. **3.** The most popular Torinos were the Gran Torino and Gran Torino Brougham two-door hardtops. **4.** Ford called the dual-purpose Ranchero its "pickup car." Rivaling Chevy's El Camino, Rancheros came in 500, GT, and Squire trim.

1

2

3

4

5

1. President Richard M. Nixon and wife Pat rode in an older Lincoln Continental on Inauguration Day in January 1973. **2.** A sub-model of the Continental, Lincoln's Town Car added even more amenities. Continental hit a sales record. **3.** This is a prototype for the Continental two-door hardtop. Production versions of the Continental hardtop and four-door sedan topped 5000 pounds. **4-6.** This Continental Mark IV hardtop coupe featured a Silver Mark decor group, including a sliding glass moonroof. Every Lincoln held a 460-cid V-8.

6

1

2

3

1. Considered a "mini ponycar," Mercury's German-built Capri 2600 coupe had a 2548-cc V-6 engine. More than 113,000 Capris were sold in '73. This one has the $169 Decor Group option, with reclining front seats, contoured rear buckets, and more. **2-3.** Despite sharing many components, the Mercury Cougar—wearing a fresh grille and with newly standard front disc brakes—was seen as more civilized and individual than Ford's Mustang. The upscale XR-7 (shown) followed a "Euro interior" theme, which exuded "class." This would be the final outing for the Cougar convertible. All Cougars had a standard 168-horsepower, 351-cid V-8.

1

2

3

1-2. Compact Comets got a bit more posh. Both the sedan and coupe pictured have the Custom decor option, with fancier interiors. **3.** Comet traded its 170-cid six for a 200-cid version in 1973. **4.** Montego MX Villager (left) and regular MX wagons carried V-8s of 302 to 429 cid. **5-6.** Montereys rode the same 124-inch wheelbase as the line-topping Marquis, but cost about $700 less.

4

5

6

The Bronze Age

and other
Precious Metals
at the sign of
the cat

February 7, 1973: The air bag–in its first non-test situation–works perfectly and prevents injury in a Los Angeles freeway crash.

"I noticed a smudge on my glasses, but my glasses didn't even come off."

Howard R. Shapiro, of Chevy Chase, Maryland, was a front-seat passenger in a U.S. Government air bag-equipped car—one of hundreds being used in on-road testing of air bags.

Mr. Shapiro was interviewed later by Ed Reimers for Allstate. Following is a condensation of that interview.

Q. Any injuries, Howard?
A. No, I seem to be all right, Ed.
Q. Did you see the accident coming and get a chance to brace yourself?
A. Well, I wasn't the driver, and I wasn't looking at the road . . . and I really wasn't braced for the accident at all.
Q. Were you aware of the fact that the car you were riding in was equipped with an air bag passive restraint system?
A. No, I wasn't.
Q. Did you hear the air bag go off?
A. No, I didn't.
Q. What did you hear during the crash?
A. Just the sounds that one would ordinarily associate with a severe crash between two automobiles.
Q. Were you wearing a lap belt?
A. I was wearing a lap belt, yes.
Q. Was there any smothering effect when the air bag deployed?
A. No, there was no smothering effect. Fact, I couldn't detect any effects directly associated with the air bag.
Q. Do you have any idea of what would have happened to you if you hadn't had the air bag?
A. I think I would have gone into the windshield.
Q. Was there any other effect you noticed from the air bag deployment?
A. The only after effect I noticed was a smudge on the outside of my glasses, but my glasses didn't even come off.

How the air bag works

Automatically inflate . . . cushions . . .   . . . and deflate, all in less than half a second.

The air bag is designed to inflate automatically, but only in a frontal crash serious enough to cause injury. A special sensing device, using space-age technology, keeps air bag from inflating accidentally. Little bumps, rough roads, panic stops don't inflate the air bag.

Allstate is convinced that a passive restraint system like the air bag can save lives, help prevent disfiguring injuries, and can help hold down the cost of your auto insurance.

For a film and brochure about air bags for your club or organization, write:

Safety Director
Allstate Insurance Company
Northbrook, Illinois 60062

Allstate®

1. A promotional folder described new bronze paint/trim combinations to help dealers "re-introduce" Lincoln-Mercury cars for spring '73. **2.** Allstate touted the merits of air bags as early as 1973. A '72 Monterey had been equipped with them by the U.S. government as a field-test vehicle. **3.** Either a 429- or 460-cid V-8 powered the big, top-of-the-line Mercury Marquis, marketed in base and Brougham editions. Despite the imminent fuel crisis, mammoth Mercurys hung on for a few more years.
4-5. Certain Lincoln-Mercury dealers marketed the exotic mid-engined De Tomaso Pantera coupe. New for '73 was a GTS version, marked by black stripes and bold lettering, which carried a 351-cid V-8 pumped up to 350 horsepower versus the L model's 266.

GENERAL
MOTORS CORP.

GM's market share keeps climbing, reaching 52.5 percent of the domestic industry

Chevrolet production sets a record at over 2.5 million

GM intermediates are fully redesigned with pillared "Colonnade" rooflines, meaning no more hardtops or convertibles; Oldsmobile's Cutlass is the best seller of the four corporate lineups

Buick's Apollo and Oldsmobile's Omega debut, both based on Chevrolet's Nova

Cadillac's Eldorado convertible paces this year's Indy 500

Chevrolet's Corvette is fitted with one the best-looking "crash bumpers" in all Detroit

Chevy's new Laguna gets a unique body-color front that also nicely hides the federally required safety bumper

Olds still lists a 4-4-2, but it's not so muscular now; a new Salon option gives Cutlass sedans the European touch, and yet another new Hurst/Olds arrives

Destined to be an icon, a wild "Screaming Chicken" hood decal is a new option for Pontiac's Firebird Trans Am

Pontiac blends Grand Prix and Trans Am to produce a sporty new mid-size coupe and sedan called Grand Am; the legendary GTO is reduced to a not-so-special package option

1

2

3

1. A mid-1973 addition to the Buick stable, the compact Apollo was essentially a rebadged clone of the Chevrolet Nova, produced in three body styles: coupe, hatchback, and four-door sedan. Early models had a standard Chevy engine, too. 2. Apollo sales never quite took off. This four-door sedan stickered for $2628, and only 8450 were built. 3. A mere $3700 drove home a Buick Century Luxus coupe in '73. "Colonnade" styling with narrow quarter windows replaced the pillarless-coupe body style. A sedan and wagon rounded out the Century line. The Century's 350-cid V-8 was rated at 150 or 175 horsepower, but a big-block 455 might be installed instead. 4. Though toned down like other performance-oriented machines, Buick marketed its new Century coupe with a $173 Gran Sport option package as well as Stage I equipment.

4

1

2

3

4

5

6

7

8

1. Photographed on December 6, 1972, the 17-millionth Buick built was a 1973 Century Regal coupe. Regal topped the Century line, with new "Colonnade" styling. **2.** Luxus was an upscale Century, in three body styles. **3.** Buick revived the Century name as a replacement for the Skylark, on a reworked mid-size platform. Mid-size ragtops now were extinct. **4.** Available for the last time, Centurions shared grilles and taillamps with LeSabre. The convertible listed for $4534. **5.** Like other big Buicks, the LeSabre Custom four-door hardtop got a fresh front end, but otherwise changed little. **6.** Limited trim cost $174 extra on a full-sized Electra 225. **7.** Rivieras had a "boattail" deck for the last time. **8.** Riviera GS buyers could order a "total roadability" package this year, separate from the Stage I performance option.

1

2

3

4

5

1. Cadillac's Eldorado continued to appeal strongly to personal-luxury coupe buyers. A new front bumper for Cadillacs integrated rather well into the styling, avoiding any "tacked-on" look. Note the Eldo's vinyl rear roof and slim rectangular quarter windows. **2.** In this photo, an Eldorado convertible looks nearly a mile long. Again holding a 500-cid V-8 engine, Cadillac's was the only true luxury domestic convertible left on the market. **3.** Powered by a 472-cid V-8, Cadillac's Sedan de Ville four-door hardtop stickered for $6500. **4.** This would be the last pillarless Coupe de Ville hardtop. **5.** A Fleetwood Sixty Special Brougham four-door sedan offered four more inches of rear leg room than a Sedan de Ville.

1-2. "Luxury" replaced "sport" as the focus for the new Camaro Type LT coupe.
3-4. Naturally, an Estate Wagon was part of the full-sized Caprice crop. Note the Glide-Away tailgate, where the window retracts into the roof and the tailgate slides under the floor 5-6. Caprice was renamed Caprice Classic, shown in two-door hardtop form. 7. Caprice Classic four-door sedans sold well, but proved less popular than their hardtop counterparts.

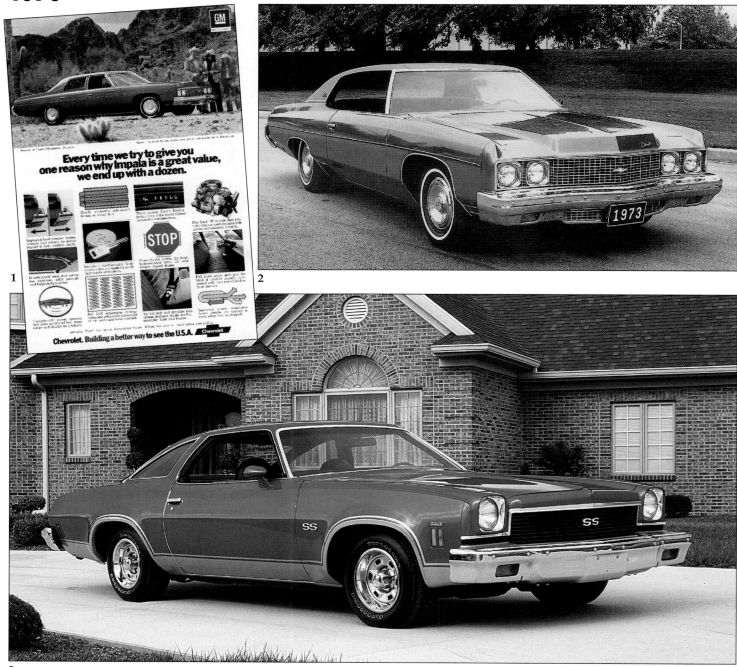

1. Ads for the Impala four-door sedan and other full-size Chevrolets employed scenic backdrops from around the country. Americans were still encouraged to "see the U.S.A. in their Chevrolets."
2. Impala was the mid-range member of the big-Chevrolet family. This Custom two-door hardtop stickered for $3836, and a whopping 176,824 were built.
3. This year's Chevelle SS coupe was actually a Malibu with a $243 SS option package. No more mid-size convertibles or pillarless hardtop coupes were built, now that the new "Colonnade" design took hold. **4.** Note the distinctive grille on this Chevelle Laguna coupe, as well as its body-colored bumpers. A new upscale model this year, Laguna came in hardtop coupe and four-door sedan form, along with twin Estate Wagons.

1

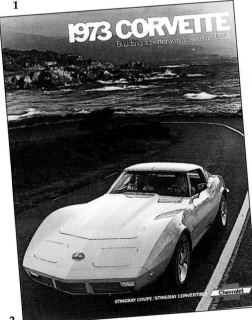

2

3

1. Corvettes managed to meet the new federal bumper standards without a major redesign. Steel-belted radial tires were new this year. **2.** Chevrolet's sports car again came in coupe and convertible form, with a new Turbo-Fire 350 V-8 or an optional 454-cid engine. Growing more civilized all the time, Corvettes gained a new cushioned body mounting system for quieter running on the road. **3.** Chevrolet's Monte Carlo coupe earned a new look, retaining its "classic" countenance. Four inches longer than before and two inches wider, the personal-luxury coupe also got a wider track dimension. Sales increased 60-percent to over 290,000.

1

2

3

1. The S was Monte Carlo's middle trim level, its higher content adding $147 to the base model's $3415 sticker. The plusher Monte Carlo Landau coupe cost $244 more than the S. **2-3.** Even in Custom trim, a compact Nova hatchback coupe or four-door sedan served mainly as practical family transportation, rather than an elegant driving experience. Novas were facelifted for 1973, adding the hatchback body style. Far more Novas had V-8 engines than sixes. **4.** A prolonged strike during 1972 had hurt subcompact Vega sales. Publicity about quality and design defects couldn't have helped, either. Customers did not seem to care, however, as more than 427,000 Vegas were produced this year—266,124 of them hatchback coupes.

4

1

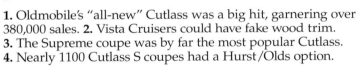

2

1. Oldmobile's "all-new" Cutlass was a big hit, garnering over 380,000 sales. 2. Vista Cruisers could have fake wood trim. 3. The Supreme coupe was by far the most popular Cutlass. 4. Nearly 1100 Cutlass S coupes had a Hurst/Olds option.

3

4

1

2

3

1-2. Hoods and fenders were revised on full-size Oldsmobiles, including the $4442 Delta 88 Royale convertible. Grilles, parking lights, and front bumpers were new. **3.** Like other Delta 88 models, the Royale two-door hardtop had a revised decklid and new integrated horizontal taillamps. All full-size Oldsmobiles were longer this year. Royale was the upscale rendition of the Delta 88. **4.** Ads for the Ninety-Eight Regency presented endorsements from businessmen whose firms were associated with comfort, style, and luxury. Previously a limited-availability option, Regency was now a full-fledged sedan model with a super-luxurious interior and 60/40 front seating. At $5418, the posh Regency cost nearly as much as a Toronado coupe. 4

1. Oldsmobile's model selection ranged from the compact Omega all the way to a sporty Toronado and massive Ninety-Eight, with Cutlass and full-sized Delta 88 in between. Full-size models got a new grille, hinged at the bottom to retract on impact. **2.** The Ninety-Eight Luxury coupe was a pillarless hardtop. Olds had been among the pioneers of the hardtop coupe body style, which was now on the way out. **3.** The only new car line from a domestic manufacturer this year, the Omega coupe was really a badge-engineered variant of the compact Chevrolet Nova. **4.** Toronado coupes earned a reworked front end, plus new back bumper and taillights.

1. Full-size Pontiacs, including this Grand Ville convertible, earned a fresh front-end appearance with new bumpers. Grand Ville was the sole remaining Pontiac soft-top. 2. Rear wheel opening covers (skirts) were now standard on Grand Villes. 3. Bonnevilles rode a wheelbase two inches shorter than comparable Grand Villes, and cost about $300 less. 4. Catalina was the least-expensive full-size Pontiac. 5. A '72 Pontiac heads down State Street in Hammond, Indiana, on January 31, 1973. Once considered dowdy automobiles, Pontiacs had developed a performance image in the Sixties—but government regulations and shifting attitudes spelled the doom of muscular models.

2

3

1. For the first time, Firebird Trans Am coupe buyers got a hood with a "screaming chicken" decal. Still available in Firebirds was the mighty Super Duty 455 V-8, producing 310 horsepower this year. **2.** Firebird coupes also came in base, Esprit, and Formula form. **3.** "The Duke" (aka John Wayne) used a '73 Firebird to run down the bad guys in the 1974 film, *McQ*. **4.** This Firebird Formula coupe packs the 455-cid V-8. **5.** This is a GTO?! Well, almost; it's a LeMans Sport Coupe with GTO option, including a scooped hood.

4

5

1

2

3

4

5

1. Although this prototype Grand Am coupe has the Super Duty 455 V-8, that engine wasn't offered in production versions. **2-3.** Based on LeMans, Grand Am was a new model for 1973, offered as a coupe or sedan. Pontiac's theme: to combine Grand Prix luxury with Trans Am performance, approximating a Euro sedan. **4.** This is Grand Am Number One, leaving the assembly line. **5.** Pontiac's LeMans Safari station wagon got a new rear-facing third-seat option, as well as swing-out rear quarter windows.

1. Skirted rear fenders added to the sleek lines of the LeMans coupe's new Colonnade styling. **2-3.** Riding a shorter wheelbase this year, the Grand Prix coupe was longer overall. The driver faced a new cockpit-styled instrument panel. **4.** This Ventura Custom coupe has the $176 Sprint option package. **5-6.** Also offered as a hatchback coupe and four-door sedan, the Ventura lost its "II" suffix this year. Custom versions are shown, but base models of each body style were available.

165

IMPORTS

Audi ousts its Super 90 for the Fox, a sly preview of Volkswagen's new-era '74 Dasher

Austin of England takes a different tack with the rear-drive Marina

BMW's 2800 sedan and CS coupe get a larger, 3.0-liter six to become "3.0" models

Buick dealers sell Opel coupes newly badged Manta

Datsun pares its winning 510 line to a lone two-door as the larger, more ornate 610 sedan, hardtop, and wagon move in

Fiat raids the parts bins to create the wedge-shaped X1/9, a low-cost mid-engine sports car using 128-series components

A little car destined for big things is Honda's new Civic hatchback, a larger, more refined four-cylinder replacement for the two-cylinder 600s

Mazda rolls out a new rotary-powered threesome called RX-3 as smaller stablemates for its RX-2s

Mercedes-Benz shifts to a new generation of senior "S-class" sedans for '73 with lower-profile styling

Britain's MGB reverts to a Sixties-style grille, but retains its classic sports-car formula

Volkswagen's Super Beetle goes Detroit with a new curved windshield; the big 411 gets a facelift to become the 412, but sales remain meager; just for fun, VW introduces "The Thing," a Beetle-based homage to the World War II "bucket car"

1

2

3

4

1. Even though the long-lived D-Series sedans were gone after 1972, Citroën remained in the U.S. market with an SM GT, introduced in '71. A Maserati V-6 engine powered the coupe, which rode on Citroën's air-oil suspension. 2. Datsun's 240Z coupe was in its final season, soon to be replaced by the 260Z. 3. Datsun chose an imaginative way to publicize the frugal gas mileage of its little 1200 series. Typically mini-compact in nature, the 1200 series was actually one of the better performers in the low end of its segment. 4. Though modest in appearance, the Datsun 510 had established quite a reputation for performance, both on the road and the race course. Only two-door sedans remained on sale, offered with four-speed manual shift or an automatic transmission.

1. Essentially identical underneath to the departing Datsun 510, the new 610 wore fresh sheet metal. Rounded contours veered the 610 away from the former boxy profile. 2. Couldn't afford a 'Vette for $5635? Buick dealers were happy to put customers into this Opel GT coupe, styled like a shrunken Corvette, for a mere $3713. 3. Seven Opel models were on sale, including this Manta Luxus coupe. Manta replaced the prior Sport Coupe. A Rallye coupe also was available. 4. Parked next to a plane, the Porsche 914/4 Targa coupe looked just right. Two engines now were available: the Volkswagen 1.7-liter, and a new 2.0-liter four.

1

2

3

4

5

6

7

1-2. Newest model from Renault was the front-drive 12-series, which hit the U.S. during 1971. The station wagon and sedan were strictly French inside. **3.** Renault's series 15 coupe had the same wheelbase and 1.7-liter engine as the 12-series. **4.** Saab's Sonett wore a fiberglass body and held a V-4 engine of 65 horsepower. From 1970-74, just 8351 were built. **5.** Turning more mainstream, Subaru had a new 1400 series, shown as a DL two-door. The flat four-cylinder engine grew to 1361-cc. **6.** Subaru's catalog used a cutaway of the GL coupe to promote technical merits. **7.** A Toyota Celica's interior looked mighty alluring with its wood-grain dash and racy steering wheel.

1

2

3

4

5

6

1. Sharp styling marked the Toyota Celica ST coupe, which wore a restyled grille and got a new instrument cluster. 2. Toyota's Carina coupe, a step up from Corolla, lasted only through the 1972 and '73 seasons. 3. A 97-cid engine went into the Toyota Corolla 1600, offered in three body styles, but the Corolla 1200 sedan had a smaller four-cylinder. 4. Topping the Toyota lineup was the Mark II four-door sedan, also available as a hardtop or station wagon. 5-6. Officially called Model 181, the Volkswagen "Thing" debuted in 1969 but did not reach the U.S. market until '73. Built in Mexico, the unique folding-topped vehicle used a Beetle engine and had removable doors.

Model-year 1974 was marked by an alarming drop in total car sales, from 9.7 million for 1973 to less than 7.5 million. The decline affected imports as well as American models. Escalating prices and fallout from the '73 gas crisis were likely culprits. Full-size cars, in particular, were hit hard—Chrysler Corporation, without a single subcompact, bit the bullet and offered rebates on its big Dodge Monaco in an attempt to spur sales.

Although OPEC lifted the oil embargo in March 1974, car-choked California initiated an odd-day/even-day gas rationing schedule. President Nixon requested service stations across the country to initiate voluntary closings to limit pleasure driving; many stations complied. By embargo's end, the average price of a gallon of gasoline was 54 cents, up from 38 cents a year earlier. The fuel crunch also propelled legislative passage of a national 55-mph speed limit.

1974

On the safety front, energy-absorbing bumpers were now mandatory front *and* rear. A federally mandated "ignition-lockout" that prevented cars from being started if seatbelts were unbuckled drove consumers crazy and was soon abandoned in favor of simple warning chimes. General Motors, after spending $80 million on airbag technology, offered the safety devices as options on 1974-76 Cadillacs, Buicks, and Oldsmobiles. Despite a hefty per-unit cost to GM of $8000, the bags retailed for less than $300. Regardless, the experiment netted only about 10,000 sales.

Johnny Rutherford drove a McLaren-Offenhauser to victory at the Indianapolis 500. This year's pace car was a 275-net horsepower Hurst/Olds. NASCAR driver Richard Petty was the 1974 Winston Cup champion.

The Automotive Hall of Fame opened its doors this year to pioneer auto manufacturer David D. Buick.

Nineteen seventy-four was a fateful year for President Nixon, who resigned in August while on the verge of impeachment over the Watergate affair. Although implicated in obstruction of justice and other offenses, Nixon was given a full pardon by his successor, Gerald Ford.

For sheer sensationalism, there was nothing like the kidnapping and subsequent bank-robbery career of 19-year-old heiress Patricia Hearst. Her abductors cum comrades were a small radical group known as the Symbionese Liberation Army.

The Godfather, Part II stood at the head of the year's most popular movies. Other hits included *Young Frankenstein, The Taking of Pelham One Two Three, The Man with the Golden Gun, The Towering Inferno, The Longest Yard,* and *Chinatown.*

All in the Family was the year's top TV show. *The Waltons, M*A*S*H, Kojak, Hawaii-Five-O,* and *The Sonny and Cher Comedy Hour* also attracted large audiences.

Top pop tunes ranged from goofy (Ray Stevens's "The Streak"), to rockin' (Bachman-Turner Overdrive's "You Ain't Seen Nothin' Yet"), to just plain peculiar (Paper Lace's "The Night Chicago Died"). Others that hit big included "Rock the Boat" by the Hues Corporation, "Can't Get Enough of Your Love, Babe" by Barry White, and "Kung Fu Fighting" by Carl Douglas—or did we already cover "goofy?"

The Miami Dolphins crushed the Minnesota Vikings, 24-7, in Super Bowl VIII. In the World Series, The Oakland A's walked all over the L.A. Dodgers, four games to one. Muhammad Ali KO'd George Foreman in Zaire to regain the heavyweight crown.

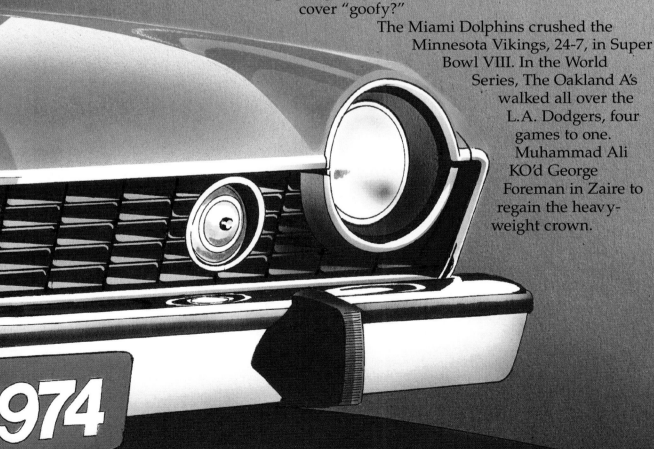

1974

AMC

Though little changed, economy cars help AMC cash in on this year's gas crunch, as sales soar past $2 billion, good for $27.5 million in earnings

Sales are up across most AMC car lines as model-year production reaches past 431,000

With that, AMC nabs 4.5 percent of the domestic market, up nearly half a point from '73

The mid-sized Matador drops its familiar hardtop coupe for a racy new fixed-pillar fastback style that will carry AMC's colors in NASCAR racing; the top-line Brougham version lists a new AMC "designer" option, this one inspired by couturier Oleg Cassini

The big Ambassador loses sales despite a heavy front-end restyle; AMC's largest car is in its final year

Javelin dies after 1974 sales of 29,536, bringing total production since debut '68 to 268,139

Jeep sheds the open-air Commando and welcomes Cherokee, a lower-priced version of the Wagoneer

1

2

3

1. Slow sales and a dated design killed AMC's Ambassador after 1974, but not before it received a completely new face to meet 5-mph bumper-impact standards. Only two models in a single Brougham trim level were fielded. Just 7070 of these wagons were called for. Base price was $4960, but most likely sold at deep discounts. **2.** Heftier rear bumpers were evident on most '74 cars, including the swan-song $4559 Ambassador Brougham sedan, which saw 17,901 copies. **3.** Helped by the continuing world fuel shortage, production of AMC's little Gremlin rose almost 50,000 units to reach over 131,000. A bigger rear crash bumper and a new grille insert were among the few changes. Base price was $2481 with 232 six, and $2635 with 304 V-8.

1

2

3

4

1-4. AMC's compact Hornet returned for '74 in Sportabout wagon, two-door sedan, hatchback coupe and four-door sedan models. All scored higher sales than in '73. **5.** Hornets weren't often seen in drag racing, but AMC had its performance partisans. The team of Maskin and Kanners ran this hatchback at the '74 NHRA Winternationals in Pomona, California. **6.** Ponycar demand was in the dumps by '74, so AMC gave up on its Javelin after a final 22,556 SSTs (shown) and just 4,980 AMX models. Both were little changed from '73.

5

6

Penske Prepared 1974 AMC Matador
1

PRESENTING THE ONLY ALL-NEW MID-SIZE CAR FOR 1974

AMC Matador
Matador X
3

2

4

1. AMC went racing with NASCAR Matadors in '74 instead of Trans-Am Javelins. Mark Donohue again did the driving. **2-4.** Racing was one reason for the new Matador coupe, here in racy "X" package trim. **5-6.** Big new front bumpers marked '74 Matador sedans and wagons. **7-8.** Couturier Oleg Cassini conjured a special trim option for the new Matador coupe. Just 6165 were sold.

5

6

7

8

CHRYSLER
CORPORATION

The Polara badge is dropped; all full-size Dodges are now Monacos

Dodge introduces rebates on the Monaco; full-size cars are not selling

Plymouth rises to third in output, followed by Oldsmobile and Pontiac

Chrysler Corporation's model-year production drops by 25 percent

Four-wheel disc brakes become standard on Imperials

Dodge produces its final Challengers as the ponycar market fades

Plymouth builds its last Barracuda—another casualty of the sinking ponycar market

An all-new Plymouth Fury debuts, a kissing cousin to the the Dodge Monaco and Chrysler Newport

The "Sundance" name appears on a Plymouth for the first time—for now as a "spring special"

The trouble-prone British-built Plymouth Cricket is dropped; the more reliable and popular Japanese-made Dodge Colts receive new styling and slightly larger dimensions

1. Chrysler Corporation's big cars got squarish new bodies for '74. This is Chrysler's $4752 Newport hardtop coupe. 2. The base '74 Newport sedan sold for $4677, but certainly couldn't be described as ornate at that price. 3. Recalling the Forties was a new cloth-and-vinyl "Navajo" trim option for '74 Newports.

1

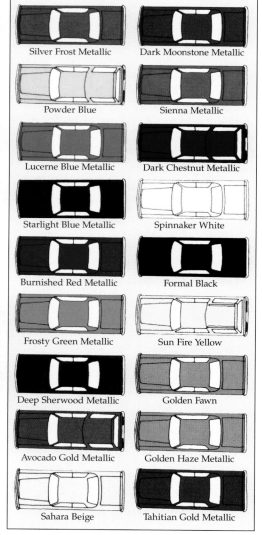

2

1-2. The '74 Chryslers introduced a look that would persist with little change for five model years. A three-model New Yorker Brougham series remained top-of-the-line, and again included a hardtop sedan. At $6063, it was Chrysler's most expensive '74, and $571 costlier than its '73 counterpart. Inflation like that,

3

plus the first energy crunch, explains why Chrysler-brand sales dropped some 50 percent for the model year, though the hardtop sedan was the best-selling Brougham at 13,165 units. A big 440 V-8 remained standard for all New Yorkers and Town & Country wagons, but it gained 15 horses this year to deliver 230 total, this despite tighter-than-ever emissions limits.
3. AM/FM stereo with eight-track tape remained a popular Chrysler option.

Silver Frost Metallic

Dark Moonstone Metallic

Powder Blue

Sienna Metallic

Lucerne Blue Metallic

Dark Chestnut Metallic

Starlight Blue Metallic

Spinnaker White

Burnished Red Metallic

Formal Black

Frosty Green Metallic

Sun Fire Yellow

Deep Sherwood Metallic

Golden Fawn

Avocado Gold Metallic

Golden Haze Metallic

Sahara Beige

Tahitian Gold Metallic

Dart Swinger Special hardtop coupe   Charger coupe   Charger SE coupe   Dart Sport coupe

Dart Swinger hardtop coupe   Charger hardtop coupe   Monaco hardtop coupe   Dart Sport 360 coupe

Monaco Custom hardtop coupe   Dart Sport Rallye coupe   Challenger Rallye hardtop coupe   Charger Rallye hardtop coupe

Monaco Brougham hardtop coupe   Dart four-door sedan   Coronet Custom four-door sedan   Monaco Custom four-door sedan

Monaco Brougham four-door sedan   Dart Custom four-door sedan   Monaco four-door sedan   Monaco Custom hardtop sedan

Monaco Brougham hardtop sedan   Coronet four-door sedan   Coronet station wagon   Coronet Custom station wagon

Coronet Crestwood station wagon   Monaco station wagon   Monaco Custom station wagon   Monaco Brougham station wagon

1

2

3

4

5

1. The broad '74 Dodge lineup would soon thin. **2.** The V-8 option for Dodge's '74 Challenger Rallye went from a 340 to a 245-bhp 360. **3.** The base '74 Challenger started at $3143. **4-5.** Base and SE Dodge Chargers got minor styling tweaks. SE retained louvered rear side windows.

1

2

1-2. "Crash" bumpers dictated revised front and rear-end styling for '74 mid-sized Dodge Coronets like this $3374 Custom sedan. **3.** Actor Joe Higgins, who played the "Dodge Safety Sheriff" in period advertising, lectures an earthbound moon walker at the Alabama Space and Rocket Center in Huntsville. Higgins himself actually logged over half a million air miles representing Dodge to promote safe driving among high-school students. **4.** The increasingly popular small Mitsubishi-built Dodge Colts gained new styling on slightly larger dimensions for '74, offering six models in three basic body styles.

4   3

1974 Dodge Colt Models

GT hardtop coupe   Custom station wagon   four-door sedan

station wagon   hardtop coupe   coupe

1

2

4

3

1. Dodge's Dart Sport fastback was little changed for '74. This standard model base-priced at $2878. 2. Full-sized '74 Dodge Monacos wore new bodies that looked larger, and wagons like this $5360 model in new top-line Brougham trim grew two inches in wheelbase to 124. 3. The new Monaco Brougham hardtop sedan started at $4999. 4. Taking note of growing demand for luxury compacts, Dodge added plush Special Edition Darts for '74. The sedan featured in this ad base-priced at $3837, a $718 premium over the Custom 4-door.

1

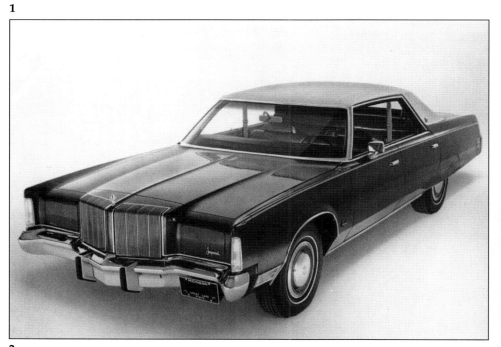

2

3

1-2. Highland Park's flagship Imperial became even more Chrysler-like with the company's 1974 big-car makeover, though a "waterfall" grille, hidden headlamps, and teardrop taillights were unique touches. Inflation helped push the price of the LeBaron hardtop sedan to $7804, a $750 increase. The coupe got a similar price hike, and was again outsold by the four-door. Overall Imperial sales were down, too, this time by 2303 units to 14,426. **3.** A specially trimmed Golden Anniversary Crown Coupe bowed at midseason to honor the very first Chryslers of 1924.

1

1. Like its Dodge Challenger sibling, Plymouth's Barracuda fell victim to fast-declining ponycar demand and would not return after '74. The swan-song models were little changed from '73, though rubber bumper "biscuits" were added to meet impact standards, especially at the rear. At least the sporty 'Cuda (foreground) remained as an echo of Barracuda's performance past, with a new emission-minded 360 V-8 option to replace the previous 340. Sales were the worst yet, however, as just 4989 'Cudas and 6745 base models (background) were built.

1

2

1-2. Like '74 Chryslers, Imperials, and big Dodges, Plymouth Furys switched from curved "fuselage" styling to a more square-shouldered look. It did nothing for sales, which suffered in the gas-crunch panic along with most other full-size cars. Top-line sedans and coupes were again badged Gran Fury. This hardtop sedan had a base price of $4675. **3.** A corporate ad from '74 addresses long-time complaints about shoddy workmanship by highlighting Chrysler's claimed lead in electronic testing for improved engine reliability. Note the "Extra Care in Engineering" headline.

3

1

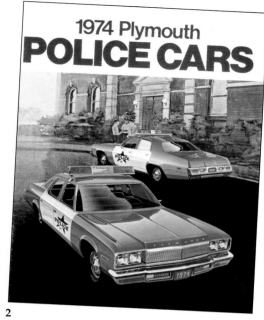

2

3

1. Big Plymouth wagons for '74 again included plain-sided Custom and wood-look Sport Suburbans, each available with six- or nine-passenger seating. 2. Plymouth Furys and mid-sized Satellites were still favored by many police departments; brochures like this '74 piece extolled their comfort and ruggedness. 3-6. Continuing the long line of "spring specials" was 1974's colorful Sundance trim option for Plymouth's mid-sized Satellite Sebring hardtop. 7. The top-line '74 Sebring Plus base-priced at $3621.

4, 5, 6

7

183

1

2

1. Plymouth's Satellite Sebring two-door hardtop enticed 31,980 customers. 2. Plaid seats were optional for the Road Runner. 3. 1974's plush $3794 Valiant Brougham hardtop. 4. The Gold Duster remained popular. 5. The first '74 Valiant leaves the line. 6. The Duster 340 became the Duster 360 for '74.

3

4

5

6

FORD
MOTOR CO.

Despite few changes to its cars, Dearborn improves its market share slightly to 16.2 percent

Just in time for the energy crisis, the smaller, lighter Mustang II takes Ford's ponycar back to basics with engineering derived from the subcompact Pintos; sales nearly equal the original Mustang's blazing first-year pace

Pinto itself benefits from some engineering improvements developed for Mustang II

Other Fords see only detail changes, but midyear ushers in the lush Gran Torino Elite, Ford's answer to the hot-selling Chevrolet Monte Carlo

While Mustang shrinks, Mercury's Cougar is upsized to become a two-door luxury edition of the intermediate Montego; the sole model is an XR-7 hardtop coupe

Aside from heavier back bumpers per federal decree, remaining Mercurys are little changed, as are Lincoln's Continental and Mark IV

1

2

Ford LTD Country Squire for '74. When you buy your wagon, make sure you can buy these features.

FORD WAGONS

Wagonmaster again in '74.

3

1. Mid-range member of Ford's full-size wagon family was the Country Sedan, part of the Galaxie 500 line. 2. Going upscale meant buying an LTD Brougham, offered as a four-door sedan, hardtop sedan, and hardtop coupe. 3. Ads for the LTD Country Squire wagon stressed its versatility and features. Standard engine was a 400-cid V-8. Imitation woodgrain trim was a $136 option. 4. This full-sized Ford two-door hardtop was destined for export. Note the lack of bodyside trim, similar to the low-priced Custom 500.

4

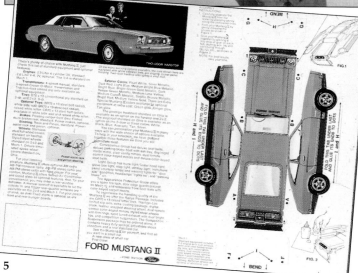

Mustang II

Mustang II...
the sporty, personal way to Free Wheel...

FORD MUSTANG II

1. Far trimmer and thriftier, the Mustang II arrived just when Americans sought slimmed-down cars. Nearly 400,000 were built for the '74 model year. **2.** Stockholder Anna Muccioli, shown with Henry Ford II, had complained at a 1968 meeting that the Mustang was getting fat. **3.** Ford Division chief Lee Iacocca posed with a new Mustang II Ghia and a '65 GT hardtop. **4.** Sales brochures pushed the Mustang II's sporty nature, but V-8 power was gone. **5.** Youthful Mustangers got a cutout version.

1

2

3

1. How far could extra-cost options go in "tarting up" an otherwise ordinary automobile? The Ford Maverick four-door sedan was dressed up to some extent by a $332 Luxury Decor package that included a vinyl top and upgraded interior appointments. But underneath, it was still an economy car. Mavericks had a choice of six-cylinder engines, or an optional 302-cid V-8. 2. Just $137 added the Luxury Decor option to a subcompact Pinto Runabout, otherwise considered basic transportation. Energy-absorbing bumpers were new this season, and engines were bigger than before—122 or 140 cubic inches. Pintos continued to sell in big numbers. 3-4. Thunderbirds now came with only one engine: the 460-cid V-8, making 220 horsepower. Either a steel sunroof or a glass moonroof might be installed. 5. Cars lined up all the way down the block at this filling station in Boston, as the fuel crisis worsened. Even after waiting for hours in gas lines, many motorists were limited in the amount they were permitted to purchase. By year's end, oil supplies began to increase and the worst was over.

4

5

1

2

1. In addition to Gran Torino (shown), Ford's mid-size came in base Torino, Sport, or Brougham form, with a choice of four V-8 engines. 2. The Gran Torino Brougham coupe topped the line—until the Elite arrived. 3. On January 21, journalists got their first look at a Gran Torino Elite, built at Ford's Chicago plant. 4. Added at midyear, the Gran Torino Elite gave Ford a response to Chevy's Monte Carlo. Elite coupes were fully loaded, including an overstuffed velour interior and "formal" grille.

3

4

1

2

1-2. Little things meant a lot when it came to luxury Lincolns, which added some sound insulation and thicker carpet to make the ride even quieter. The price of the Continental Mark IV shot past $10,000, but the hardtop coupe far outsold the regular Continental. Still, overall sales fell by about 34,000, mostly because of the ongoing fuel shortage. No big cars were exempt from the after effects of the OPEC oil embargo, and double-digit inflation pushed sticker prices higher and higher. The Mark's 460-cid V-8 engine developed 220 horsepower, but had to push around a whopping 5362 pounds. Mark IV buyers could choose Luxury Group packages in Silver or Gold to personalize their coupes. Options included velour or leather upholstery, a power sunroof, and dual exhausts.

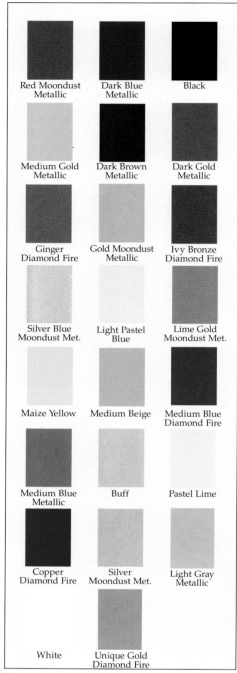

Red Moondust Metallic

Dark Blue Metallic

Black

Medium Gold Metallic

Dark Brown Metallic

Dark Gold Metallic

Ginger Diamond Fire

Gold Moondust Metallic

Ivy Bronze Diamond Fire

Silver Blue Moondust Met.

Light Pastel Blue

Lime Gold Moondust Met.

Maize Yellow

Medium Beige

Medium Blue Diamond Fire

Medium Blue Metallic

Buff

Pastel Lime

Copper Diamond Fire

Silver Moondust Met.

Light Gray Metallic

White

Unique Gold Diamond Fire

1

2

1. Lincoln Continental buyers could pick from a palette of 23 body colors. Continentals got a mild facelift, with a new vertical-bar grille and wrap-around signal lights. Rear bumpers bulked up, to match the fronts in meeting 5-mph impact standards. Lincolns were big beasts, riding a 127.2-inch wheelbase. **2.** Plenty of luxury automobile buyers liked the look of the tufted seat cushions and broad dashboard in a Continental Mark IV. Either velour or leather upholstery cost an extra $179. **3.** Prices edged past $8000 for the Continental two-door, reaching $8238 for a four-door sedan. Lincoln's 460-cid V-8 developed 215 horsepower. A Town Car package with vinyl roof was available for two- or four-door models.

3

1. Ordering the GT option for a Mercury Comet two-door brought high-back bucket seats, dual racing mirrors, and a color-keyed hood scoop. 2. This two-door Comet has the Custom decor option. 3. For 1974, Mercury moved the Cougar to the mid-sized Montego platform, dubbing it a "new breed." 4. Montego's Sports Appearance Group included a tachometer and full gauges, as well as tape striping and big tires.

THE FIRST OF THE NEW BREED 1974 COUGAR

1

2

4

3

1. Offered only in XR-7 trim, Mercury's enlarged Cougar wore a wider grille. 2. Full-size pillarless hardtop sedans appeared for the last time. Topping the line, the Marquis Brougham featured pillar lights and door pull straps. Sales were meager. 3. The big Colony Park wagons found only half as many buyers as the year before, much like the rest of the full-size Mercs. 4. Those who couldn't afford a Marquis might drive home a Monterey Custom, which was about just as big. 5-10. Mercury station wagons offered quite a choice of interiors. The Colony Park could get a luxury trim (5) or Grand Marquis option (6). The standard interior in a Monterey (7) or Marquis (8) was decent by '74 standards. The Montego MX Villager could have a Custom trim option (9) instead of the standard interior (10).

5

6

7

8

9

10

GENERAL
MOTORS CORP.

Being top-heavy with gas-guzzlers in a fuel-crisis year costs GM nearly three points of market share, which slips to just under 50 percent

With Congress still threatening to enact rollover standards, GM begins replacing some full-size hardtops with sturdier fixed-pillar styles; other models sport squared-off rooflines

Buick restyles Riviera with a blockier look, pillared roof, and nary a trace of "boattail"

Chevrolet's Corvette puts on a reshaped tail done in body color; like '73's new "soft" nose, it artfully conceals a "crash" bumper

Chevy's Camaro and Vega adopt slanted fronts to meet impact standards with style; Camaro wears a new rear end too

Oldsmobile helps keeps performance alive with another limited-edition Hurst/Olds; a one-off H/O convertible paces the Indy 500, but 380 replica coupes are sold to the public

It's strictly a test, but a few big Oldsmobiles are built with an embryonic dual airbag system to gauge consumer reaction, a portent of the Nineties

Once a mean midsize, Pontiac's GTO becomes a mere cosmetic option for the compact Ventura two-door; it's the end of the line for the hallowed "Goat"

Like Camaro, the Pontiac Firebird adopts a new "shovel" nose that handsomely meets bumper-impact standards

1

2

'74 Buick Apollo
'74 Buick Electra
'74 Buick LeSabre
'74 Buick Riviera

3, 4, 5, 6

1. Launched in mid-1973, Buick's compact Apollo—a clone of the Chevrolet Nova, offered in three body styles—earned a fresh hood and grille. 2. Performance options weren't quite extinct, despite tighter emissions standards. This Gran Sport coupe has Buick's "Stage I" equipment. For $558 extra, the buyer got a modified 455-cid V-8 with dual exhausts and a dual-snorkel air cleaner. 3-6. Buicks ranged in size from the compact Apollo to massive LeSabre and Electra 225 models.

1

2

3

4

1. Regal was part of Buick's mildly facelifted Century lineup. Instead of the standard 350-cid V-8, a 455 might be found—with up to 245 horsepower. 2. Regals came in hardtop coupe and hardtop sedan form. 3. The biggest and poshest Buick was the Electra 225, in base, Custom, or Limited trim. 4. Like the Electra 225, Buick's LeSabre got a significant facelift. Included in the LeSabre Luxus group was Buick's only convertible. 5. Abandoning its controversial boattail back end, the Riviera had a new roofline and vertical grille.

5

195

1

2

3

4

1. Hefty but heroic in stature, Cadillac's Eldorado convertible tipped the scales at more than 5000 pounds and stickered for $9437. Biggest in the industry, the 500-cid V-8 produced 210 horsepower. **2.** Would you expect anything but GM's best inside a soft-top Eldorado? Leather was standard. **3.** Eldorados also came in hardtop coupe form. **4.** John Wayne obviously has been busy—and wet—after a chase in a '73 Sedan de Ville. This scene is from the 1974 film, *McQ*.

1

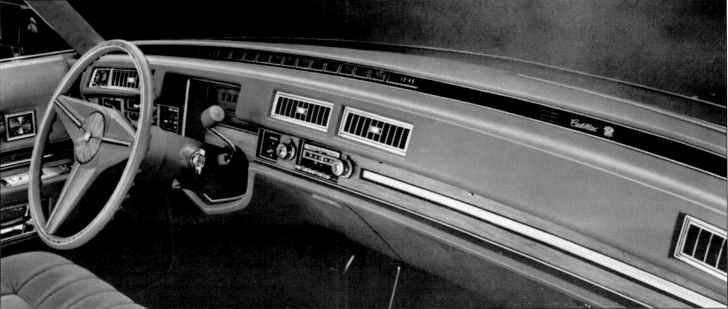

2

3

4

1. No Cadillac was more opulent than a Fleetwood with the Talisman option, seating four in Medici crushed velour armchair-style seats. 2. Cadillacs got a sweeping, slightly curved dashboard. 3. Sedan de Villes retained the pillarless design, unlike the pillared Coupe de Ville. 4. An AM/FM radio with eight-track tape deck cost $426 extra, while airbags were available for $225.

1

2

3

1. The U.S. Bicentennial was still two years off, but Chevrolet came up with a "Spirit of America" Impala—white with red and blue striping. 2. Even with the high price of gasoline casting a shadow over the market for big cars, Chevy dipped into its past to remind shoppers of the long-term value of its family cruisers like the Impala Custom coupe. 3. Except for Corvette, the $4745 Caprice Classic was Chevrolet's sole convertible. Just 4670 were built. 4. More than 35,000 folks drove home a new Caprice Estate Wagon. 5. Priced at $4162, the Impala Sport Coupe was a true pillarless hardtop. Full-size Chevrolets carried anything from a 250-cid six to a 454-cid big-block V-8.

4

5

1

2

3

4

5

1. Chevrolet pushed both appearance and performance in this ad for the Camaro Type LT, which came only with a V-8 engine. Close to 49,000 rolled off the line, stickered at $3713. Base-model Camaros sold better than the LT. This year's output also included 13,802 Z28 Camaros, which wore bolder graphics but did not exactly thrill ardent ponycar enthusiasts with their performance. **2.** Notable restyling gave the Camaro a "shovel" nose as well as new large, wraparound taillights to replace the previous round units. Both ends of the car now held 5-mph impact bumpers that were made of spring-mounted aluminum, with resilient impact strips. New "sugar scoop" headlights set the style for the rest of this Camaro generation. Camaro prices shot dramatically upward during this period of rampant inflation. Production increased by 56 percent, however, now that Chevrolet and Pontiac essentially had the ponycar market to themselves. **3.** Mid-sized Malibu Classic coupes stuck with the pillared "colonnade" two-door styling, introduced a year earlier. Standard engines included a 250-cid six and 350-cid V-8. **4.** A step up from basic Malibus, the Malibu Classic sedan had such extras as a stand-up hood ornament. **5.** A Malibu Classic Estate Wagon stickered for $4291 with two seats, or $4424 with three. Joining the mid-sized Chevelle team this season was a new sport-luxury Laguna Type S-3 coupe, featuring a body-colored urethane front-end that resisted cracks, dents, and scratches. Hydraulic cylinders supported its bumper/fascia assembly to reduce impact damage.

1

2

CORVETTE

3

1. Corvette sales kept climbing; 5474 convertibles and 32,028 coupes were built. Corvettes got a matching body-color tail, to meet new bumper-impact standards. **2.** Corvettes could still have a 454-cid big-block V-8 engine, packing 270 horsepower, or the 350 V-8 with 195 or 250 horses. **3.** In "S" trim alone, the Monte Carlo attracted more than 184,000 customers. The Monte Carlo Landau sold almost two-thirds as well.

1

2

3

1. Chevrolet created a limited-edition "Spirit of America" Nova hatchback.
2. Top Novas wore Custom trim, and used a six-cylinder or V-8 engine.
3. Five models of the subcompact Vega went to dealerships, including the Estate Wagon. Vega's four-cylinder engine made 75 or 85 horsepower.
4. Vega hatchback buyers could choose their own "Spirit of America" edition.

4

1

2

3

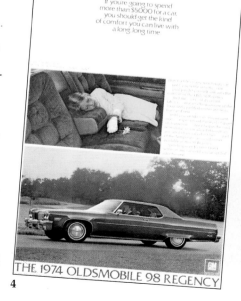

4

5

1. Fancier than the base model, Oldsmobile's Delta 88 Royale two-door hardtop had an abundant glass area, with twin quarter windows. Focusing on upper-middle-class luxury carried Olds through the Seventies. 2. Oldsmobile's only convertible was the Delta 88 Royale, priced at $4799. Just 3716 were built, with a 350- or 455-cid V-8.
3-4. Biggest and poshest of the lot, the Ninety-Eight Regency two-door hardtop stuck with the old pillarless style. All Ninety-Eight models, including Regency, carried a 455-cid V-8 engine, which made 210 or 230 horsepower. 5. Textured Bravado nylon cloth upholstery was standard in the Ninety-Eight Luxury Sedan.

THE 1974 OLDSMOBILE 98 REGENCY

If you're going to spend more than $5000 for a car, you should get the kind of comfort you can live with a long, long time

1

2

3

4

1-2. In the Seventies, Oldsmobile's Cutlass Supreme coupe established itself as a true American favorite, helping to keep the company coffers full. More than 172,000 Supreme coupes were built for '74. Olds also launched a Salon package, to attract buyers who favored European touring sedans. **3.** Smaller than a Delta 88, the Cutlass Supreme Cruiser wagon could have two or three bench seats. **4.** A special Olds convertible paced the Indianapolis 500 race. To mark the occasion, Oldsmobile collaborated with Hurst—known for specialty gearshift systems—to create a Hurst/Olds pace car coupe. Not everyone would feel at ease driving a car that flaunted its origin so boldly, but 380 were sold.

1

2

4

3

1-2. Oldsmobile's Omega compact was in its second model year. It was powered by a six-cylinder or V-8, and could be equipped with bucket seats and a console. 3. Pushing secondhand biggies in '74 was no picnic at this Wisconsin dealership. 4. Olds buyers could choose styled steel wheels (lower right), or a variety of wheel covers. 5. The pricey Toronado coupe still managed to find 27,582 buyers in '74.

5

1

2

3

4

1. Like other big cars in '74, Pontiac's Bonneville had a harder time attracting buyers. **2-3.** Those who thought $4572 was too much for a Bonneville could turn to this Catalina instead. For $294 less, it was similar in dimensions, nearly as plush, and came in the same three body styles. **4.** Firebirds earned a styling update. The most popular model was the base coupe, followed by the Esprit, Formula, and Trans Am. **5.** This Trans Am has the optional 290-horsepower Super Duty 455-cid V-8 installed in just 943 cars.

5

1

1. Despite a sticker price $385 higher than a regular Grand Prix, the SJ edition attracted close to 14,000 buyers. 2. More than 99,000 Grand Prix coupes left the factory this year. 3. Grand Am four-door sedans sold less strongly than two-door models—but neither model really took hold. 4. A GT option package gave this mid-sized LeMans coupe greater eye appeal, even if it held nothing startling under the hood. 5. Not everyone stayed home, even during the worst of the fuel shortages that resulted from the OPEC embargo. Traffic keeps flowing easily over Hammond Indiana's, Indianapolis Boulevard bridge in January 1974.

2

3

4

5

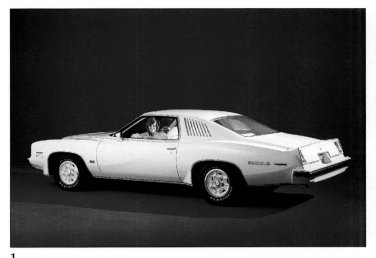

1

2

3

4

5

1-2. Pontiac sent a sporty "All American" Grand Am onto the auto-show circuit in 1974. It had white paint with red and blue striping, and carried a bold wedge spoiler. Show cars inevitably lured people to GM dealerships, where they might be induced to purchase a production model. **3-4.** What else but red, white, and blue could upholster the interior of the "All American" Grand Am? But even with such attention-getting measures, Grand Ams didn't sell well; people seemed to want either low-budget cars or glitzy models. **5.** The name's the same, but the image is gone. Based on the ho-hum Ventura compact, the GTO coupe was a mere shadow of its one-time self by '74. Only 7058 pillared coupes were built with this $195 option package, which included a distinctive grille, hood scoops, and 350-cid V-8 engine. Purists bemoaned the loss, recalling the days when GTO stood for driving excitement. The designation quickly vanished into Pontiac history.

IMPORTS

Citroën withdraws from the U.S. market after 1974, a victim of slow sales and the rising cost of complying with federal requirements

Datsun's small 1200 gives way to the more ambitious B-210; the 710 arrives to succeed the late 510

Power-sapping emissions gear prompts a larger engine for Datsun's sports car, which becomes the 260Z; a stretched 2+2 companion arrives during the year

Jaguar brings restyled Series II XJ sedans Stateside after a fall '73 European debut; "safety" bumpers and a more crash-friendly interior headline the changes

Mazda moves upscale with larger RX-4 models, but the relative thirst of Mazda's near all-rotary-engine lineup produces sharp sales declines in gas-pinched '74

Porsche's mid-engine 914 switches to a 1.8-liter four as base power and offers a zippier new 2.0-liter model; a larger 2.7-liter six highlights this year's 911s, where the first of the now-famous "whale tail" Carerras makes its U.S. debut

What looks like a sedan but packs like a wagon? Saab's new 99 "Wagon Back," a hatch-tail "three-door" with cavernous cargo room

Toyota emphasizes five-speed manual transmission in the new, racy-looking Corolla SR-5 coupe, Corona SR hardtop, and Celica GT

Volkswagen introduces the Dasher, beginning the company's shift to front-wheel drive and water-cooled front engines

1

2

3

4

5

6

1. American versions of the BMW 2002 weighed an extra 200 pounds and stood 9.5 inches longer, due to 5-mph bumpers. 2. Launched in '73, the Datsun 610 got a bigger (1952-cc) four-cylinder engine this year. 3. Cheapest member of the Datsun family was the new subcompact B-210. 4. Datsun's 240-Z became the 260-Z when its six-cylinder engine grew in displacement. A 2+2 coupe arrived in midyear, one foot longer. 5. Smaller than the 610, Datsun's midyear 710 promised to blend spirited driving with miserly gas mileage. 6. Troublesome they could be in the real world, but the Fiat 124 Spyder 1000 was both attractive and fun to drive.

1. Honda's little Civic began to make a real dent in the U.S. market. The initial engine grew to 1237-cc. **2.** Mazda used a rotary (Wankel) engine in its RX-3 station wagon and sport coupe, as well as in the RX-2 series. **3.** Six-cylinder engines powered the Mercedes-Benz 280C coupe and 280 sedan. **4.** Porsche's lineup included a 911 Targa (left), high-performance S coupe, and new Carrera with "ducktail" spoiler. **5.** A badge on the Subaru 1400 DL says "Front Drive," which was hardly the norm in 1974.

1

2

3

4

5

1. A five-speed gearbox went into the Toyota Corolla SR5. **2.** Toyota's Corona got new styling. **3.** Higher up Toyota's scale stood the Mark II. **4.** In its final season, the Triumph TR6 wore new bumper guards. **5.** This was VW's last year as the best-selling import in the U.S. **6.** Volkswagen's "Thing" lured folks who craved something different.

6

ETC.

Sales of the Avanti II remain steady, despite now being saddled with bulky 5-mph bumpers and reduced power

Checker builds the last of its wagon models; sedans struggle, against changing consumer taste and increased competition from the big three

Bricklin introduces the SV-1, which it touts as a "safety sports car"

A neo-classical fad emerges; cottage-industry automakers with names like Blakely, Panther, and Royale come out of the woodwork to produce old-timey replicars; despite the competition, sales are good for Excalibur, the first and best regarded of them

1. This is a 1974 model? Sure, it's an Excalibur Series II phaeton—rekindling memories of 1930s cars, with modern running gear. **2.** The Bricklin SV-1 looked exotic, but was quite conventional mechanically, with AMC V-8 power and a live rear axle. **3.** Styled by Virgil Exner, the Stutz Blackhawk borrowed only its name from a Twenties model.

211

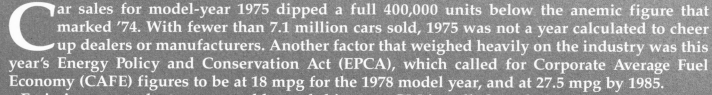

Car sales for model-year 1975 dipped a full 400,000 units below the anemic figure that marked '74. With fewer than 7.1 million cars sold, 1975 was not a year calculated to cheer up dealers or manufacturers. Another factor that weighed heavily on the industry was this year's Energy Policy and Conservation Act (EPCA), which called for Corporate Average Fuel Economy (CAFE) figures to be at 18 mpg for the 1978 model year, and at 27.5 mpg by 1985.

Emissions controls, too, were addressed this year: GM installed catalytic converters on all its cars; Chrysler on 75 percent; and Ford on 70 percent. American Motors, already a major player in the sub-compact market, added the Pacer, a rounded bubble of a car that some likened to an upside-down goldfish bowl. But let 'em laugh, for with first-year production in excess of 72,000 units, the Pacer outsold both of its import-fighting stablemates.

The Automotive Hall of Fame welcomed Charles Nash, who resigned as General Motors president in 1916 to build a car under his own name.

1975

Top dog at the '75 Indy 500 was second-time winner Bobby Unser. Rain caused the race to conclude after 435 miles. A Buick Century Custom, modified to produce 325 net horsepower, served as the pace car. This year's NASCAR Winston Cup champion was again Richard Petty, who claimed his sixth season title since 1964.

President Ford faced a couple of scary days in California: In Sacramento on September 5, a Charles Manson groupie named Lynette "Squeaky" Fromme pointed a .45 automatic at Ford but did not fire. In San Francisco just 17 days later, an unassuming-looking woman named Sara Jane Moore mounted a more assertive assassination attempt, pulling the trigger of her .38. She missed.

In May, 38 U.S. sailors and Marines died in a successful re-taking of the American merchant ship Mayaguez, which had been seized by Cambodia.

Box office turnstiles spun to *The Rocky Horror Picture Show, Three Days of the Condor, Jaws, One Flew Over the Cuckoo's Nest,* and *Rollerball. All in the Family* continued to dominate TV's Nielsen ratings, and was closely followed by *The Jeffersons, Chico and the Man, Rhoda, The Rockford Files,* and *Good Times.* NBC launched a comic-sketch show called *Saturday Night Live.* Pop charts were awash by this time with a highly syncopated dance music: disco. The much-publicized "Queen of Disco" was former stage singer Donna Summer, who had a tremendous smash with her overtly sexy debut single, "Love to Love You Baby." Van McCoy's richly orchestrated "The Hustle" was another enormous disco hit. Other top records that you might have popped into your eight-track player included "Fire" by the Ohio Players, "Lady Marmalade" by (Patti) LaBelle, "Jive Talkin'" by the Bee Gees, "Get Down Tonight" by K. C. & the Sunshine Band, and "Mandy" by Barry Manilow. The Pittsburgh Steelers slipped by the Minnesota Vikings, 16-6, in Super Bowl IX. In the World Series, the Cincinnati Reds got past the Boston Red Sox, four games to three.

AMC

AMC loses $27.5 million on sales of $2.3 billion in a generally soft year for the U.S. industry, yet its market share actually inches up

America's number-four producer turns out nearly 324,000 cars for the calendar year; Jeep production hits a record 105,833

The all-new Pacer debuts in February as "America's first wide small car"; its unusual two-door hatchback styling sparks plenty of debate

Other AMC models see little change, but electronic ignition becomes standard linewide to help fight smog; overdrive is newly offered in Gremlins and Hornets in an effort to boost fuel economy

The Matador coupe lineup is scaled back as the luxury Brougham and sporty "X" versions are reduced to option packages; overall demand for AMC's two-door intermediate drops drastically to slightly more than 22,000 units

On the NASCAR racing circuit, the news about the Matador is a little cheerier: Driver Bobby Allison nabs victories in three 500-mile races while at the wheel of the Roger Penske-owned coupe, including the prestigeous Southern 500

Although a small number of mid-size cars are believed to have been built with 401-cid V-8s, AMC's biggest engine is formally withdrawn from the options list

Following a strong 1974 season, Gremlin sales also take a sharp tumble, a fall no doubt helped by the arrival of a competing subcompact in AMC showrooms

1

2

3

4

5

1. AMC's penchant for cosmetic option groups was demonstrated by this Gremlin, equipped with both Levi's and "X" packages costing $220 and $201, respectively. **2.** In base form, the Gremlin sold for $2798 with a six-cylinder engine, which outsold the V-8 version by about 14-1. **3.** Like the Gremlin, the more conventionally shaped Hornet hatchback coupe could have either six-cylinder or V-8 power. **4.** This Hornet Sportabout wagon is equipped with the newly optional Touring Package. **5.** Compact Hornet sedans came in two- or four-door form. Half a dozen Hornet trim packages were available, including a sporty "X" option.

1

2

INTRODUCING THE 1975 PASSENGER CARS.

GREMLIN · HORNET · MATADOR

AMC

3

4

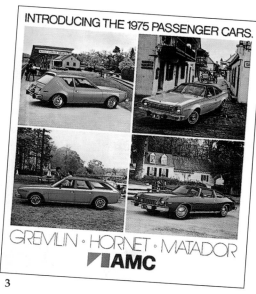

5

6

1. With Ambassadors now extinct, the Matador, shown in Brougham four-door sedan form, became the biggest AMC model. **2.** The Brougham option added $145 to the price of a Matador station wagon. **3.** In addition to the new bubble-look Pacer, AMC continued three models from the past for 1975: Gremlin, Hornet, and Matador. **4.** The Matador X was actually a $199 option for the coupe, including front disc brakes and radial tires on restyled wheels. Officially, Matadors came with a six-cylinder engine or a choice of two V-8s. **5.** A Roger Penske-built Matador won three NASCAR Winston Cup races in '75, the top season for factory-backed AMC stockers. **6.** Driver Bobby Allison (left) talks with car owner Penske.

215

1

2

3

4

1-2. Pacer debuted in February with scads of glass and a short nose ahead of its wide hatchback body. Some loved the look; many did not. Sales failed to approach those of Vega or Pinto, but Pacer was the top-selling AMC model. This one has the $339 "X" option. **3.** All Pacers were two-doors, and many had the $289 D/L group. Two six-cylinder engines were available. **4.** D/L trim included an upgraded interior. **5.** Pacer X was the sporty edition. Note the floor-mounted gearshift lever.

5

CHRYSLER
CORPORATION

Chrysler joins the other major automakers in installing catalytic converters

A "Fuel Pacer" option warns when the driver hits the gas pedal too hard

After years of publicly steering clear of "junior editions," Chrysler introduces the Cordoba personal-luxury coupe, the smallest postwar Chrysler yet

The new Cordoba and similarly restyled Dodge Charger SE are built in Canada

The "final" Imperial is built on June 12, but the car itself continues as the Chrysler New Yorker Brougham

Plymouth's full-size car is now called Gran Fury; mid-size models adopt the Fury badge

Among the offerings in the Plymouth Fury line is the last Road Runner built on an intermediate platform; engine choices top out at 235-bhp V-8 of 400 cubic inches

A Custom model joins the Plymouth Duster roster

Plymouth slips to sixth in production

Chrysler Corporation's model-year output skids another 19 percent, but industry auto sales are down just eight percent

GM's market share tops 53 percent, Ford's 28 percent, and Chrysler's 14 percent

John Riccardo becomes the corporate chairman, replacing Lynn Townsend on October 1st; Eugene Cafiero is president

1

2

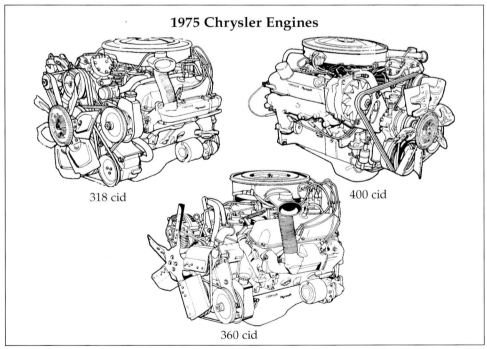

1975 Chrysler Engines

318 cid

400 cid

360 cid

3

1. Big as a New Yorker, Chrysler's Newport Custom came in three body styles, with a 360-cid V-8 standard. **2.** Opulent was the word for the New Yorker Brougham hardtop sedan, the top-selling New Yorker. More than 12,700 found customers, despite declining interest in big cars. Standard fittings included leather, velour, or brocade upholstery. **3.** Four V-8 engines were available in Chryslers. What's missing? The big-block 440, newly downrated to 215/260 bhp.

217

1

2

3

1-5. Chrysler tried a new tack with the Cordoba personal-luxury coupe—its smallest model since World War II. Suave actor Ricardo Montalban touted the car's "fine Corinthian leather," but that option pushed the $5072 base price higher. Three V-8 engines were offered. Cordoba accounted for three-fifths of Chrysler sales, with 150,105 produced.

4

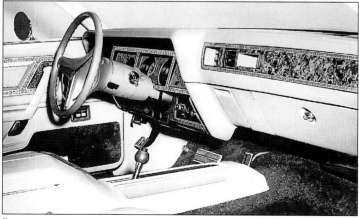

5

1

2

1-2. Similar in structure to the new Chrysler Cordoba, the Dodge Charger SE coupe featured slim-louvered quarter windows. Formal styling included a padded roof. Priced at $4903, SE was the sole Charger model, and 30,812 were produced. Standard enine was a 360-cid V-8, with 318- and 400-cid versions available. The Cordoba and Charger were built in Canada. **3.** Six versions of the Mitsubishi-built Dodge Colt could be found at dealerships in '75, including a new Carousel hardtop.

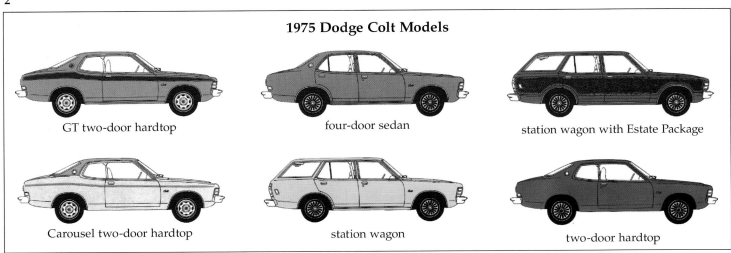

1975 Dodge Colt Models

GT two-door hardtop

four-door sedan

station wagon with Estate Package

Carousel two-door hardtop

station wagon

two-door hardtop

3

1

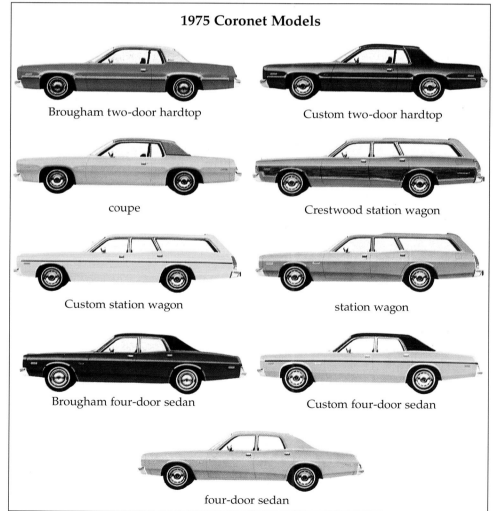

1975 Coronet Models

Brougham two-door hardtop

Custom two-door hardtop

coupe

Crestwood station wagon

Custom station wagon

station wagon

Brougham four-door sedan

Custom four-door sedan

four-door sedan

4

2

3

1-3. Mid-sized Dodge Coronets earned a heavy facelift for 1975, and welcomed two-door models back into the fold. The Brougham two-door hardtop was the raciest member of Coronet's top line. Broughams got such extras as vinyl-insert bodyside moldings, a stand-up hood ornament, padded vinyl top, and turbine-style wheel covers. **4.** Beyond the Brougham, Coronets came in base and Custom form, in three body styles: sedan, wagon, and hardtop/coupe. A Slant Six and 318-cid V-8 were standard.

1

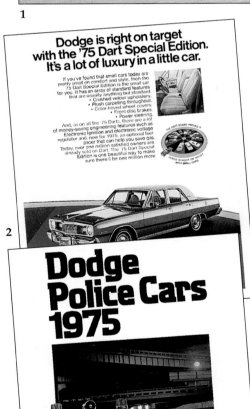

2

1. Like all '75 Darts, the Dart Sport coupe wore a new grille. **2.** A padded vinyl top and velour seating added poshness to the Dart Special Edition. **3.** Dart Swinger hardtops exuded a breezy personality. **4.** Dodge Monacos served plenty of police departments. **5.** A full-sized Royal Monaco Brougham coupe commanded $5460.

4

5

Though plush and loaded with comfort and convenience equipment, there was less interest than ever in the Imperial LeBaron, shown with the Crown Coupe roof option. Its 440-cid V-8 produced a modest 215 bhp. Imperials faded in name in June 1975, but returned in spirit as the '76 Chrysler New Yorker Brougham.

1975 CHRYSLER CORP. *PLYMOUTH*

1

2

3

1. Plymouth shuffled its lineup for 1975, giving the existing mid-size platform a taste of squared-up sheet-metal and a new nameplate. Billed as the "small Fury," sales ranked as so-so. This Fury Custom two-door hardtop, which started at $3711, might have held anything from a mild 225-cid Slant Six engine to a 400-cid V-8. The wheelbase of two-door Furys was set at 115 inches. 2. Fury came in four body styles and three trim levels, including this $3704 Custom four-door sedan, which turned out to be the best-selling model with 31,080 deliveries. Sedans and wagons rode a 117.5-inch chassis. 3. Only V-8 power went into the $4105 Fury Sport two-door hard-top, which could be ordered with turbine-style wheels.

1

3

1. While refining its lineup this year, Plymouth kept just one old name for a mid-sized model: Road Runner. The two-door hardtop differed from other Fury models by including a blacked-out grille, as well as beltline tape striping that reached all the way over the roof. Road Runners got a heavy-duty suspension, dual exhausts, and a choice of five V-8 engines—from two-barrel 318 all the way to a four-barrel 400-cid mill that developed 235 bhp. Note the newly optional "tunnel" decal on the decklid, boldly spelling out the car's name. As actual performance dwindled, optional items sometimes took strange forms in the Seventies. This one was a reminder of Road Runner cartoon shorts, in which fake tunnels often played prominent roles. 2. Optional Sundance-pattern cloth-and-vinyl bucket seats could give the Road Runner a little extra pizzazz. Plymouth produced 7183 Road Runners this year, stickering at $3973.

223

1

2

3

1. Now called Gran Fury, the full-sized Plymouth coupe could be ordered in Brougham trim, with a 360-, 400-, or 440-cid V-8. **2.** Gran Fury Custom four-door hardtops were a little less posh than Broughams, and had a standard 318-cid V-8. **3.** Gran Fury Plymouths were still big cars, measuring almost 220 inches long on a 121.5-inch wheelbase. Interior space was a trifle smaller than in today's full-size automobiles.

1. "Mean Mary Jean" served as Plymouth's spokestomboy during the mid-Seventies. 2. Duster 360 was the performance member of the Valiant team. 3. The Gold Duster trim package added a pebble-grain vinyl roof to the basic coupe. 4. A Silver Duster coupe highlighted Plymouth's display at the '75 Chicago Auto Show.

225

FORD
MOTOR CO.

Dearborn's market share slips to 28.1 percent despite a fair helping of new models and features

Ford Granada and Mercury Monarch arrive as upscale compacts offering Mercedes-Benz looks and Detroit-style luxury at K-Mart prices

Full-size Ford and Mercury hardtops switch to fixed center pillars, with big rear-quarter windows on two-doors

Ford's Mustang II powers up by adding a 302-cid V-8 option

The Ford Gran Torino Elite is now merely Elite, but remains a "junior T-Bird"

Thunderbird marks its 20th birthday with new Silver and Copper Luxury Group options

Lincoln Continentals adopt fixed-pillar rooflines in a major facelift

Mercury trots out the Bobcat, an upscale Pinto with a square, Lincolnesque grille

Smog-reducing catalytic converters feature on most '75 Detroiters; Ford highlights the switch at midyear with converter-equipped "MPG" versions of the Pinto and Mustang II

Pinto's base engine is upgraded to the formerly optional 140-cid four, and a 171-cube V-6 borrowed from the Mustang is offered for the first time; Bobcat shares this same choice of power plants

Lincoln-Mercury goes without a '75-model Capri, but an improved '76 with cleaner looks and hatchback versatility goes on sale in March

1

2

1975 Ford Models

LTD coupe

LTD Landau coupe

LTD four-door sedan

LTD Landau four-door sedan

LTD Brougham coupe

LTD station wagon

LTD Brougham four-door sedan

LTD Country Squire station wagon

3

1. With the fuel crisis gone—but not forgotten—sales of full-size cars bounced back to a degree, but the days of bigness were numbered. High-back Flight Bench seats and a vinyl roof added some distinction to Ford's full-sized LTD Landau four-door sedan. **2.** The cheapest two-door big Ford was the $4753 base LTD coupe. **3.** Eight models comprised Ford's LTD series, including two station wagons. Coupes had fixed B-pillars and abundantly sized quarter windows.

1

2

1. Ford Motor Company President Lee A. Iacocca poses with a Granada Ghia four-door sedan—the new upscale compact that became the company's best seller. More than 302,000 were built, with six-cylinder engines or a choice of 302- or 351-cid V-8s. 2. Few realized that the Granada's underpinnings came from the modest Maverick. 3-4. Ford ads and sales literature tried to show that the Granada was really different, in theme as well as size.

What looks like the newest Cadillac and is priced like the newest VW?

Ford Granada. 1975's best-selling newcomer.

Ford Granada—with Cadillac's $12,000-look at a price like VW—is a real engineering achievement. But it's only one of the reasons Granada is 1975's best-selling newcomer.

What so many people like about Granada is the efficient way it brings together features they are looking for today. This distinctive new-size design provides full-scale room for five. Granada combines a smooth, quiet ride with precise, sure handling and a high level of elegance. The engine choice ranges from a 200 CID Six to an action-packed 351 CID V-8. There's lots more you'll like about Granada. Check it out at your Ford Dealer soon.

*Base sticker prices excluding title, taxes and destination charges. Dealer prep extra on Granada and VW. Price comparison based on sticker prices excluding title, taxes and dealer prep which may affect comparison in some areas. Granada shown with optional WSW tires ($33) and paint stripes ($24).

Look close and compare. Ford means value.

Ford Granada 4-Door $3,756*

Cadillac Seville $12,479*

VW Rabbit 4-Door $3,800*

And your local Ford Dealer can show you.

FORD GRANADA
FORD DIVISION

3

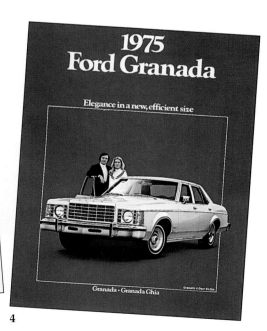

1975 Ford Granada

Elegance in a new, efficient size

Granada · Granada Ghia

4

227

1975 Mustang II Models

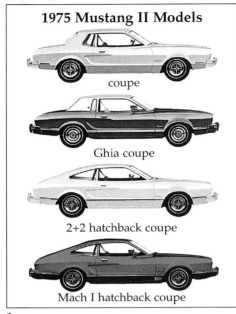

coupe

Ghia coupe

2+2 hatchback coupe

Mach I hatchback coupe

1

2

1. Four models made up the Mustang II family in 1975, the second year of the scaled-down redesign. Sales dwindled, despite a new V-8 option. **2.** The 302-cid V-8, rated at 122 bhp, sits beneath the hood of this Mustang II Ghia coupe. **3.** Whether equipped with a standard V-6 or optional V-8, the Mustang II Mach 1 hatchback wore black paint on its lower bodysides and rear fascia. **4.** Compact Mavericks continued to attract a fair share of interest —far more for the basic model than for the sporty Grabber. **5.** Despite well-publicized problems, Pintos—including this Runabout hatchback—scored high on the sales charts. Almost 224,000 were made. **6-7.** Birthday finery for the Thunderbird, which turned 20, included a special Copper Luxury Group (pictured) and a comparable Silver Luxury Group.

3

4

5

The 1975 Thunderbird. Could it be the best luxury car buy in America?

Decide for yourself. Besides the very specialness of Thunderbird itself, and the superb feel of Thunderbird's ride, there's more to consider. All those lavish extras that come standard: Air conditioning. An AM/FM multiplex radio. Opera windows. Steel-belted whitewall radial ply tires. Deluxe bumper group and cornering lights. Choose the optional Moonroof, and you can have it in silver or gold color. Be sure to see the two new 20th Anniversary Thunderbird Editions for 1975. They're in Silver and Copper.

The closer you look, the better we look.

Shown: 1975 Thunderbird with optional Copper Luxury Group, and convenience group.

THUNDERBIRD
FORD DIVISION *Ford*

6

7

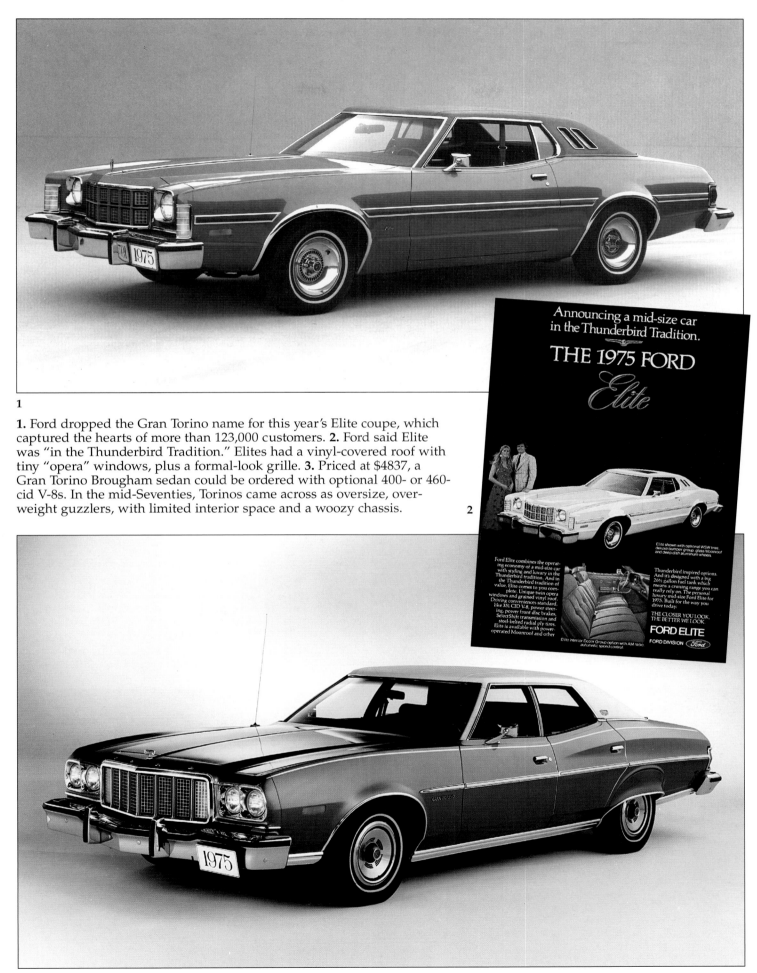

1

1. Ford dropped the Gran Torino name for this year's Elite coupe, which captured the hearts of more than 123,000 customers. **2.** Ford said Elite was "in the Thunderbird Tradition." Elites had a vinyl-covered roof with tiny "opera" windows, plus a formal-look grille. **3.** Priced at $4837, a Gran Torino Brougham sedan could be ordered with optional 400- or 460-cid V-8s. In the mid-Seventies, Torinos came across as oversize, over-weight guzzlers, with limited interior space and a woozy chassis.

2

Announcing a mid-size car in the Thunderbird Tradition.

THE 1975 FORD

Elite

3

1

3

2

1-4. The Blue Diamond Luxury Group was one of the new decor choices for the Lincoln Continental Mark IV coupe. The glass moonroof was an extra-cost option. 5-6. Standard at first on the Continental Town Car, opera windows later became optional. 7. Continentals could be quite colorful.

4

5

6

1975 Lincoln colors

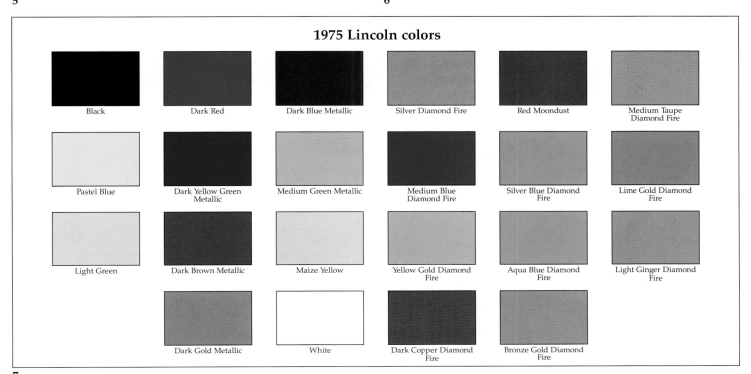

Black	Dark Red	Dark Blue Metallic
Silver Diamond Fire	Red Moondust	Medium Taupe Diamond Fire
Pastel Blue	Dark Yellow Green Metallic	Medium Green Metallic
Medium Blue Diamond Fire	Silver Blue Diamond Fire	Lime Gold Diamond Fire
Light Green	Dark Brown Metallic	Maize Yellow
Yellow Gold Diamond Fire	Aqua Blue Diamond Fire	Light Ginger Diamond Fire
Dark Gold Metallic	White	Dark Copper Diamond Fire
Bronze Gold Diamond Fire		

7

1975 FORD MOTOR CO.

MERCURY

1

2

1. Mercury took Ford's Pinto and turned it into the upscale Bobcat. Marketed as a Runabout or a Villager wagon (shown), Bobcat got a four-cylinder engine or small V-6. **2.** Cougars still drew from a loyal crop of customers who favored a little more plushness than they might find in a Thunderbird. Sole model was the XR-7, selling for $5218 with the standard 351-cid V-8. **3.** Many small gauge dials greeted the Cougar XR-7 driver.

3

1-2. No Mercury Capris were officially sold in the U.S. as 1975s, but a new Capri II debuted in March, as an early '76 model. It displayed smoother bodyside lines and hatchback versatility. The Ghia coupe was billed as a "sexy European road car." Capris could be equipped with either a 140-cid four-cylinder engine or a 171-cube V-6. **3.** A leather-wrapped steering wheel for the compact Comet was one of the features of the Custom Option package. The $408 option group for Comet sedans included dual body paint striping, a tan interior, Odense-grain vinyl roof, improved insulation, and DR78×14 whitewall tires.

1

2

3

1. A Comet sedan holds down a precious on-street parking space along Cedar Street, on Chicago's North Side, in 1975. (Chicago Historical Society/Sigmund J. Osty) 2. Looking for practical transportation with at least a whiff of luxury? Mercury dealers had an answer, in the form of a Comet four-door sedan, for a mere $3270. Some 31,000 went on sale. 3. Like most sporty-sounding options at mid-decade, the Comet GT was more "show" than "go." With high-back seats, dual racing mirrors, and a blacked-out hood, GT equipment added $244 to a Comet's sticker. 4. Ford President Lee Iacocca poses with Ford Granada Ghia (left) and Mercury Monarch Ghia sedans, both new for 1975. 5. This Monarch Ghia instrument panel features an optional AM/FM stereo tape player ($347) and air conditioning ($416).

1

2

3

4

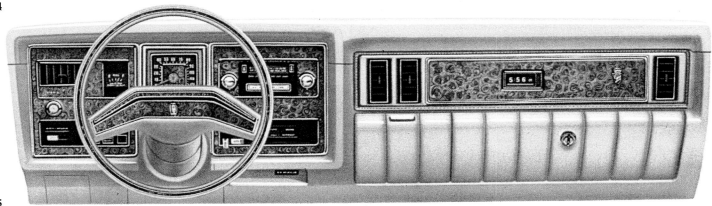

5

1

2

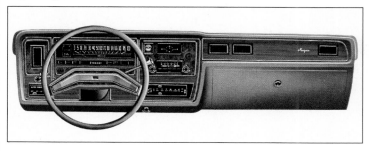

3

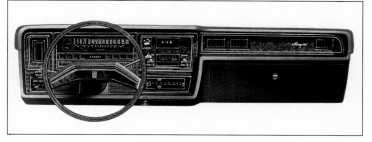

4

1. Mercury launched the Monarch as an upscale counterpart to Ford's new compact Granada. Monarchs came in base, Ghia (shown), and Grand trim levels. 2. The Monarch Ghia also came as a four-door sedan. Standard engine was a 250-cid six (200-cid on the base model), with 302- and 351-cid V-8s optional. Sales trailed well behind those of Ford's Granada. 3. Fewer than 8,300 Mercury buyers opted for a Montego MX Brougham four-door sedan. 4. Montego MX Brougham coupes could get an optional Landau vinyl roof. Both base and Brougham Montegos came in three body styles: coupe, sedan, and station wagon. 5. Comfort and convenience options like an AM/FM stereo, air conditioning, and a clock were lodged on the Montego MX instrument panel. 6. Grand Marquis topped Mercury's big-car line, which also included Marquis and Marquis Brougham models. The Grand Marquis four-door sedan stickered for $6469, with its standard 460-cid, 216-bhp V-8. 7. The driver of a Marquis coupe, sedan, or wagon faced this instrument panel. 8. The more posh Grand Marquis brought with it a tonier dash, including a digital clock.

5

6

GM again claims more than 50 percent of the market as the gas crunch begins to subside and big-car sales recover; still, car output slips to 2.9 million units.

It's the last year for remaining GM convertibles except the Cadillac Eldorado

A heavy redesign gives GM's N-O-V-A compacts a more European look, plus better handling via chassis improvements from the Camaro and Firebird

Chevrolet musters Monza, a small 2+2 "fasthatch" coupe with Ferrari-like lines on the Vega chassis; Buick's Skyhawk and Oldsmobile's Starfire arrive within months as close variations on the theme, as does a notchback Monza Towne Coupe

After an eight-year lapse, Buick returns to V-6 power for a new mileage-minded mid-sized Special coupe; a big-block 455 V-8 powers a special Buick Century Custom for Indy 500 pace-car duty

Cadillac goes compact with Seville, an "international size" sedan based on the N-O-V-A platform; it's the smallest Caddy in decades, but tops the line in base price

Wraparound rear windows freshen Chevy Camaro and Pontiac Firebird appearance, but Camaro loses its Z28

In April, Chevrolet introduces the Cosworth Vega with twin-cam power and other performance-oriented upgrades

Pontiac brings its Vega-clone Astre down from Canada to take advantage of booming small-car demand in the U.S.

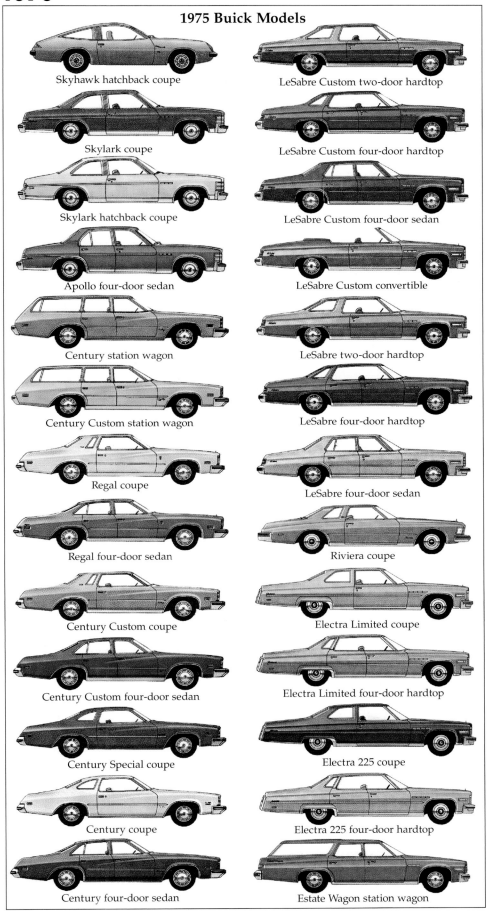

1975 Buick Models

Skyhawk hatchback coupe

Skylark coupe

Skylark hatchback coupe

Apollo four-door sedan

Century station wagon

Century Custom station wagon

Regal coupe

Regal four-door sedan

Century Custom coupe

Century Custom four-door sedan

Century Special coupe

Century coupe

Century four-door sedan

LeSabre Custom two-door hardtop

LeSabre Custom four-door hardtop

LeSabre Custom four-door sedan

LeSabre Custom convertible

LeSabre two-door hardtop

LeSabre four-door hardtop

LeSabre four-door sedan

Riviera coupe

Electra Limited coupe

Electra Limited four-door hardtop

Electra 225 coupe

Electra 225 four-door hardtop

Estate Wagon station wagon

Buick's 1975 lineup ranged from the new subcompact Skyhawk, evolved from Chevrolet's Monza, to the big LeSabre and Electra 225. The old Skylark name returned to Buick's fold, topping the list of models in the Apollo compact series.

1. Regal gained a degree of distinction from other members of the intermediate Century family via its vertical-bar grille and fascia-mounted upright parking lights. This Regal coupe, with the Landau vinyl half-roof option, could have the new 231-cid V-6 engine, rated at 110 bhp, or an extra-cost 350-cid V-8 that yielded 165 horses. A total of 56,646 Regal coupes were built, along with 10,726 sedans. 2. Shown here in posh Limited trim, the line-leading Electra four-door hardtop also came in Park Avenue guise. 3. Electra Limited coupe sales were only about half as brisk as those of four-door hardtops. The Electra wheelbase was 127 inches. 4. End of the line for soft-roofed Buicks was the 1975 LeSabre Custom convertible. Some 5300 ragtop fans paid at least $5133 to drive one home.

1

2

3

1-2. Even with a Landau roof option, the Riviera failed to capture as many hearts as in the past. A GS option appeared for the last time. 3. The Skylark name was applied to compact coupes. 4-5. The new Skyhawk hatchback yielded decent performance with its 231-cid V-6, but ho-hum sales.

4

5

1

2

3

1. If a regular Cadillac Coupe de Ville didn't provide enough opulence, an extra $350 fetched the d'Elegance decor option. The two-door De Ville was the most popular '75 Caddy, with more than 110,000 going to customers. **2.** Stepping up a notch over the De Villes, the posh Fleetwood Brougham four-door sedan cost $10,414. **3.** The Sedan de Ville four-door hardtop was no piker in the annual sales race; more than 63,000 were produced. All Cadillacs (except the new, smaller Seville) adopted the Eldorado 500-cid V-8, now downrated to a tame 190 bhp.

1

2

3

1-3. Eldorados inevitably attracted a certain kind of Cadillac buyer—one who liked a little bit of flash along with his or her luxuries. Only 8950 Eldo convertibles rolled off the line, versus 35,802 coupes. **4.** Cadillac as a compact? Yes, the new "international size" Seville gave Cadillac a serious contender against such European sedans as Mercedes-Benz. Styling relied more on good taste than high drama, and the Seville look influenced GM designs for more than a decade. A fuel-injected, Oldsmobile-built 350-cid V-8 engine, rated at 180 bhp, produced brisk acceleration. Seville owners enjoyed a pillowy ride as well as impressive handling. At $12,479, only long-wheelbase Seventy-Five limousines cost more.

4

1

2

3

4

1. An era was ending as Chevrolet produced its last full-sized convertible: a
Caprice Classic. Only 8349 examples
went to customers in '75. **2.** Ads for the
Caprice Estate Wagon pushed practicality along with lower maintenance
costs—which freed up money for plenty
of pricey fuel. Twice as many were sold
with three seats as two. **3.** Full-size
Chevrolets, like this Caprice Classic
hardtop sedan, epitomized middle-class
American motoring. **4.** Five versions of
the Impala went on sale, the cheapest
and most popular being the four-door
sedan. Two Bel Airs were offered, too.

240

1

2

3

4

Selected 1975 Chevelle Models

Malibu Classic Landau coupe

Malibu Classic four-door sedan

Laguna Type S-3 coupe

Malibu coupe

Malibu four-door sedan

1. The Impala lineup still included a four-door hardtop. New for the year was the addition of small rear-quarter windows. **2-3.** Issued in base and Type LT trim, Camaros gained a wraparound back window. The performance-oriented Z28 was gone, but a Rally Sport option returned. Hottest engine was now a mild-mannered 145-bhp, 350-cid V-8. **4.** Deeper-pocketed buyers of mid-sized Chevelles could step up to a Malibu Classic coupe. **5.** Among the members of the Chevelle coupe and sedan family was the sporty Laguna Type S-3 coupe with its sloping urethane nose.

5

241

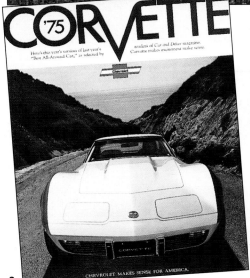

1. Step by step, Corvettes had become more balanced and even more pleasant to drive. Performance was another story, with no more than 205 bhp available from the 350-cid V-8. A convertible—the last such 'Vette for several years—stickered for $6537. **2.** The catalog still proposed the Corvette as *the* car for the open road. **3.** Though the Corvette coupe cost more than the convertible, it dominated in sales. **4.** Evolved from the subcompact Vega, the new Monza 2+2 hatchback scored high in sales. Almost 113,000 were built. A 140-cid four-cylinder engine was standard, with two V-8s available. **5.** Late arrivals included the Towne Coupe and Monza S. **6.** The best-selling Monza was the notchback Towne Coupe.

1

1. Monte Carlo coupes seemed to move like magic off dealer lots, to the tune of almost 259,000 for 1975. 2. Restyling gave the popular compact Nova—including this LN coupe—more glass and a new roofline. 3. LN (Luxury Nova) topped Chevy's compact lineup. 4. A hot Vega arrived in April. Painted black with gold striping, the Cosworth Vega had a 111-bhp twin-cam engine with an aluminum head designed in England by Cosworth Engineering. At about twice the tab for an ordinary Vega, 2061 were built. 5. GT gear added $425 to the cost of a Vega wagon. 6. Vega trim choices grew more extensive.

2

3

4

5

Selected 1975 Vega Models

Kammback station wagon

GT hatchback coupe

LX two-door sedan

hatchback coupe

panel delivery

6

1

1. Nothing from Oldsmobile could beat a Ninety-Eight Regency for size and comfort. Built on a 127-inch wheelbase, these were truly big cars—in an era when size had become less of a selling point. Their 455-cid V-8 made 190 bhp. "Luxury" variants of the coupe and four-door hardtop cost less. **2.** Custom Cruiser full-sized station wagons came in two- and three-seat styles **3.** Royale was the upscale branch of the Delta 88 family. The series included this hardtop sedan. **4.** The four-door Town sedan was the price leader of the three-model Delta 88 series. **5.** The intermediate Cutlass Supreme coupe proved to be Oldsmobile's best-seller by far, with nearly 151,000 customers drawn to its formal style. V-8 models came with a new standard 260-cube engine.

2

3

4

5

1

2

1. High-performance was thought to be dead in American cars, but Oldsmobile again worked with the Hurst company—known for its slick specialty gearshift setups—to produce a Hurst/Olds Cutlass Supreme coupe. Available only in white or black, the H/O coupe had a newly standard T-top and W-30 equipment. People liked those T-roofs, so Hurst began to install them on plain Cutlasses. **2.** A sign of the times, the left-hand needle of the optional fuel economy gauge in a Cutlass indicated degree of fuel efficiency. The right-hand needle was a regular gas gauge. **3.** The new Salon edition of the compact Omega sedan cost lots more than its base-model counterpart, so customers tended to avoid it. A 250-cid inline six-cylinder engine was standard, but a 260- or 350-cid V-8 might be installed in its place.

3

1

2

3

1. Despite new styling and an improved chassis, sales of the Nova-based Oldsmobile Omega fell this season. 2-3. Olds joined the subcompact parade with its new Starfire 2+2 hatchback coupe. It shared a 231-cid V-6 engine with the Buick Skyhawk. 4. Front-drive Toronado coupe loyalists now had two flavors to choose from: Custom or Brougham.

4

1

2

1. Astre, Pontiac's version of Chevy's Vega, migrated down from Canada for '75. Bodystyles included a hatchback coupe, station wagon, and notchback sedan. Three trim levels were offered. This is the Custom hatchback. 2. The SJ Safari carried a more robust standard four-cylinder engine than did other Astre wagons. 3. Bonnevilles, such as this coupe, drew closer in looks to the top-line Grand Ville. 4. Similar in size to a Bonneville, the Catalina four-door sedan cost less. 5. Grand Safari wagons joined the Bonneville family. 6. High hopes for the Euro-style Grand Am coupe (and sedan) came to naught when the line was dropped after 1975.

3

4

5

6

1

2

3

4

5

1-2. Optional Rally II wheels helped enhance the look of Pontiac's base Grand Prix coupe. Sales were off, though. **3.** Firebirds wore a new roofline. As usual, they came in four varieties: base (shown), Esprit, Formula, and Trans Am. **4.** Either a 400- or 455-cid V-8 might be found in a Trans Am, now the top-selling Firebird. **5-6.** Luxury LeMans became Grand LeMans, again in coupe, sedan, and Safari wagon.

6

1

2

3

4

1-2. Based on the compact Ventura, Pontiac's Phoenix concept car had a four-cylinder engine and made extensive use of lightweight materials. Built during 1975, it toured the '76 auto-show circuit. **3.** Ventura restyling was in line with that of similar-sized GM compacts, and included a modified roofline, more glass area, and a revised front end. One of 10 Ventura models, the SJ hatchback (shown) sold for $3961. Standard power came from a 250-cid six-cylinder, but a 260- or 350-cid V-8 drove more than three-fifths of Venturas. **4.** In addition to base models, Venturas came in SJ and Custom form, in three body styles—plus a low-budget Ventura S coupe. This season's redesign failed to help sales, which dwindled noticeably. Marginal assembly quality and inept marketing doubtlessly played roles in the compact Pontiac's sagging popularity.

IMPORTS

Led by small economy jobs, including a growing horde from Japan, import cars capture nearly 18.3 percent the U.S. market, a new record; it's a sign of the times as Japan's Toyota passes Germany's Volkswagen for sales supremacy among imports

Alfa Romeo eyes better U.S. sales with the new Alfetta sedan and GT coupe with rear transaxle

Buick dealers sell a reduced line of German-built Opels with first-time fuel injection, but imports end after '75 due to price pressure from a fast-strengthening Deutsche mark

Fiat replaces its venerable 124 sedans and wagons with the more modern, but still orthodox, 131 series

Honda makes history with its new Civic "CVCC" engine as mandatory in California and available in other states; it combines low emissions with good drivability

While Detroit ditches hardtops, Jaguar brings over a pair of pillarless XJCs; Series III E-Type production ceases early in the year

Mazda emphasizes piston power by adding a sedan and wagon to its four-cylinder 808 coupe while sales of rotary-engine RXs continue plunging

Mercedes-Benz stresses fuel-thrift with the usual 240D diesel sedan, plus a new 3.0-liter 300D model and a smaller 2.8-liter gas-engine option for the big four-door S-class

At VW, the water-cooled, front-drive Scirocco hatchback coupe replaces the Karmann-Ghia

1

2

3

5

1. The Datsun 610 appeared in three body types, including this two-door hardtop. **2.** The smallest member of the Datsun crew was the B-210, shown as a hatchback coupe. **3.** Smaller than a 610, Datsun's 710 station wagon used the same 2.0-liter four-cylinder engine. **4.** Sales of rotary-engine cars fell, but Mazda kept two series with that powerplant. This RX-4 station wagon stickered for $4697. **5.** Mazda's RX-3 coupe was cheaper, but shoppers were turning to piston-engine models instead.

1. Honda had something new for its sub-compact Civic: the Compound Vortex Controlled Combustion—or CVCC—engine. With an auxiliary combustion chamber, it promised improved emissions control without a catalytic converter. A regular-engine Civic remained available. 2. The Opel Manta got a new fuel-injected engine. This coupe wears optional dealer-installed side stripes. 3. Unlike most Porsches, the 914 had a mid-mounted engine. 4. More traditional Porsches were the 911, 911S, and Carrera, in coupe or Targa form. 5-6. Subaru's DL offerings included a wagon and coupe.

1

2

TOYOTA
Mark II

See how much car your money can buy.

3

4

1. Subaru launched a new GF hardtop to augment the DL/GL. **2.** Also new this year: a Subaru DL four-wheel-drive wagon. **3-4.** Toyota's Mark II came three ways. **5.** A Celica GT hardtop was the sportiest Toyota. **6.** A five-speed gearbox went into Toyota's Corolla SR-5 hardtop. **7.** Woodgrain siding was a Corolla wagon option. **8.** Toyota said its Corolla two-door sedan was the lowest-priced car in the U.S.

5

6

7

8

2

1. Now in its second year, Volkswagen's front-drive Dasher, with a water-cooled 1.5-liter engine, started at a rather hefty $4295. 2. With the Beetle's days numbered in the American market, Volkswagen needed something new to attract its budget-minded buyers. The answer was the front-drive Rabbit hatchback sedan, with two or four doors, a transverse 70-bhp engine—and a $2999 base price.

ETC.

Prices for the Avanti II sports coupe soar by $1300 to $9945, but production hits 125 cars, the most since 1972; horsepower is down, though, with the car's 400-cid Chevrolet V-8 backsliding to 175 bhp

Only slightly more prolific is Checker, which continues making its taxi-like Marathon sedans on a 120-inch wheelbase and a Marathon Deluxe on a 129-inch stretch; station wagons disappear from the catalog, though

A new Series III Excalibur incorporating styling, emissions, and safety improvements hits the road for $18,900 a copy; an SS roadster (eight built) and SS phaeton (82 built) make up the model lineup

In Inglewood, California, the Duesenberg Company ceases its attempted revival of the classic marque; a 440-cid Chrysler V-8 powers the final versions

1

1. On sale for one season, the Leata was produced in Idaho by Stinebaugh Manufacturing Company. Evolved from an all-terrain vehicle, the Leata was said to be inspired by the early Lincoln Continental, complete with outside spare, but hints of a prewar Willys can be seen in its shape. Leatas had a tiny 70-inch wheelbase and a fiberglass body. 2. Available for the last time, the Bricklin SV-1 now held a Ford 351-cid V-8. Prices shot upward and sales rose, but the company faltered in September.

2

A relatively serene White House, an end to double-digit inflation, and plentiful gasoline encouraged a dramatic comeback of car sales, to 9.96 million units. But American buyers were flocking back to large and intermediate cars, suggesting that whatever lessons might have been learned from the 1973 OPEC oil embargo had been forgotten.

Regardless of improved sales, the auto industry still felt unfairly pressed by the federal government. General Motors warned that all domestic car production may have to be halted some time in 1977 unless emissions requirements were eased.

The federal government did do the auto industry some good this year with passage of the Federal Highway Act of 1976, which earmarked tax money for repair and upgrades to the Interstate highway system.

1976

Johnny Rutherford won the Indy 500 for the second time in three years; his ride was a Hy-gain McLaren-Offenhauser. The year's pace car was a Buick Century with a turbocharged V-6 rated at 306 net horsepower. The NASCAR crown went to Cale Yarborough.

In this, the nation's bicentennial year, Georgia governor Jimmy Carter was elected president, defeating the incumbent (but never-elected) Gerald Ford. The Supreme Court ruled that the death penalty was not cruel or unusual punishment, and in a mystifying incident in Philadelphia, 29 American Legion members attending a convention died from a yet-to-be-named ailment.

The year's movies included three with cars as centerpieces: *Death Race 2000*, *The Gumball Rally*, and Martin Scorsese's darkly disturbing *Taxi Driver*. *The Shootist*, *Marathon Man*, *Network*, *Silver Streak*, and *Carrie* were other releases.

Top television shows of 1976 were *Laverne and Shirley*; *Happy Days*; *S.W.A.T.*; *The Six Million Dollar Man* and its spinoff, *The Bionic Woman*; and *Starsky and Hutch*.

The music industry promised that five fellows from Scotland, the Bay City Rollers, were "the new Beatles." That was pure hype, but the band's first single, "Saturday Night," did become the year's top record. Other hit-makers in 1976 were Paul Simon ("50 Ways to Leave Your Lover") and Rhythm Heritage ("Theme From S.W.A.T."). Then there were musical crimes committed by L.A. deejay Rick Dees ("Disco Duck") and C. W. McCall ("Convoy," inspired by the CB-radio craze).

Super Bowl X was a nail-biter, with the Pittsburgh Steelers edging the Dallas Cowboys, 21-17. In the World Series, the Cincinnati Reds walked all over the New York Yankees in a four-game sweep. The year's biggest athletic hero may have been Bruce Jenner, who won the Olympic decathlon at Montreal, Canada.

AMC

AMC's market share takes a dive, dropping below three percent for the first time in five years

All car lines receive only detail, trim, and mechanical changes

The Cassini option is no longer available for Matador coupes, but two-door Broughams can be ordered with a Barcelona decor package; plush upholstery and carpeting are included, as are color-keyed wheel covers and a stand-up hood ornament

Gremlin gets a new upgraded Custom model

Of the nearly 53,000 Gremlins built for 1976, just 826 have the 304-cid V-8, which makes its last appearance in AMC's pioneering subcompact

There's more action at Jeep, which adds a four-door Cherokee, an off-road-ready "wide-track" Cherokee Chief, and the CJ-7, a longer version of the veteran CJ-5, which continues

1

2

3

1. Wearing a fresh grille, AMC's Gremlin came in base or Custom trim. Gremlin trailed subcompact rivals in fuel economy, partly due to the lack of a four-cylinder engine. **2.** For a bit more sportiness, the Gremlin X wore full-length side markings and slotted wheels. Unique styling helped Gremlins sell passably well. **3.** AMC's four model lines, Gremlin, Pacer, Hornet, and Matador, leaned toward the smaller end of the scale—a shrewd strategy in the fuel-conscious Seventies.

1

2

3

4

5

6

1. Hornets came in four body styles, including a four-door sedan—shown with D/L option. 2. Hatchbacks gained favor during the Seventies giving Hornet an edge over some competitors. 3. Unlike other models, Hornets displayed a conventional design. 4. The Hornet Sportabout wagon had new compact rivals in the Dodge Aspen/Plymouth Volaré. 5. Whether because of, or in spite of, its odd profile, Pacers sold far beyond expectations. More than 117,000 rolled off the line. Only six-cylinder engines were available, with overdrive an option. This Pacer has the D/L package. 6. Pacer's unusual shape lent itself to exotic striping patterns. Abundant glass area was not a bonus in hot weather, but owners liked the wide Pacer's stability and spaciousness.

257

1

1. Originally planned as a style leader, AMC's Matador Brougham coupe failed to sell well. Bulky outside and lacking space inside, the two-door wore a new grille in '76. **2.** All Matador station wagons had V-8 engines. **3.** The Barcelona option added black or tan wheel covers and knap-knit fabric trim to a Matador Brougham coupe. **4-5.** Despite an aging design, the Matador Brougham four-door sedan offered more room than many mid-size rivals.

2

3

4

5

CHRYSLER CORPORATION

1

Chrysler announces an agreement to purchase engines and transaxles from Volkswagen for its 1978 front-drive subcompacts

The compact Dodge Aspen and Plymouth Volaré debut, but the pair soon sets a sad record for the number of safety recalls

Aspen is advertised as the "family car of the future"

Aspen/Volaré have cross-mounted torsion bars up front

After a long and successful run, the final Valiants and Darts are built

The New Yorker Brougham assumes Imperial's role—a good example of badge engineering

Plymouth Arrow hatchbacks are imported from Mitsubishi in Japan

An electronic Lean Burn System is fitted to the corporation's biggest V-8s for cleaner exhaust

The economy-tuned Dart Lite and Feather Duster are introduced by Dodge and Plymouth, respectively; aluminum parts are key components of the package

2

3

1. Actor Ricardo Montalban touted the Chrysler Cordoba, pronouncing the word with his sensually suave intonations. 2. Cordoba sales soared far beyond predictions. 3. Standard Cordoba upholstery was velour, not the rich Corinthian leather praised by Mr. Montalban. 4. Next to the svelte Cordoba, a full-sized New Yorker Brougham looked immense.

4

259

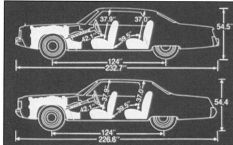

1-2. Chrysler Newport buyers had an often-bizarre choice of interior fabrics. 3. Highlander plaid seat upholstery could be installed in a Newport Custom. 4. Velour was the standard fabric in a New Yorker Brougham. 5. Dimensions of the New Yorker Brougham (top) and less-costly Newport Custom were similar. New Lean Burn 400- and 440-cid V-8s promised better mileage. 6. Newports, like the two-door hardtop, came with a standard 360-cube V-8.

1

2

3

4

5

1. New Dodge Aspens came in three body styles and three trim levels, including this mid-range Custom coupe. **2-4.** Buyers could step up to a Special Edition (SE) Aspen, in any body style, with a Slant Six or V-8. **5.** An Aspen served as the basis for an experimental Gas Turbine Special, for the Energy Research & Development Administration. **6.** With a new front suspension, Aspen promised a big-car ride with small-car handling. **7-8.** Aspen ads featured British actor Rex Harrison.

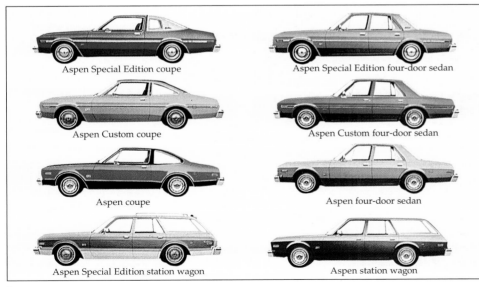

Aspen Special Edition coupe

Aspen Special Edition four-door sedan

Aspen Custom coupe

Aspen Custom four-door sedan

Aspen coupe

Aspen four-door sedan

Aspen Special Edition station wagon

Aspen station wagon

6

1

2

4

3

1. Long known for performance, the Dodge Charger got a modified image in 1976. In fact, all mid-size two-door models were renamed Charger. Similar to the popular Chrysler Cordoba in appearance, Chargers did not sell nearly as well. Wearing sheetmetal different from basic Chargers, this SE coupe rivaled the Chevrolet Monte Carlo and Ford Elite, and handily outsold its base-model companions. **2-3.** More than 17 percent of Charger SE coupes had the $345 Daytona option, featuring two-tone paint and special body taping, plus a black-textured grille and "Charger Daytona" bodyside lettering. **4.** Charger Daytonas got all-vinyl bucket seats and an optional "Tuff" steering wheel. Base engine was a 318-cid V-8, with 360- and 400-cid engines and a floor-shifted TorqueFlite transmission optional.

1

2

1. Four-door mid-size Dodge sedans and wagons kept the Coronet designation, focusing on interior space and practicality. This upscale Brougham four-door sedan sold nearly as well as its base-model Coronet mate. With a Slant Six engine, the Coronet earned a frugal 18/30-mpg mileage rating from the EPA, but V-8 engines were available in three sizes. 2. Despite Coronet fender badging, this is a Charger Sport coupe. In 1975, this design carried a Coronet badge, and would again in '77, making the Charger Sport a one-year-wonder. Just 13,826 were built.
3. Promoted as "the value car," the compact Dart came in four versions: four-door sedan, Sport fastback coupe, Swinger hardtop coupe (shown), and Swinger Special. Engines ranged from the 225-cid Slant Six to a 360-cid V-8.

3

1

2

3

4

5

1. Eking out a little extra gas mileage helped draw customers in 1976. Dodge's Dart Lite was a Sport coupe with a special fuel-economy package, weighing 150 pounds less than its standard compact companions, and equipped with overdrive. Aluminum was used for bumper reinforcements, and for hood and decklid inner panels. **2.** Previously offered in more variations, Dart had been Dodge's top seller—but the rapidly aging compact was about to be overtaken by the new Aspen. Fewer than 35,000 four-door sedans were built this year, in contrast to 98,000 in '75. **3.** Not many families drove home a Royal Monaco Brougham station wagon in 1976, as popularity of traditional American behemoths continued to wane. **4.** Opera windows, a vinyl roof, and individually adjustable 50/50 front seats failed to lure many buyers to the top-of-the-line Royal Monaco Brougham coupe. Hidden headlights made the big Dodges easy to spot. V-8s of 360, 400, or 440 cid could be installed. **5.** Occupying the mid-level position in Dodge's full-size lineup, the Royal Monaco was offered in three body styles with a standard 360-cid V-8. Royal Monacos outsold the lower-priced regular Monacos, which had a standard 318-cid V-8 and came in only two body styles: sedan and station wagon. Unlike other coupe models, which sported opera windows, two-door Royal Monacos retained the traditional roll-down quarter windows—making them true hardtops.

1-3. Like the Dodge Colt, the new Plymouth Arrow was made by Mitsubishi, but came only as a two-door hatchback. A new "Silent Shaft" 2.0-liter four was available. **4.** Mid-sized Fury sedans started at $3733. **5.** Fury Sport coupes had opera windows, tape stripes, and styled wheels.

1

3

6

4

5

7

1. Plymouth's Fury Salon sedan had bodyside trim and a hood ornament that were absent on the base Fury. 2. A cloth/vinyl interior was optional in full-sized Gran Fury Sport Suburban wagons. 3. Once the top Plymouth seller, the big Gran Fury now had trouble finding customers. 4. Hood ornaments were used to mark many top-trim cars, including the Valiant Brougham. 5. Police departments favored big sedans, even if other buyers shunned the guzzlers. 6. This Gran Fury (with Dodge wheel covers) was used by the Hammond, Indiana, police traffic division. 7. Bright bodyside stripes helped identify a Duster coupe with the Silver Duster decor option.

1

2

3

5

4

1. Plymouth's Feather Duster was a lightweight version of the Duster coupe, with aluminum components and over-drive transmission. **2.** Two-tone paint could decorate the new Volaré Custom coupe, kin to Dodge's Aspen. **3.** Once a synonym for sizzling performance, the Road Runner option moved from Fury to the new Volaré coupe, and included a 318-cid V-8 and heavy-duty suspension. **4.** Volaré station wagons came in either base (top) or Premier trim. **5.** Premier was the dressiest of the three Volaré sedans.

267

FORD
MOTOR CO.

1

Dearborn loses nearly two points in market share, to 26.2 percent, as its car lines offer little new of substance

Saleswise, full-size Fords finish fourth among full-size cars, but Granada is number-one in compacts, Lincoln records its second best model-year sales ever, and the Mercury line returns to pre-energy-crisis volume

Jazzy Stallion trim options arrive for non-wagon Ford Pintos and the two-door Maverick; Pinto gets a new close-checked grille and a no-frills, budget-priced Pony two-door

Ford's Mustang II fastback offers its own Stallion package, as well as a white-and-blue Cobra II option that nods to the great Sixties Shelby-Mustangs

Thunderbird's major happening is another round of paint-and-trim packages called Creme/Gold, Bordeaux, and Lipstick

Fashion provides profit as Lincoln introduces its first Designer Series Marks, special models with color and trim inspired by (Hubert) Givenchy, (Emilio) Pucci, Bill Blass, and jewelry house Cartier

Other FoMoCo model lines see only detail changes

2

3

1. Ford's "precision-size" Granada Ghia coupe sported more ornamentation than the base model. Granada sales soared past their impressive 1975 totals. 2-3. A 250-cid six-cylinder engine was standard in the Granada Ghia, with V-8 optional. 4. CB radio still was popular, as evidenced by this 1976 bank promotion.

4

1

2

4

3

5

6

7

8

9

1-2. Hidden headlights set the LTD Landau apart from other big Fords. **3.** Pinto led in subcompact sales. **4.** Pinto, Maverick, and Mustang each offered a Stallion edition. **5.** Runabout was one of 11 Pinto models. **6-7.** A Mustang II hatchback might have a T-top and V-8. **8.** Venom might be missing from the Cobra II, but louvers and lettering made it noticeable. **9.** Mustang II notchbacks came in base or Ghia trim.

1

2

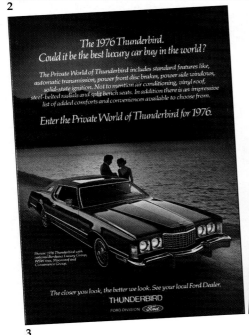

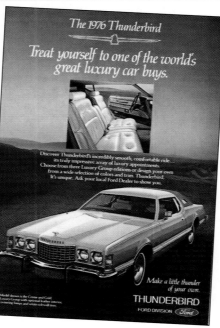

3   4

1-2. Ford Thunderbird scored high in ride comfort and quietness, but a soft suspension made it wallow on winding roads. This would be the last of the really big 'Birds. 3. A Thunderbird with the Bordeaux Luxury Group got Bordeaux glamour paint, a padded vinyl roof, and matching wide bodyside moldings. 4. Specifying a Creme/Gold Luxury Group for Thunderbird brought gold paint with creme accents and a gold padded half-vinyl roof. A Lipstick T-Bird also went on sale.

1

2

3

4

1-4. Ford's designers focused on flexibility when creating the four-in-one Prima concept vehicle for 1976. At a glance, the Prima appeared to be a two-seat compact pickup truck (1), equipped with a tailgate that displayed a Ghia badge—because Ghia stylists in Italy frequently worked with Ford on its concept creations. Adding and removing clip-on plastic panels could transform the show vehicle into a hatchback coupe (2), a station wagon (3), or a two-seat coupe (4). Dimensions were similar to the mini-sized Ford Fiesta. Invariably popular with auto-show audiences, concept vehicles demonstrated the unfettered skills of a company's design staff, but few wound up in actual production. Even so, certain elements would occasionally be adapted for real-world automobiles.

1

3

2

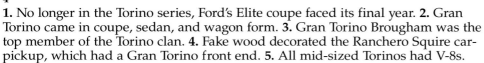

4

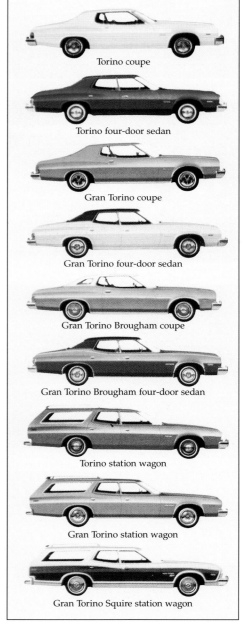

Torino coupe

Torino four-door sedan

Gran Torino coupe

Gran Torino four-door sedan

Gran Torino Brougham coupe

Gran Torino Brougham four-door sedan

Torino station wagon

Gran Torino station wagon

Gran Torino Squire station wagon

1. No longer in the Torino series, Ford's Elite coupe faced its final year. **2.** Gran Torino came in coupe, sedan, and wagon form. **3.** Gran Torino Brougham was the top member of the Torino clan. **4.** Fake wood decorated the Ranchero Squire car-pickup, which had a Gran Torino front end. **5.** All mid-sized Torinos had V-8s. **5**

271

2

3

4

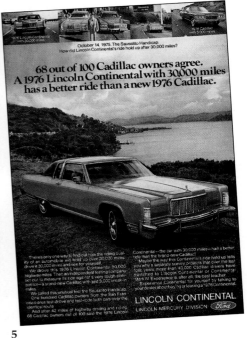

5

Introducing the Mark IV Designer
Series and Lincoln Continentals for 1976

6

1-4. Were these cars or gowns? New Designer Series editions of the Lincoln Continental Mark IV personal-luxury coupe carried the names of fashion designers Bill Blass (1), Givenchy (2), Cartier (3), or Pucci (4). Each had tiny oval opera windows and hidden headlights. **5.** Packing 460-cid V-8 engines, Continentals promised a comfortable ride—but miserable gas mileage. **6.** The Lincoln catalog cover played up the new Designer Series. **7.** Big Continentals came in coupe or four-door sedan form, with available Town Coupe and Town Car packages.

1

2

1. A dramatic black/gold color scheme marked the new Mercury Capri II S coupe, available with an optional 2.8-liter V-6 engine or the standard 2.3-liter overhead-cam four-cylinder. Seating surfaces were gold-colored cloth with black vinyl trim. A white S coupe was also available. **2.** Introduced in mid-1975, the Capri II served as an upgrade of the original (1970-74) Capri, and was built in West Germany or Great Britain. European sport coupes had a certain panache that was absent from American-built cars. Sleek and sporty, the four-passenger Capri II came in three trim levels: base hatchback, S, and Ghia, the latter with high-back bucket seats and cast-aluminum wheels. Capris with the 109-horsepower V-6 engine got a heavy-duty four-speed manual transmission, bigger clutch and brakes, and dual exhaust system. Sales of the original Capri had been sagging, and its Capri II replacement failed to reverse that trend—due in part to the car's hefty sticker price, which started at $4117.

1

2

3

4

5

6

7

1. Replacing the GT, a Sports Accent Group for the two-door Mercury Comet included two-tone paint, styled steel wheels, and racing mirrors. **2.** This Comet sedan has the Custom option, with new bucket seats, door trim, and tinted glass. **3.** Comets got a new front end, and could have a six-cylinder or 302-cid V-8 engine. **4.** Kin to Ford's Pinto, the Bobcat Runabout wore a distinctive vertical grille and domed hood. **5.** Simulated wood trim was a new option for the Bobcat Runabout. **6.** Bobcats also came in Villager wagon form, with either a four-cylinder engine or a 2.8-liter V-6. **7.** Cousin to Ford's Granada, the Monarch Ghia was the upscale edition of Mercury's compact.

1

2

3

1. Mercury's Cougar XR-7 coupe was essentially a two-door Montego with different grille and interior trim. 2-3. Offered as a sedan or coupe, the Marquis Brougham was the mid-level version of the full-sized Marquis group. 4. Colony Park station wagons could have two or three seats. 5. A ghost view of the line-topping Marquis shows the sliding rams that held the energy-absorbing bumpers.

4

5

GENERAL
MOTORS CORP.

GM's market share swells by 2.5 points to 55.8 percent

Most mid-size GM cars switch to rectangular headlamps; so do Chevrolet Caprice and Oldsmobile Toronado

Buick supplies a special turbocharged V-6 Century as Indy 500 pace car; it's only the second time in Indy history that the same make has paced the race two years running

Cadillac trumpets its ragtop Eldorado as "America's last convertible," and ups production to cash in on rabid "instant collectible" speculation

Chevrolet unveils the rear-drive Chevette, a subcompact two-door hatchback based on GM's European T-car platform; sales are good, but not as good as forecast

Pontiac marks its half-century with two limited editions: a 50th Anniversary Firebird clad in black paint with gold accents, and a Golden Anniversary Grand Prix with an available T-bar roof

Pontiac also introduces Sunbird, a close cousin of Chevy's Vega-based Monza Towne Coupe

1

2

3

4

5

6

1. Mid-size Buicks, including the new price-leader Century Special coupe, got a new look. 2. Century Customs came in sedan, coupe, and wagon form. 3. A turbo V-6 went into the Century Indy 500 pace car. 4. The Electra 225 line included a hardtop sedan and coupe. 5. This up-scale Electra 225 Limited wears Custom Landau trim. 6. A bit smaller than Electra, the LeSabre Custom coupe is shown with Landau vinyl roof.

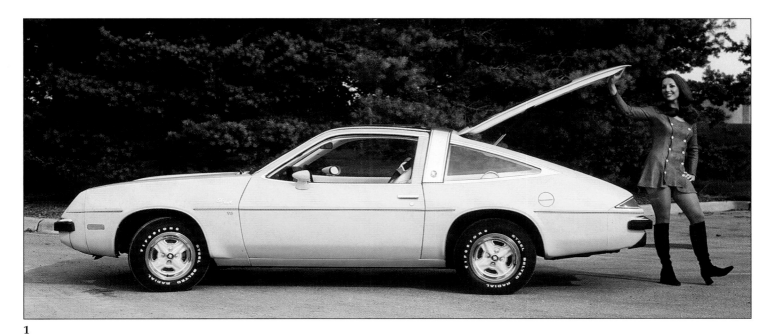

1

2

3

4

1. A glass Astroroof could be installed on the subcompact Buick Skyhawk hatchback for $550 extra. 2. The sporty Riviera GS was gone, but an S/R option cost $276. 3. Skylark S/R models were offered in sedan, coupe (shown), and hatchback form, but combined production totaled only 8371. 4. Buick's sales catalog cover featured a wood carving created with a "free spirit" theme.

1

2

4

3

5

6

7

1. A 500-cid V-8 engine again went into all Cadillac models, except for the compact Seville. An optional fuel-injected version produced 215 horsepower. 2. Next to a Coupe de Ville, the Seville looked modest in size. 3. Sedan de Villes weren't quite as popular as the equivalent coupes. 4. The Coupe de Ville attracted 114,482 buyers. 5. A big Fleetwood Sixty Special Brougham four-door sedan topped 5200 pounds—but other Cadillacs weren't far behind. 6-7. The last Eldorado convertibles went on sale in 1976—at least until ragtops were revived in the early Eighties. Speculators snapped up many of the final examples. 8. GM's response to Mercedes-Benz, the Seville four-door sedan, had a strong sales year. Equipped with a 350-cid V-8, the Seville was loaded with power accessories.

8

1

2

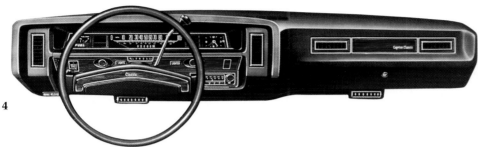

3

4

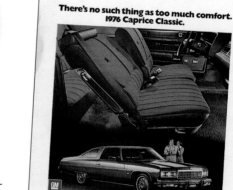

1-2. Chevrolet's full-sized Impala came in four body styles with any of four V-8 engines. **3.** Second-best Impala seller was the Custom coupe. **4-5.** Full-size Chevy buyers could step up to a Caprice Classic, which promised plenty of comfort. **6.** For $306 extra, fake wood trim could dress up the new mini-sized Chevette hatchback. **7.** Chevettes could get Rally equipment for as little as $230 extra. **8.** Weighing under a ton, the rear-drive Chevette was the smallest Chevrolet ever, and the only all-new GM model for '76. The minicar was derived from the Opel Kadett.

5

6

7

Chevette coupe

Chevette Sport coupe

Chevette Rallye coupe

Chevette Woody coupe

Chevette Scooter coupe

8

1

2

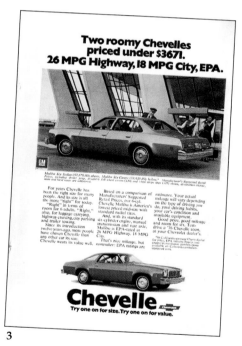

3

1. Stylish and sporty, the Chevelle Laguna Type S-3 coupe got a redesigned rear panel for its final season on the market. 2. A six-cylinder engine was standard in the Chevelle Malibu Classic sedan, or the lower-cost base Malibu. 3. Chevelle Malibus promised ample interior space and fuel economy. 4. Round dials went into the Laguna S-3 dashboard. This one has an optional four-spoke steering wheel.

4

1

2

3

4

5

6

1-3. No more Corvette convertibles were produced, but engine outputs for the Stingray coupe rose this year and sales set a record. More than 46,000 coupes were built. Their 350 V-8s were rated at 180 or 210 horsepower. **4.** The formal-windowed, notchback Chevrolet Monza Towne Coupe had debuted in 1975. This one has the optional 4.3-liter V-8 and special roof treatment. **5.** Evolved from the Vega, Monzas also came in 2+2 hatchback coupe form, with the Vega's four-cylinder engine or a V-8. **6.** In addition to the V-8 engine, a Monza Towne Coupe might be equipped with a performance/handling package.

282

1

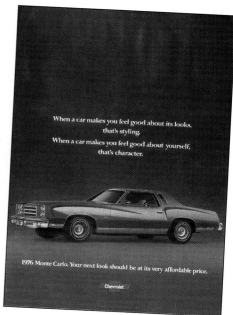

1976 CHEVROLET POLICE VEHICLES

3

When a car makes you feel good about its looks, that's styling.
When a car makes you feel good about yourself, that's character.

1976 Monte Carlo. Your next look should be at its very affordable price.

Chevrolet

2

4

5

1-2. Most popular of the personal-luxury coupes, Chevrolet's Monte Carlo Landau got a fresh front end but lost its 454-cid V-8 option. **3.** Some police departments favored the compact Nova. **4.** A Nova Concours sedan replaced the prior Nova LN. **5.** An SS package for the Nova hatchback cost only $187, including a heavy-duty suspension. **6.** Chevrolet promoted reliability of its Vega and Monza four-cylinder engines, which had suffered serious mechanical problems. **7.** Available for the last time, the potent Cosworth Vega, with Twin Cam engine, sold in small numbers.

6

7

283

1

2

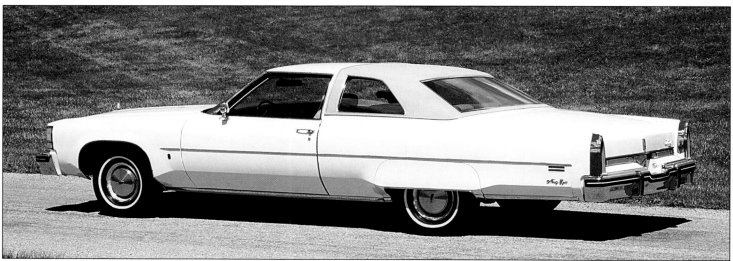

3

4

5

1. Cutlass S was the new base model in the mid-size Oldsmobile line. 2. Vista Cruiser wagons were members of the Cutlass family. 3. Cutlass S coupe buyers could specify a 4-4-2 appearance/handling option for $134, but performance didn't come with the package. 4-5. Could a fellow feel like a king behind the wheel of a Ninety-Eight Regency four-door hardtop? Ad writers wanted people to think so.
6-8. Biggest of the Olds models, Ninety-Eights came in hardtop coupe or sedan form.

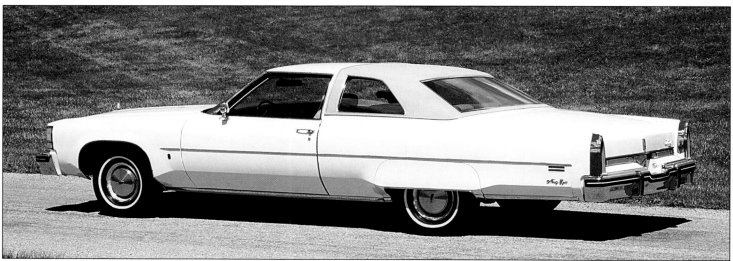

6

7

8

1

2

We built this Delta 88 for John Andersen, who needed a car that could stand up to his ultimate endurance test.

His three kids.

1976 DELTA 88
Oldsmobile
Can we build one for you?

3

4

1-2. An Oldsmobile Ninety-Eight Regency coupe had a few more posh extras than the lower-priced Luxury series. **3.** Olds targeted families with the Delta 88 hardtop sedan, which was full-size but smaller than a Ninety-Eight. **4.** This Delta 88 Royale has the Crown Landau option, with padded vinyl roof and 6-inch stainless steel roof band.

1

2

1. Oldsmobile's Delta 88 four-door hardtop came in base (shown) or Royale trim. **2.** An Omega Brougham replaced the Salon edition. **3.** A special hood and wide stripes marked the Starfire GT. **4.** Toronado's 455-cid V-8 made 215 horsepower.

3

4

1

2

4

3

5

6

1. In its second season, the subcompact Pontiac Astre hatchback could get a five-speed gearbox, as well as a GT option. Evolved from Chevrolet's Vega, Astre used the Vega's four-cylinder engines. **2-3.** The Bonneville, offered in coupe (shown) and hardtop sedan, was similar to the Bonneville Brougham, Pontiac's new flagship. **4.** Yes, the times were changing. Pontiac pushed gas mileage with its "performance" Formula Firebird, not just the economy-minded Sunbird and Astre. **5.** Firebirds got new body-colored Endura bumpers, front and rear. Concealed wipers helped identify the luxury Esprit (shown). **6.** Bold graphics on the "shaker" hood gave an impression of vigor, but the Trans Am's 400-cid V-8 made a modest 185 horsepower. The optional 455-cid V-8 got a 200-horse rating. Trans Ams had an air dam and decklid spoiler, rally gauges, and rode Rally II wheels.

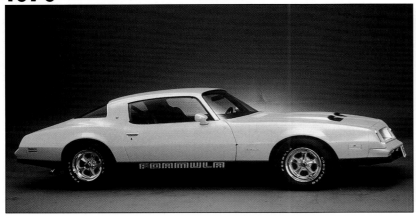

1

2

3

4

5

6

1. A 350-cid V-8 was standard in the Firebird Formula coupe. **2.** Pontiac created this Trans Am Type K to demonstrate the possibility of a kammback body. **3.** Half a century of Pontiacs had passed, as suggested by this Grand Prix SJ anniversary model, posed next to a 1926 Pontiac coupe. SJ was the upscale Grand Prix. **4.** This 50th anniversary emblem decorated the hood of the special '76 Grand Prix. **5.** An LJ luxury appointment group could be installed on the Grand Prix coupe that included velour buckets and two-tone paint. **6.** Pontiac's Grand Prix could have a 350-, 400-, or 455-cid V-8.

1

2

3

1. Grand LeMans topped the LeMans lineup, with a newly available 260-cid V-8 engine or the option of a 455. **2.** LeMans Safari wagons came in standard or Grand guise. **3.** The LeMans Sport Coupe—seen here without the usual quarter window louvers—sold for $3,916. A five-speed manual transmission was newly optional. **4.** New for '76, the subcompact Sunbird coupe was related to Chevrolet's Monza. **5.** A new 260-cid V-8 and five-speed failed to stimulate sales of the compact Ventura, shown in SJ trim.

4

5

IMPORTS

Perhaps buyers are more patriotic in America's Bicentennial year, but foreign-car market share drops over three points to 14.8 percent

Buick tries an end-run around price inflation by replacing German Opels with a Japanese-built "Opel by Isuzu" coupe

Datsun has a busy year, adding a low-priced Honey Bee version of its two-door B-210 sedan and, at midseason, oddly styled F-10 subcompacts; topping the line are a new six-cylinder 810 sedan and wagon

Honda makes history anew by introducing the Accord two-door hatchback at midyear; it's an instant hit

Jaguar's respected XJ sedan sires the XJ-S, a grand touring coupe with standard V-12 power

Lancia returns to the U.S. with the front-drive Beta sedan and coupe powered by Fiat's dohc 1.8-liter four; sales suggest the Italians shouldn't have bothered

With fuel flowing again, Mercedes-Benz brings a new version of its high-performance "super sedan" to the U.S. market, the $50,000 450SEL 6.9

Porsche drops the base-model 914, revives the four-cylinder 912, and brings in the awesome 911 Turbo Carrera

Toyota turns its sporty Celica notchback into a mini-Mustang called Celica GT Liftback

Triumph makes a controversial transition, abandoning its classic six-cylinder TR6 roadster for a wedgy new TR7 coupe with four-cylinder power

1

2

THE LIMITED EDITION 41 MPG* HONEY BEE.

3

4

5

1. The 100 LS sedan topped Audi's front-drive line. 2. Fox was the smaller Audi, offered in three body styles. 3-5. Datsun added sport to frugality in the subcompact B-210 Honey Bee two-door. 6. An F-10 hatchback and wagon arrived late as the lowest-cost Datsuns.

6

1

2

3

4

1. Datsun's 280Z sports car came as a two-seater, or a longer-wheelbase 2+2 coupe. **2.** A Mercedes-Benz 450SL two-seat coupe/roadster (left) and a bigger 450SLC coupe are seen on the test track at company headquarters in Stuttgart, Germany. Each held a 4.5-liter V-8 cranking out 180 horsepower. **3.** The Mercedes-Benz sedan lineup included a six-cylinder 280S (left), and the 450SE and 450SEL with V-8 power. Top-selling mid-Seventies model was the diesel-powered 240D sedan, with one-fourth of sales. **4.** Renault launched a new low-budget R-5 subcompact. Later known as Le Car, the front-drive R-5 was billed as "the incredible little car a million Europeans drive."

1

2

3

4

1. Even in the shrinking-horsepower Seventies, Porsche never let up on performance and handling talents. Wearing a "whale tail" spoiler, the 911 Turbo Carrera (type 930) reached America in 1976, to become the swiftest Porsche ever. A turbocharged flat-six engine sent 234 horsepower to its four-speed manual transaxle. The Turbo could reach 60 mph in 4.9 seconds. **2.** Front-wheel-drive Subarus, including this GF hardtop coupe, were gaining in popularity, partly due to their impressive fuel-economy figures. A 1595-cc four-cylinder engine became optional in 1976, later replacing the 1361-cc version. **3-4.** Subaru offered the DL as a station wagon, four-door sedan, and two-door sedan.

1. Toyota's Mark II came in coupe or four-door sedan form. The top-selling Toyota was the subcompact Corolla, which helped the company overtake Volkswagen as Number One in import sales. 2. A Toyota Corona station wagon could be purchased with optional woodgrain trim. 3. Toyota Corona buyers had three body styles to consider, including this four-door sedan. 4. Volkswagen's front-drive Scirocco hatchback used the Rabbit's running gear, but wore a low-roofline Karmann body, styled by Ital Design. Stiffer springing gave it a sporty character.

1

2

3

4

Model-year output of American cars again topped 9 million units, and there was good news for makers of imports, too, which hit the 2-million sales mark for the first time. That was encouraging, but Detroit knew it would have few friends in Washington when President Carter appointed Joan Claybrook, a colleague of autophobic consumer advocate Ralph Nader, as head of the National Highway Traffic Safety Administration. Consumers were in for a bad time, as well, as real income began to slide dramatically.

American Motors, which had been doing pretty well with its subcompacts, particularly the Pacer, took a big hit this year, with sales of Pacer—AMC's most popular car—sliding to about 58,300 units on the heels of 117,200 sold for model-year 1976. Hornet sales held steady, but Gremlin and Matador, like Pacer, saw dramatic drops. AMC appeared to be on the verge of going up in smoke.

This year's inductee into the Automotive Hall of Fame was legendary GM engineer and corporation president Ed Cole, whose vision helped produce cars as disparate as the original Corvette and the right-for-the-Seventies Chevette.

A. J. Foyt won his fourth Indy 500, this time in a Gilmore Coyote-Foyt. The great race was paced by a

1977

185-net-horsepower Oldsmobile Delta 88 driven by actor James Garner. NASCAR's Winston Cup champ was Cale Yarborough, in the middle of a Winston Cup three-peat.

In national news, President Carter pardoned Vietnam-era draft evaders, which raised the hackles of conservative Americans. Fifteen nations, including the United States and the USSR, signed the nuclear-proliferation pact to curb the spread of deadly weapons. And in China, a major political shakeup purged the Communist government of the so-called "Gang of Four," which included the widow of dictator Mao Tse-tung, who had died in 1976.

A high-profile Hollywood release, *Bobby Deerfield*, grafted Grand Prix racing onto a hey-my-girlfriend's-dying-of-some-weird-disease plotline, and was a complete mess. Other, more satisfying '77 releases included *Star Wars, Saturday Night Fever, Close Encounters of the Third Kind, Slap Shot, A Bridge Too Far*, and *Greased Lightning*, the story of Wendell Scott, the first African-American stock-car racer.

Small-screen winners included *Charlie's Angels, Baretta, Three's Company, Little House on the Prairie*, and *Barney Miller*.

Top records included "Car Wash" by Rose Royce, "Torn Between Two Lovers" by Mary MacGregor, "Dancing Queen" by Abba, "Hotel California" by the Eagles, and "Rich Girl" by Hall & Oates.

This year's Super Bowl was the 11th—make that the XIth—and was won by the Oakland Raiders, who defeated the Minnesota Vikings, 32-14. In the World Series, Billy Martin's New York Yankees got by Tommy Lasorda's Los Angeles Dodgers, four games to two.

AMC

It's another down year for America's number-four automaker, as market share slips to just above two percent

Gremlin supplements its usual six with a newly optional 2.0-liter overhead-cam four-cylinder engine built under license from Audi of Germany; it's a mileage-minded legacy of the energy crisis

Pacer adds a three-door wagon to its familiar bubble-shaped hatchback two-door, yet combined production isn't even half that of the '76 model run

The AMX name returns on a jazzy option package for the Hornet hatchback coupe; AMC's 304 V-8 remains a Hornet option, but the reborn AMX is far more show than go

Still clinging to late-Sixties engineering, Matador is a virtual rerun, and sales continue declining

1

2

3

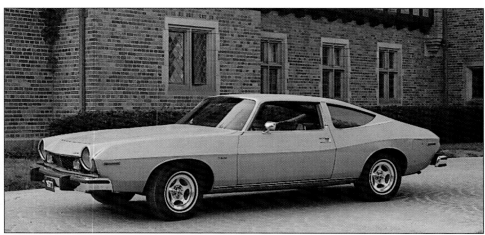

4

5

1. Again available in sporty "X" trim, AMC's Gremlin got a front/rear restyling and new optional engine. 2. The youth-oriented, limited-edition Hornet AMX included a front sway bar, fender flares, and window louvers. 3. Hornet buyers who wanted luxury could order a D/L edition. 4. A Hornet Sportabout wagon lured the practical-minded. 5. Aluminum wheels and a vinyl top could dress up a Matador coupe.

1

2

3

4

5

1. AMC's Matador station wagon held a standard 304-cid V-8, or optional 360-cid V-8. **2.** Matador sedans gained some standard equipment—and an ample price hike. **3.** Pacer hatchback buyers could go upscale by specifying the D/L option. **4.** AMC even offered a combination of "Levi's" trim and "X" equipment for the Pacer. **5.** A station wagon joined the Pacer lineup, but failed to spark sales.

AMC designers came up with a diverse assortment of concept vehicles, evolved from existing models (top to bottom): a Pacer-based four-wheel-drive AM VAN, complete with curious porthole; the Jeep II; a wedge-shaped Concept Electron; plus the Concept II; Concept Grand Touring; and Concept I.

297

CHRYSLER CORPORATION

The industry's model-year output tops 9.1 million cars; Chrysler Corporation production is up 25 percent

Imported-car sales hit the 2-million mark

Plymouth is sixth in output—behind Oldsmobile, Pontiac, and Buick

General Motors begins its downsizing wave, but Ford and Chrysler cling longer to their large cars

The LeBaron and Diplomat "senior" compacts arrive, built off the Aspen/Volaré platform

LeBaron and Diplomat exhibit a boxy Mercedes-like look, with square headlights

Dodge renames its mid-size models Monaco, displacing Coronet; the former full-sized Monaco becomes the "Royal Monaco"

Dodge and Plymouth get their last 440-cid V-8 engines

1

2

1. Wearing a fresh grille and horizontal taillights, Chrysler's Newport four-door hardtop was still a pillarless design—unlike most rivals. The Custom version was gone, but its trim went on base Newports. 2. Topping the Chrysler line, the New Yorker Brougham came in two- or four-door hardtop form, with a 400- or 440-cid V-8 engine. Other manufacturers were abandoning their big-block V-8s, but Chrysler kept them around a while longer. 3. This ad for the Newport hardtop coupe touted the car's Lean Burn V-8 engine, dubbed "the engine that thinks." One of several methods of reducing emissions, the Lean Burn system was available on all three V-8 engines installed in full-size models: 360-, 400-, and 440-cid.

3

1

2

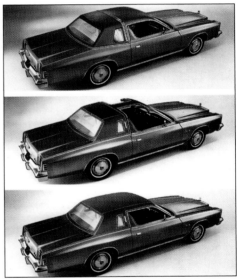

3

4

5

1-2. Chrysler's strong-selling Cordoba could get a new optional T-top for $605 extra. **3.** Cordobas came with a choice of optional roof treatments, including (top to bottom): "Crown" padded elk grain vinyl, new T-top, or "standard" style Halo vinyl roof. **4.** Cordobas got fresh front/rear styling, with a formal-look grille and a choice of three V-8 engines. **5.** Midyear brought a new LeBaron Medallion sedan (and coupe), a "senior" compact with a 318-cid V-8. Cleanly styled, LeBarons sold well.

299

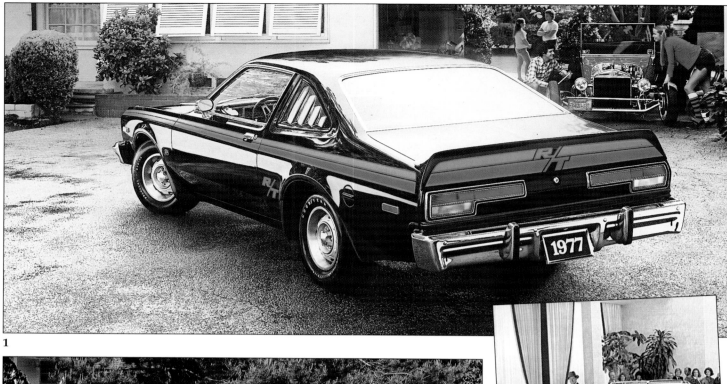

1

2

3

1. An R/T option, including Super Pak equipment, added pizzazz to a Dodge Aspen coupe. 2. For those who didn't care to be noticed, an Aspen R/T coupe could omit some flamboyant trim. 3. The Special Edition (SE) wagon topped the compact Aspen lines. Introduced a year earlier, in three body styles, Aspen had become the hottest-selling Dodge—by far. A new Super Six engine was available, with two-barrel carburetion. 4. Compact dimensions aside, some Aspens saw service as taxis. 5. Kin to Chrysler's new LeBaron, the "senior" compact Diplomat debuted in mid-season. Upmarket buyers might favor a Medallion coupe (shown). 6. Diplomat sedans also came in Medallion trim, but didn't sell as well as coupes.

4

5

6

1

4

2

5

6

3

1. A Dodge Charger Limited Edition coupe emerged after the start of the model year. 2. A T-top could be installed on the Charger SE coupe, which stick-ered for $5098. 3. Daytona trim added only $166 to the Charger's price. Note the curious two-tone paint pattern. 4. A Colt GT was a lot tamer than its name might suggest. 5. This Mitsubishi-built Colt wagon has a woodgrain Estate package. 6. Rear-drive Colts got "silent shaft" four-cylinder engines.

1

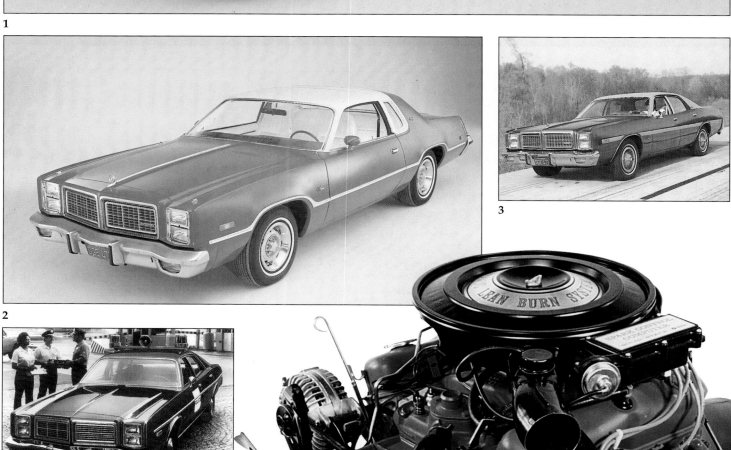

2

3

4

1-2. A new Monaco coupe, shown in Brougham trim, replaced the Coronet as Dodge's mid-size. Restyling included stacked headlights. 3. The Monaco Brougham sedan could have a Super Six, or any of four V-8 engines. 4. Plenty of four-door Monacos went into service with police departments, which liked the car's dimensions and V-8 power. 5. Even the 318-cid V-8 got a Lean Burn engine management system.

5

1

2

3

4

5

1-2. Dodge renamed its full-size cars Royal Monaco. **3.** This Royal Monaco was in the opening credits for the Eighties TV drama, *Hill Street Blues*. **4.** Street vans were promoted as "Adult Toys." **5.** Dodge even had a Ramcharger sport-utility vehicle.

1

2

3

4

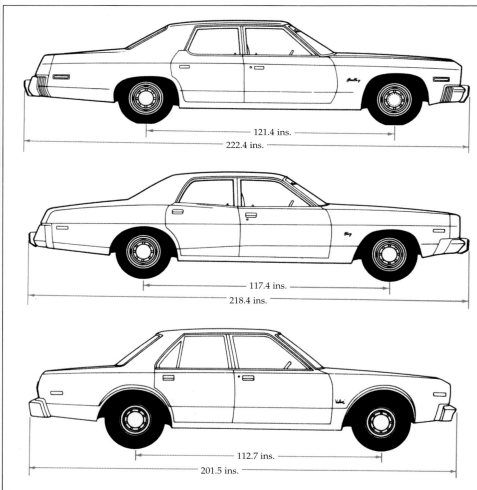

5

1. Selling well in the mid-Seventies, Plymouth's sporty Japanese-built Arrow hatchback added a mid-level GS edition. 2. Facelifting of the mid-sized Fury Sport coupe included stacked headlights. 3. Loaded with luxury and convenience features, Salon was the top-of-the-line Fury sedan. 4-5. More and more Plymouths—including the mid-sized Fury and big Gran Fury—were purchased for police and other fleet use, rather than going to retail customers. Police departments liked the still-strong V-8 engines and roomy interiors.

1

2

3

4

5

6

1. A 318-cid V-8 was standard in the full-sized Gran Fury Brougham coupe, but even the big-block 440 V-8 remained available. 2. Not much was new for the $4948 Gran Fury Brougham sedan, but its Custom companion was dropped. 3. Traffic was a growing problem even in smaller cities, as revealed by this scene in Green Bay, Wisconsin, on January 25, 1977. 4. Sport Suburban station wagon came in mid-sized Fury and full-sized Gran Fury form, but neither leaped off showroom floors. Once a staple of suburban life, the big wagon was waning in popularity. 5. Plymouth's Trail Duster Sport utility vehicle—that's right, an SUV of the Seventies—could have two- or four-wheel drive and a host of options. 6. Like the Dodge Sportsman, Plymouth's Voyager sport van came in three weight ratings, on a short or long wheelbase.

305

1

2

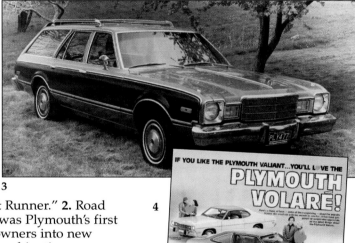

3

1. Extras transformed a Volaré (left) into a Road Runner "Front Runner." 2. Road Runner with optional T-top. 3. Volaré, shown in Premier trim, was Plymouth's first compact wagon since '66. 4. Plymouth worked to lure Valiant owners into new Volarés. 5. Volaré coupes were offered in nine two-tone paint combinations.

4

5

FORD MOTOR CO.

Dearborn does well this year, tacking on nearly two points in market share to just over 28 percent

The mid-sized Ford Torino gets crisp new lines and a name trading on big-Ford prestige: LTD II

Thunderbird is dramatically downsized by becoming a high-line mid-size; price is down dramatically too and sales soar, the Bird outselling all LTD IIs combined; a lush Town Landau joins the standard model in January

A like transformation turns Mercury's Montegos into Cougars, with a top-line XR-7 as a sister to the smaller new T-Bird; sales here are up too, but not as much as Ford's

Ford's Pinto adds a sloped "soft" nose and a sporty Cruising Wagon model with bold graphics and porthole rear side windows

Planned for the chop in '75, Ford Maverick and Mercury Comet reach the end of the line after '77

Ford Mustang II offers a bevy of new options: T-bar roof, Rallye Package (replacing Stallion), and louvered windows for the Cobra II group

Lincoln ushers in a new Continental Mark V that's a full 500 pounds lighter than the Mark IV; sales set a new record for the model

Meantime, Lincoln gilds a Granada to create Versailles, a belated luxury-compact reply to Cadillac's Seville

1

2

3

1. GM downsized its full-size cars this year, but no one could accuse Ford of shrinking its LTD Landau sedan—the top-of-the-line model, with a $5742 sticker. 2. LTD station wagons came in plain or Country Squire trim. 3. A four-speed overdrive transmission became standard in Granada, shown in upscale Ghia guise. 4-6. Ford's admakers did not hesitate to compare their Granada to the luxury European Mercedes-Benz, or the LTD to a Cadillac. Comparison-type ads were in vogue, but the one that set the LTD wagon against an equivalent Chevrolet might have made more sense.

How did an American Ford Granada compare in tests of smoothness and quietness of ride with a $20,000 German Mercedes?

4

5

6

1

2

3

1-2. Keeping its big cars ample in size for a while longer, Ford had several selling points that gave them an edge. Heavyweights with V-8 engines were admittedly better for heavy-duty hauling and towing. This LTD Landau coupe sold fairly well at $5717, though the base-model LTD proved to be stronger yet when the annual totals were counted. A 351-cid V-8 was standard, but many buyers opted for a 400- or 460-cid V-8, the latter pumping out 197 horsepower. 3. Actor Karl Malden hit the pavement with a Ford police car in the 1972-77 TV series, *The Streets of San Francisco*. 4. Lynwood, Illinois, Police Chief Peter DeMaio directs traffic away from a closed road after a heavy snowstorm in January 1977. The chief could count on rolling through wintry roads in that big Ford. Only Ford and Chrysler continued to sell traditional-size models.

4

1

2

3

4

5

6

1977 Ford Mustang II
Sweet handling.

If you think it's time
you put some fun
in your driving...
think Ford.

Ford.
A giant step for vankind.
Ford pioneered the van. And who's still out in front? You guessed it.

Mustang II for 1977.
Sweet-handling SuperCoupe.
Some people consider driving a kick. We had these people in mind when we began building the five new sweet-handling Mustang II's.

Ford pickups.
The haul of fame.
There are some people who think Fordpickup is all one word. That's because Ford has built so many that lasted so long.

4x4xFord.
Ever wish you could head off the road for the wide open spaces? Ford's four-wheel drive vehicles will get you there—and back. They work hard all week, play hard all weekend.

'77 Pinto. Changed.
But not just for the sake of change.
New styling, new features, new options add up to more fun in America's best selling subcompact.

Granada. LTD II. Thunderbird.
Three for the road.
Head for the horizon in one of Ford's stylish, 2-door coupes. They're what road machines are all about.

7

1. Ford reskinned the Torino this year and called it the LTD II, shown here in Brougham sedan form. Sales were good, beating the previous year's Torino by over 40,000. 2. The simple Maverick compact was in its final season. 3. Spotting a Mustang II Cobra II hatchback wasn't difficult—not with those broad full-length twin stripes and louvered windows. Turning a tame Mustang into a flamboyant Cobra cost $535.
4. Planners rejected this Stallion II paint scheme for the Mustang II. 5. T-tops joined the Mustang II option list. 6. A $4119 Ghia was more plush inside, but base Mustang II coupes sold somewhat better. 7. This ad mixes Ford cars with trucks, vans, and SUVs as "sport" vehicles—shades of things to come.

1

2

1. The Pinto Runabout gained a new all-glass hatch. 2. Ford boasted of extensive standard features on its redesigned Thunderbird. 3. T-Birds lost 10 inches of length and 900 pounds. Result? Super sales. 4. Youth-oriented Cruising Van was based on the Econoline E-150 in Chateau trim. 5. This was the last year for the original Bronco design, shown here as a half-cab.

3

4

5

1

2

1-2. Facelifted and downsized modestly, but wearing all-new sheetmetal, the new Continental Mark V coupe again wore concealed headlights and tiny oval portholes. Sales quickly set a new record. A 400-cid V-8 engine now was standard, with the 460-cid V-8 offered as an option. Posh designer editions remained available, too.

1

3

Introducing the 1977 Lincoln Continental.
Judge any luxury car by this standard.

The 1977 Lincoln Continental sets a high standard for luxury cars. Full-sized, full-luxury, to give you the pleasures of space, of comfort, of superb handling on the highway. That's because it's a Continental. Unmistakable from its redesigned front end to its winning Lincoln ride.

For 1977, some luxury cars are smaller than last year. For 1977, Lincoln Continental retains its traditional luxury car size. We believe it's a luxury car that meets your standards.

Lincoln Continental. A standard by which luxury cars are judged.

LINCOLN CONTINENTAL
LINCOLN-MERCURY DIVISION *Ford*

2

1. The "Mark" Continentals, from the 1940-41 Mark I (upper left), to the '77 Mark V (bottom). **2.** Lincoln ads stressed the Continental's full size, against now-smaller rivals. **3.** Special editions included the two-tone Williamsburg Town Car. **4-5.** The Town Car or Town Coupe added $913 to the price of a Continental sedan or coupe.

4

5

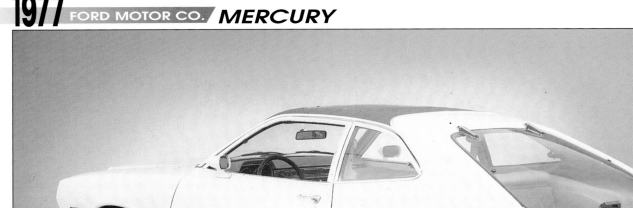

1

2

1. Little-changed this season, Mercury's subcompact Bobcat hatchback got a new all-glass hatch, as a $13 option. New bumpers helped reduce weight. A Sports Group included a tachometer, front stabilizer bar, and higher-rate springs for improved handling. Either a four-cylinder or V-6 engine could be installed.
2-3. Still sold by Lincoln-Mercury dealers, the snappy European-built Capri II coupe had a standard 2.3-liter engine, but a V-6 was optional. Rust-prone early models had given the Capri a bad reputation, but sharp looks helped attract buyers. A Ghia edition added such extras as cast aluminum wheels and flip-out quarter windows.

3

1

2

4

3

1-3. As the Cougar badge moved onto plain old Montegos, the Cougar XR-7 coupe became a specialty model on its own. Redesigned for '77, but still relatively large in size, the XR-7 had a sporty flair and ranked as the flashiest domestic Mercury model. Vertical slots in rear quarter windows were exclusive to the XR-7, which did not share its roofline with other Cougars. A new decklid was similar to the one used in Lincoln's Mark V coupe. Ride and handing were improved, courtesy of a new rear stabilizer bar and heavier front bar. A 302-cid V-8 was standard; 351- and 400-cid V-8s optional. **4.** Facing its final season with little change, the compact Comet came only in base trim—but this coupe has the optional Sports Accent Group. Engine choices remained 200- and 250-cid six-cylinders, or a 302-cid V-8.

1

2

3

1. Flaunting the same front end as the XR-7, the Cougar Brougham was essentially a modified Montego. 2. Lincoln-Mercury ad manager John Vanderzee hangs a Cougar medallion around the neck of "spokesbabe" Farrah Fawcett-Majors. 3. The $5363 Cougar Villager wagon outsold its base-model mate. 4. Mercury's big Grand Marquis sedan came in base or Brougham trim. 5. Now equipped with a "Mod-4" four-speed manual gearbox, Monarch edged past the XR-7 as top-selling Mercury.

4

5

The General wants 60 percent of the market, and inches closer to it in '77 by taking 56.6 percent

GM's biggest cars from Chevy to Cadillac shrink by many inches and hundreds of pounds to near intermediate size, yet sell better than ever thanks to improved fuel mileage and no loss of interior room

Among Buick's trim new LeSabres is a distinctive Sport Coupe with a standard V-8; in subsequent years, a turbocharged V-6 powers the Sport Coupe

Buick's Riviera is also downsized, shifted to the smaller new B-body used by LeSabres

After a two-year absence, the Chevrolet Camaro Z28 returns at midyear, but with the emphasis now on handling, not acceleration

Chevrolet drops the Cosworth Vega after two disappointing seasons

A special open-top version of Oldsmobile's new Delta 88 paces this year's Indy 500; a few replicas are offered with the normal coupe bodywork

Pontiac's Astre subcompacts offer a tough new "Iron Duke" four in most models to replace the trouble-prone Chevy Vega engine

Pontiac's Sunbird also offers the Iron Duke, and adds a "SportsHatch" fastback coupe late in the season

Pontiac's Firebird adopts a new "bird beak" face; a special 10th Anniversary Edition marks the birth of the hot Trans Am

1

2

3

4

5

6

7

8

9

10

1. Skylark continued as Buick's compact. 2. Regal Landau with its new grille. 3. Century dropped its Collonade name. 4. Electra Limited in Park Avenue trim. 5. Electra 225 was now smaller. 6. Estate Wagon in Limited trim. 7. LeSabre Custom outsold the base sedan. 8-9. The downsized '77 Riviera. 10. Skyhawk got a new grille. 11. By '77, any street was a mix of domestics and imports.

11

1

2

3

4

1. Cadillac touted its dramatically downsized Fleetwood Brougham, now closer in appearance and dimensions to the lower-priced Sedan de Ville, as a car "for very special people." This one has the $885 Brougham d'Elegance package, including contoured pillow-style seats trimmed in Florentine velour, plus turbine-vaned wheel covers. Standard engine was now a 425-cid V-8, sending the old 500-cid engine into the history books. Broughams had all-disc brakes. **2.** The Sedan de Ville lost a whopping 900 pounds, and 9.5 inches of overall length. The 425-cid V-8 was available with fuel injection, for a 15-horse-power difference. One Cadillac model departed this year: the Calais. While most automakers suffered in the sales department following the 1973-74 fuel crisis, Cadillac continued to attract plenty of tradition-minded buyers. As improved energy supplies and a revived economy arrived, Cadillac fared even better when the annual totals were calculated. **3.** Even the Fleetwood limousines shrunk in size, to a mere 144.5-inch wheelbase. Prices began at $18,349, or $19,014 for a Formal Limousine with black leather up front. **4.** Newly elected president Jimmy Carter and wife Rosalyn stroll down the street, near the U.S. Capitol in Washington, D.C., on Inauguration Day, January 1977. A formal Cadillac parade car follows the couple as they wave to the assembled crowd. Inaugural Balls were held all over the city to commemorate the occasion—including one in Amtrak's Union Station. Since the Thirties, various Cadillacs and Lincolns have been used for presidential parades and other ceremonial occasions.

1

2

1-2. Unlike its downsized companions, the Eldorado coupe stuck to its overly abundant dimensions, selling even better than before. Still front-wheel drive, promising a super-cushiony ride, the Eldo gained new all-disc brakes, but was otherwise falling behind the times. Convertibles were now a part of Cadillac history, leaving only the coupe. 3. Seville sedans displayed only minor changes, including a new grille that some considered akin to Rolls-Royce. Amber turn-signal lenses also contributed to its European-like demeanor. Because big Cadillacs had shrunk so sharply, a Seville now weighed almost as much as a De Ville.

3

Z28 The Camaro's Camaro

You remember this car. Low and lean. Born to run. It's back. The Z28. Take one Camaro and add the blackened grille • Body-colored bumpers • Extra-wide body-colored 15 x 7 wheels • White-lettered GR70 steel-belted radial tires • High performance dual exhausts • Double sport mirrors • Tachometer • Power disc brakes • Spoilers, front and rear • "Z28" spelled out loud and clear, front, sides and back • F-41 sport suspension • Stowaway spare • 350 4-barrel V8 connected to a performance axle • Heavy duty Borg-Warner 4-speed manual transmission*. And there's more.
Z28. We won't build many.
So, if you want to move "Z" style, you better get moving.   **Chevrolet**
*Turbo Hydra-matic required in California.

1. Little-changed for '77, the sleek Camaro—close relative to Pontiac's Firebird—still appealed to a certain breed of buyer. A 250-cid six-cylinder engine now was standard in the Type LT coupe, which got fresh knit cloth and puffed vinyl upholstery. Two V-8 engines were optional—either 305 or 350 cubic inches. **2-4.** Chevrolet revived the Camaro Z28 at midyear, after a two-year absence, launching its sportiest coupe in midseason at the Chicago Auto Show. Rather than raw power, as in the past, the modernized Z28 promised refined road manners, helped by tauter springs, bigger tires, and improved anti-sway bars. Bold exterior graphics decorated the hood, which sat atop a special 350-cid V-8 engine. A four-speed Borg-Warner gearbox sent its horses to wide-profile tires, and steering was quicker than usual.

1

2

3

4

5

1-2. After their aggressive downsizing, a Chevrolet Caprice Classic sedan weighed less than a comparable mid-sized Chevelle—complicating the 1977 model lineup a bit. Though smaller outside, a Caprice was as roomy as before. 3. This pre-production mockup of a Caprice Estate wagon wears an Impala grille. 4. For economy-minded buyers, a six-cylinder engine was standard in the Impala, Chevrolet's less-costly full-size model. Stylists snipped away at front and rear overhangs to reduce the car's length by close to 11 inches, and width by four inches. 5. Ads for "The New Chevrolet" promoted the merits of the freshly shrunk full-size models, including improved gas mileage—no small matter in 1977.

1

1. Changes were subtle for the Chevette in its second season, and sales of the rear-drive subcompact hatchback faltered noticeably this year. Intermittent wipers joined the option list, and a back seat became standard in the bare-bones Scooter. Both engines gained a little bit of power, but not enough to send the Chevette beyond the econocar league. **2.** Subcompact Chevrolet models included (top to bottom): base Chevette, Chevette Sport, Chevette Scooter, and a new "Sandpiper" appearance package with white or yellow-gold paint and foot-long quarter-panel decals. Fuel economy was the car's foremost selling point. **3.** Stingray badging departed from the Corvette's body, but new crossed flags sat between the headlights as well as on the fuel filler door. A Euro-style control stalk was installed, and power window switches moved to the console. Corvettes had plenty of avid fans who loved its handling and performance, but also more than a few detractors who disdained the fiberglass-bodied coupe as a pretender to the sports car category.

2

3

1

2

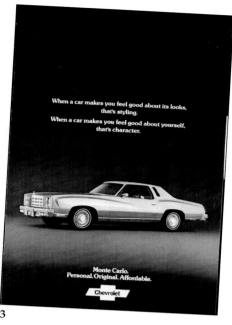

3

1. The Landau Coupe was one of five Chevelle Malibu Classic models.
2. Monte Carlos also came in Landau coupe form. 3. Ads emphasized Monte Carlo's unique character. 4. Engine choices dwindled for the Monza 2+2 hatchback, which could be equipped with a new Monza Spyder option.
5. Concours was the upscale member of the compact Nova family. 6-7. The Vega soldiered on for one more season.

4

5

6

7

1

2

4

3

1. Like other GM full-size models, the Oldsmobile Ninety-Eight Regency sedan earned a massive downsizing, losing 800 pounds and nearly a foot of length. Doors were narrower, seats thinner, for greater rear legroom despite reduced dimensions. **2-3.** A 350-cid V-8 was standard in the Ninety-Eight Luxury (LS), with a 403-cid engine optional. Even in their newly shrunken form, full-size Oldsmobiles were hardly lilliputian, capable of carrying six in comfort. **4.** Fully restyled in the new "family size," the Delta 88 Royale came in coupe and sedan body styles, selling far better than their base-model mates.

1. Oldsmobile Custom Cruiser wagons were downsized along with the full-size coupes and sedans, but could still carry plenty out back. **2-3.** A new two-way tailgate on the Custom Cruiser opened like a regular door, or could drop down (with glass lowered) for a flat loading area. **4.** Base engine for the Delta 88 Royale was now a 231-cid V-6, but three V-8s were optional. **5.** A Cutlass Supreme was the millionth '77 Olds built. **6.** Allegedly mid-sized, a Cutlass Supreme coupe now weighed more than a two-door Delta 88, and nearly as much as the Ninety-Eight.

1

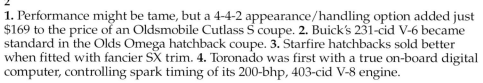

3

1. Performance might be tame, but a 4-4-2 appearance/handling option added just $169 to the price of an Oldsmobile Cutlass S coupe. **2.** Buick's 231-cid V-6 became standard in the Olds Omega hatchback coupe. **3.** Starfire hatchbacks sold better when fitted with fancier SX trim. **4.** Toronado was first with a true on-board digital computer, controlling spark timing of its 200-bhp, 403-cid V-8 engine.

4

1

2

1. Big letters made it hard to miss the Astre's new Formula package. 2. Astre Safari wagons got the new "Iron Duke" four-cylinder engine. 3. Downsizing cut 14 inches from big Pontiacs, like the Bonneville Brougham sedan. 4. Valencia cloth was a Brougham option. 5. A Bonneville coupe cost $5411. 6. Grand Safari was the top Pontiac wagon. 7. Catalinas got a standard 231-cid V-6.

3

4

5

6

7

1

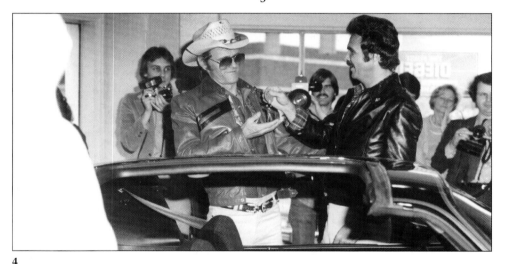

2

3

1. A new 301-cid V-8 went into the Firebird Formula coupe. No more 455-cid V-8s powered Firebirds. 2. A Special Edition coupe marked the 10th anniversary of Pontiac's performance Trans Am, now packing a choice of two 6.6-liter V-8 engines below a "shaker" hood. A four-speed was standard.
3. One step up from a base Firebird, the Esprit sold a bit better—yet both were beaten by the popular Trans Am.
4. Actors Jerry Reed and Burt Reynolds favored Pontiacs in the 1977 film, *Smokey and the Bandit*. 5. A 180-bhp, 400-cid V-8 powered the Grand Prix SJ, the sportiest member of Pontiac's personal-luxury coupe family.

4

5

1

2

3

4

1. Unique two-tone paint marked the GT edition of Pontiac's LeMans Sport Coupe. 2-3. Grand LeMans models cost about $600 more than a regular LeMans. 4. An Enforcer package prepared LeMans for police duty. 5. A new Formula package dressed up the subcompact Sunbird but didn't make it sell any better. 6. Venturas could now get four-cylinder power. 7. In upscale SJ form, Ventura sales were meager.

6

5

7

IMPORTS

BMW introduces a swank new coupe, the 630CSi, plus a car destined to be the definitive "yuppiemobile," the new entry-level 320i sedan

Existing Dodge Colts are reduced to hardtop and wagon models; two- and four-door sedans are switched to a newer and slightly smaller Mitsubishi design

Ford Division returns to "captive imports" for the first time since 1971, as the new German-built front-drive Fiesta two-door hatchback arrives in August as an early '78 model

Honda regroups its Civics into "1200" and CVCC series; the larger Accord is little changed except for sales, which keep heading up

Mazda eyes better days by supplementing its quick but slow-selling rotary models with a conventional new two-door hatchback, the four-cylinder GLC ("Great Little Car")

Porsche abandons the mid-engine 914 and brings a new "budget" model to America: the front-engine, water-cooled 924, which sells far better

Toyota drops its top-line car, the six-cylinder Mark II, but still can't build enough Corollas, Coronas and Celicas to satisfy U.S. buyers

Volkswagen tweaks cosmetics on the Dasher while preparing for U.S. production of Rabbits at a recently acquired Chrysler plant in Pennsylvania

Volvo rolls on with only detail refinements to its 240 and 260 series

1

2

3

4

1. With three models, Honda saw record sales. 2. *Motor Life* named Honda Accord "Car of the Year." 3. Smallest Datsun was the B-210. 4. Datsun had a new 200SX sport coupe. 5. A luxury Datsun 810 debuted at midyear. 6. Datsun offered Li'l Hustler and King Cab pickups, too. 7. Datsun's 280Z had six-cylinder power.

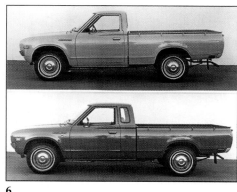

5

6

7

1

2

3

1-2. Mazda's RX-3 SP coupe was the last remaining RX-3 model, featuring sport trim, a blackout grille, spoiler, and five-speed gearbox. A spirited performer with its 95-bhp Wankel rotary engine, this RX-3 handled well. **3.** Mazda launched a new GLC DeLuxe hatchback at midyear. Instead of rotary power, this one got a conventional piston engine. **4.** Porsche inserted a water-cooled engine up front in its new 924 coupe, which incorporated many Volkswagen components.

4

1

2

3

1. Subaru responded to complaints about sluggishness in prior models by installing a 1600-cc flat four-cylinder engine in its 1977 models, including this front-drive DL station wagon. The new powerplant made 67 horsepower. **2.** Subaru's standard two-door sedan started at just $2974. **3.** Toyota's sporty Celica GT Liftback coupe was similar in specs to a Corona sedan. **4-5.** On sale in the U.S. for a decade, Toyota Coronas came in three DeLuxe body styles, plus a Custom two-door.

4   5

1

2

3

1-2. Toyota's Corolla SR-5 was the upper-level subcompact coupe. **3.** All Volkswagen Rabbits now had fuel-injected engines. **4.** Volkswagen station wagons held seven or nine passengers, for a $50 price difference. **5.** Volkswagen Beetle sedans reached the U.S. for the last time in '77, but convertibles stayed a bit longer.

4

5

The biggest automotive story of the year actually turned out to be a *pair* of stories. Neither meant a great deal to the general public, but they shook industry insiders—and stock-watchers—to the core: In July, Ford Motor Company president Lee Iacocca was given the heave-ho by company chairman Henry Ford II.

In November, Iacocca was installed as president of Chrysler Corporation, which had been sliding toward bankruptcy. Inefficiency, overemphasis on big cars, a lack of internal communication, lax financial controls, poor product quality, government mandates—all of these were bedeviling Chrysler when Iacocca stepped in.

Chrysler and every other automaker selling cars in the U.S. was challenged this year because the federal government's new Corporate Average Fuel Economy (CAFE) requirements took effect. Failure to comply with CAFE's complicated formulas for all cars and light trucks sold domestically meant heavy fines.

Despite these executive-suite and government-induced upsets, model-year 1978 turned out to be the third-best in Detroit history, with 9.4 million units sold.

In a nod to the industry's past, this year's inductee into the Automotive Hall of Fame was Rudolf Diesel, who developed the diesel engine and founded the Diesel Motor Co. of America.

Al Unser won his third Indianapolis 500 of the decade, this time in a 1st National City Lola-Cosworth. Pace car was a Chevy Corvette. The pace 'Vette was unique in that it was the first Indy pace car in modern times to run with a completely stock drivetrain: a three-speed automatic mated to a 350-cid ohv V-8 producing 220 net horsepower. The pace car was piloted for the fifth time by 1960 Indy winner Jim Rathmann.

The NASCAR Winston Cup champion for the third straight year was Cale Yarborough.

1978

In other news, Israel and Egypt signed a historic peace accord after a 13-day conference chaired at Camp David by President Carter. The Supreme Court barred quota systems for U.S. college admissions, but held also that preferential admissions programs for minorities are constitutional. In California, voters overwhelmingly approved Proposition 13, a ballot measure designed to slash state property-tax revenues by 60 percent. The U.S. Senate voted to turn control of the Panama Canal over to Panama no later than the year 2000.

Moviegoers enjoyed *The Boys From Brazil, Blue Collar, Hooper, Pretty Baby, The Deer Hunter, National Lampoon's Animal House, Grease,* and *Superman.*

The year's top TV shows included *Three's Company, Charlie's Angels, Little House on the Prairie, Soap,* and *Fantasy Island,* the last starring Chrysler spokesman Ricardo Montalban.

The Bee Gees had a monster pop hit with "Stayin' Alive"; other winners included Yvonne Elliman's "If I Can't Have You," Andy Gibb's "Shadow Dancing," Nick Gilder's "Hot Child in the City," and—for all the world's car fanciers and moonlight romantics—Meatloaf's "Paradise By the Dashboard Light."

The New York Yankees outlasted the L.A. Dodgers, four games to two, in the World Series, and Dallas triumphed over Denver, 27-10, in Super Bowl XII.

AMC

AMC's market share slips to just 1.83 percent, its lowest level of the decade

Company veteran Roy D. Chapin, Jr., is replaced as president by Gerald C. Meyers, who begins laying plans for a turn-around

Hornet is restyled, plushed up, and renamed Concord; the AMX logo returns for a sporty Concord hatchback coupe that's more show than go

Concord's advertising banner is "The luxury Americans want. The size America needs"

Pacer adopts a starchy formal grille with raised center section and adds a 304 V-8 as a new option, plus a luxury-oriented Limited trim level

Gremlin and Matador carry on little changed in their final season; the former does add an optional GT package and the latter extends the Barcelona decor to sedans

1

2

3

4

1978 AMC
CONCORD·PACER·GREMLIN·AMX·MATADOR

5

6

1. Restyling of AMC's compact Hornet yielded a new Concord, but the difference wasn't as great as the change of name would imply. 2. Concords came in four body styles, including this D/L two-door sedan. A 232-cid six was standard, with a bigger six or 304-cid V-8 optional 3. A two-door hatchback continued in the Concord line. 4. An AMX badge went on a sporty hatchback offshoot of the Concord, wearing a blacked-out grille and full fender flares. 5. AMC's lineup consisted of five models, but Gremlin and Matador faced their final year. 6. The little-changed Gremlin could now get a $649 GT package, with fiberglass body components.

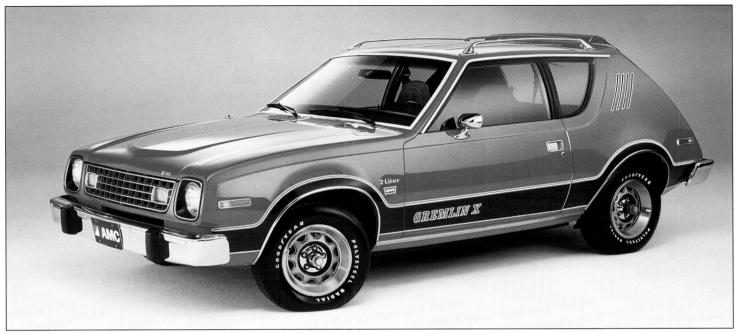

1

2

3

4

5

6

1. Special striping helped identify an AMC Gremlin with the "X" option, including a "Levi's" bucket-seat interior. Based on the Custom hatchback, this one has the 2.0-liter four engine rather than a six. **2.** Matador sedans could get the Barcelona decor option, previously limited to coupes. **3.** Not much was new for Matador wagons. A 304-cid V-8 was standard. **4.** Note the distinctive quarter window on this Matador coupe with Barcelona decor. **5.** A D/L option with special upholstery could be ordered for the Pacer station wagon, but the "X" package was deleted. **6.** Wearing a new eggcrate grille, Pacers (hatchback shown) could now be equipped with a 304-cid V-8 instead of just a six.

CHRYSLER CORPORATION

The domestic auto industry enjoys its third-best year ever, but Chrysler Corporation's output sinks

Chrysler launches the first domestically built front-drive subcompacts: Dodge Omni and Plymouth Horizon

The initial Omnis and Horizons get an enlarged 1.7-liter Volkswagen engine

After only one year, Dodge drops the Royal Monaco, and Plymouth ditches the Gran Fury

It's also the final season for the intermediate Monaco and Fury

The 400/440-cid V-8s are available for the last time

Chrysler builds its last "big" Newports and New Yorkers on a 123.9-inch wheelbase

The mid-sized Chrysler LeBaron has a standard Slant Six; two V-8s are optional

Dodge adds the sporty Magnum XE to sell alongside the Charger SE; a metal sunroof and T-top are newly optional

Chrysler sells all its European subsidiaries to Peugeot-Citroën

Lee Iacocca is fired from the Ford presidency by Henry Ford II, but is soon hired to head Chrysler

The inevitable happens: Chrysler Corporation nears bankruptcy

1

2

1. Chrysler Cordoba coupes could again have an optional Crown roof (shown), or the choice of a new T-bar roof or a sunroof. Stacked rectangular headlights flanked a new fine-mesh grille. Cornering lights joined the option list. 2. Still a sizable automobile in an era of serious downsizing, Cordoba earned praise from fashion photographer Anthony Edgeworth. 3-4. A 400-cid V-8 powered the standard Cordoba, while a 360-cid engine went into the "S" edition, which cost $200 less. Economy-minded buyers might select a Lean Burn 318-cid V-8 instead, with four-barrel carburetion.

3

4

1

2

3

4

5

6

1-2. Chrysler promoted the new LeBaron Town & Country station wagon as a "new size" replacement for the big New Yorker wagon, which was discontinued this year. Weighing almost 1500 pounds less than its full-size predecessor, the LeBaron wagon had a one-piece rear liftgate and came only in the two-seat configuration. **3-4.** In addition to the upscale LeBaron Medallion sedan (shown), a budget-priced LeBaron "S" went on sale. **5.** A Slant Six engine was standard in LeBarons, including this Medallion coupe, with 318- or 360-cid V-8 optional. Automatic transmissions gained a new lock-up system to improve fuel economy. **6.** Newport was one of the last true two-door hardtops left on the market—and one of the last big cars. The pillared four-door sedan was gone, leaving only a hardtop coupe and sedan. Most examples had the standard 400-cid V-8, but the big 440 was still optional, as was a more miserly 360 V-8. Because it had so much heft to haul around, gas mileage remained meager even with the transmission's new lock-up feature.

1

2

1-2. For as much as $642 extra, a St. Regis decor package added a padded canopy Seneca-grain vinyl roof to the Chrysler New Yorker Brougham coupe. Formal-style opera windows were part of the package. A Salon package also was available, for a similar price, featuring high-gloss crystal metallic body paint and a silver vinyl roof. New Yorkers had a minor grille change and new tape striping.
3. Still unabashedly full-size, the New Yorker Brougham four-door hardtop and its two-door mate, each riding a lengthy 123.9-inch wheelbase, went on sale for the last time. So did Chrysler's 400- and 440-cid V-8 engines.

3

1

2

3

4

5

6

1. As its name suggests, the Dodge Colt M/M (Mileage Maker) sedan aimed at extreme economy. 2. A sporty Challenger coupe with louvered pillars and wraparound back window joined the group of Mitsubishi-built Dodges. A 1.6- or 2.6-liter engine could be installed. 3. A Colt wagon cost $848 more than the sedan. 4. Colorful striping, louvered side windows, rear spoiler, and heavy-duty suspension made the Aspen R/T package worth $289. 5. Aspen Super Coupes had similar features on a brown body with wheel flares and black trim. A 360-cid V-8 was standard. 6. An Aspen could be dressed up with Special Edition trim.

2

3

5

4

1. In this ad, Sherlock Holmes and his cohort, Dr. Watson, discover that the lovely new Dodge Diplomat wagon has "car-napped" Ford and GM owners. **2-3.** Diplomats cost more in Medallion trim (shown), but the new budget-priced "S" model failed to sell well. **4.** A Monaco Brougham sedan, now Dodge's biggest model, might hold a Slant Six or V-8 up to 440 cid. **5.** The sporty new Magnum XE coupe could have a T-top (shown) or sunroof. **6.** An eye-catching front end on the Magnum XE helped strengthen Dodge's image. **7.** This was the final season for Monaco, and the big Royal Monaco was already extinct.

6

7

1

1-2. Following the lead of the trend-setting Volkswagen Rabbit, the new Dodge Omni four-door hatchback even used a VW-based 1.7-liter engine at first. Omni and the nearly identical Plymouth Horizon were the first domestically built front-drive subcompacts, a response to economy imports. Up-front space rivaled that of some big cars, and wet-weather traction beat rear-drive models. Multi-purpose control stalks helped give the Omni a European flavor. **3-4.** Base-priced at $3976, an Omni could look quite spiffy with optional woodgrain trim and a roof rack. First-year sales weren't huge, but Omni/Horizon soon turned into stars in Chrysler's otherwise-dismal sales picture of the late Seventies.

2

3

4

1

2

3

4

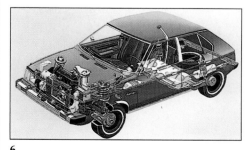

5

6

7

8

1. Made by Mitsubishi, the Plymouth Arrow hatchback could have a Jet decor package (top) in flat black and orange, or come as a GT hatchback (bottom) with full gauges. 2. In its final season, the Fury Sport coupe had a choice of six engines. 3. Now that full-size Plymouths were gone, the $4568 Fury Salon sedan topped the line in size and price—though Suburban station wagons cost even more. 4. The new Horizon four-door hatchback was the smallest Plymouth ever, shaped and structured like a Volkswagen Rabbit but a bit bigger. 5. Optional woodgrain trim and a roof rack turned the $3976 Horizon into an appealing people/cargo carrier, more roomy than expected. 6. Phantom view shows Horizon's transverse-engine layout. 7-8. Early ads promoted the Horizon's front-drive traction and fuel mileage.

1

2

3

4

1-2. Nearly identical to the Dodge Challenger, Plymouth's new rear-drive Sapporo sport coupe had a choice of two "silent shaft" engines: 1.6 or 2.6 liters. A gauge cluster around its steering wheel included a tachometer.
3. Enthusiasts liked their Volaré coupes spiffed up. That could mean paying an extra $289 for a basic Road Runner package (rear), or going all the way to Super Coupe status, with all the sporty and flashy goodies installed for no less than $1348. Those were just two of the many option groups offered in '78, including a Fun Runner. 4. Sedan buyers could perk up their $3899 Volarés with a Premier package. More than 100,000 Volaré sedans were built.

1

2

3

4

♪Introducing the
wagon that has America singing♪

You guessed it.
After all, you don't find people singing about ordinary wagons. Just extraordinary ones. Which, we modestly propose, is precisely the category the 1978 Plymouth Volaré wagon fits into.

Reason number one is the most obvious. That cavernous space you see below. Where those kids could lug home about 60 bushels of shells, or fish, or something else suitably exotic. (Parental guidance suggested.)

Of course, the nice thing about lugging anything around in a Volaré is that you never lug around a lot of car. Because Volaré is a trim, compact wagon. Maneuverable. Easy to park. And, a pure joy to drive. Thanks to the Isolated Transverse Suspension. An ingen-

tion system designed to keep life's bumpy road as far away from you as possible.

Other comforts also abound in Volaré. Like a gas pressurized liftgate that opens part way on its own. And two optional lockable storage compartments to keep "out-of-sight" valuables out of sight.

Volaré. People have been singing its praises since the day we brought it out. So much so, in fact, that last year, they helped make it the No. 1 selling wagon in America.

And if we're hearing it right (ah, what a great sound) that's exactly where it's going to remain. Buy or Lease a Volaré at your Chrysler-Plymouth Dealer today.

New 1978 Plymouth Volaré.
The car with the accent on value.

5

1. Depending on personal taste, a Volaré Road Runner coupe could be plain or flamboyant. 2. Quarter-window louvers and bold striping marked a Volaré Road Runner coupe with Sport Pak decor. 3-4. Volaré coupe buyers could even order a $1085 "Street Kit Car" option—right from the factory—to get the look of a stock-car racer. 5. Value was the theme in ads for the Volaré Premier wagon. A Slant Six was standard, but the 318- and 360-cid V-8s gave a little more oomph.

FORD
MOTOR CO.

Dearborn celebrates its 75th anniversary, but market share is no cause for joy, easing back to 27.8 percent

There's turbulence in the boardroom, as chairman Henry Ford II abruptly fires president Lee Iacocca in October, citing "insubordination"

Ford Division's big news is Fairmont, a clean, modern, more efficient compact to replace Maverick

Mustang II enters its final season with a gaudy new King Cobra package for the fastback

As part of Dearborn's birthday bash, Ford Thunderbird offers a limited-edition Diamond Jubilee model; new for other T-Birds is a Sports Decor Group

Ford's full-sized LTDs tout the advantages of "road-hugging weight" in an appeal to traditional buyer tastes against GM's smaller big cars

Other Fords change little for '78, but LTD II wagons are dropped

The Bronco sport-utility, introduced in 1966, is replaced by an upsized F-Series-based model

Lincoln makes mainly detail changes, but offers a Diamond Jubilee Mark V, another low-volume birthday special

German-built Capri is dropped

Zephyr replaces Comet

Cougar loses its wagons, but the XR-7 gets Midnight/Chamois Decor option

1

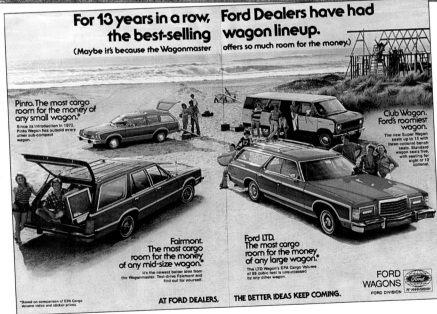

2

3

1. Ford offered its true full-sized LTD series for the last time. Coupe fanciers could step up to the $5970 LTD Landau edition, or pay $5398 for a base car that promised the same quiet boulevard ride. LTDs could have a 302-, 351-, 400-, or 460-cid V-8. 2. New this year and replacing the Maverick, the compact Fairmont family included two- and four-door sedans, plus a station wagon. Flaunting a modern, boxy profile, Fairmonts were the first downsized Fords, offered with a four-cylinder, inline six, or 302-cid V-8 engine. 3. Ford stocked station wagons in three sizes, including the still-huge LTD—plus an Econoline-based Club Wagon.

1

2

3

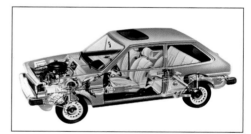

4

5

1. Fairmonts sold well in all three body styles, and the "Fox" platform led to a series of Eighties models. **2.** A Fairmont Squire cost $4428, versus $4063 for a plain-bodied wagon. **3.** Police agencies got specially equipped Fairmonts. **4.** A rakish Fairmont Futura coupe debuted during 1978. **5.** Space, mileage, and price drew shoppers to Fairmont. **6-7.** A cut above most minicars, the German-built, front-drive Fiesta had a transverse engine. **8.** Fiestas were made for easy maintenance.

6

7

8

1

2

3

4

5

6

1-2. A chrome vertical rib turned the Granada's opera windows into "twin-dows." **3-4.** Trying for a frisky image, the new Granada ESS (European Sports Sedan) got louvers, blackout trim, and a heavy-duty suspension. Shoppers saw through the ruse. **5-6.** Whether in Brougham (5) or base trim, the LTD II failed to catch on. Wagons were gone. **7.** A Mustang II Ghia with V-8 mixed tastefulness and a touch of action. **8.** Buyers of a Mustang II King Cobra paid $1253 for a wild mix of stripes, decals, black accents, and body cladding. **9.** A Mustang II IMSA Cobra toured the auto-show circuit. **10.** Final Mustang IIs are shown on display at the '78 Chicago Auto Show.

7

8

9

10

1

2

3

1. Small businesses on a budget might have liked the Ford Pinto panel delivery van. **2-3.** Pintos were down to one series, in three body styles, but dress-up options included stripes and aluminum wheels. Variable-assist power steering could now be installed. **4.** Imitation luggage straps on the decklid marked a Thunderbird coupe with the Sports Decor Group, featuring a blacked-out grille and paint stripes. A 302-cid V-8 was standard. **5.** This T-Bird has Sports Decor as well as the new T-top. While other models faltered, more than 352,000 Thunderbirds went on sale.

4

5

1

2

3

1-2. Ford Motor Company's 75th anniversary prompted the debut of a Lincoln Continental Mark V Diamond Jubilee Edition. Sprayed in Diamond Blue or Jubilee Gold paint, the limited-edition coupe had a Valino grain Landau vinyl roof and twin coach lamps. Beveled-glass opera windows contained a simulated diamond chip, laminated into the glass. Padded vinyl covered the trunk lid. Sculpted bucket seats and "Tiffany" carpeting added to the plush experience. Extravagant it was—and also overweight and wasteful of fuel. **3.** Designer editions of the Continental Mark V continued to spark interest among the posh-minded. This Cartier Edition coupe sported a champagne-colored body and vinyl roof, but a plain painted roof was available at no extra charge. Pucci, Givenchy, and Bill Blass also continued to contribute their Designer editions. **4-5.** Not many Continentals of this sort sat in upscale-neighborhood driveways. Wild exposed exhaust headers on this Bordinat Custom Continental Mark V coupe looked ready to snarl like a hot rod as the big-block V-8 engine roared to life.

4

5

1. This Lincoln Continental Williamsburg Town Car combined two distinct option groups, loading the four-door sedan with just about every comfort/convenience and dress-up feature that might be desired. **2.** To no one's surprise, ads for the Continental Town Car—a $1440 option—emphasized its luxury appointments. For Ford Motor Company, at least, "bigger is better" remained the rule when it came to luxury models. Continental sedans outsold two-door coupes by a 3-to-1 margin. Either a 400- or 460-cid V-8 engine could be installed, the latter delivering 210 horsepower. **3.** Introduced during 1977 to great hoopla, the smaller Versailles four-door sedan failed to meet sales expectations. Intended as a rival to Cadillac's Seville, the $12,529 Versailles (by comparison, a Continental sedan cost $10,166) was actually an offshoot of the Ford Granada, albeit with a passel of lavish features. Borrowing traditional Lincoln touches, a simulated spare tire was integrated into the decklid and the grille resembled that of the Continental. A fully padded vinyl roof had a "frenched" back window. Initial models had carried a 351-cid V-8 engine, but a 302-cid V-8 became standard fare for '78.

Lincoln Continental is a standard for luxury cars. In 1978, we have not compromised that standard in any respect.
Lincoln Continental continues to offer full luxury. Full comfort. Full pleasure.

"Luxury car owners have their standards."

LINCOLN CONTINENTAL
LINCOLN-MERCURY DIVISION

2

3

1

1978 Cougar Models

XR-7 coupe with Midnight/Chamois decor

Brougham four-door sedan

XR-7 coupe

coupe

Brougham coupe

four-door sedan

2

1. Plagued by recalls and lack of interest, Mercury's little Bobcat hung on with three models, including base and Villager (shown) station wagons. Only 8840 wagons were built. Variable-ratio power steering was new. **2.** Still abundant in size, the Cougar family lost its wagon but again included a sporty XR-7 coupe, which led the pack in sales—by far. Two- and four-door Cougars came in base or Brougham trim. **3.** This Cougar XR-7 has the Midnight/Chamois Decor option, with a half vinyl roof and crossover strap, a padded rear deck, and paint striping.

3

Grand Marquis four-door sedan

Grand Marquis coupe

Marquis Brougham four-door sedan

Marquis Brougham coupe

Marquis four-door sedan

Marquis coupe

Marquis station wagon w/Colony Park option

Marquis station wagon

1

2

3

1. The full-size Mercury lineup included Grand Marquis, Marquis Brougham, and Marquis. **2.** A fair number of folks remained loyal to big guzzlers like the Grand Marquis, which still offered a 460-cid V-8. **3.** Who fared worse in this nasty collision between a 1974 Marquis Brougham and a later-model Cadillac? Even in a clash between equals, somebody has to lose. **4.** Monarchs earned a fresh front end, plus an available ESS option group for a European flavor. **5.** A Ghia option gave the Monarch cast spoke wheels and paint stripes.

4

5

1

2

3

4

1. At the start of the season, the new Mercury Zephyr family included a two-door sedan, four-door sedan, and station wagon. Replacing the outmoded Comet, the less-hefty Zephyr—like its Ford Fairmont cousin—promised frugal fuel usage, without compromising on comfort. 2. This Zephyr has the Luxury Exterior Decor Group. An inline six or 302-cid V-8 could replace the standard four-cylinder engine. 3. Woodtone trim in medium cherry tone identified a Zephyr wagon with the Villager option. 4. Midseason brought a sporty Zephyr Z-7 coupe, comparable to Ford's Fairmont Futura, featuring a wrapover roof design with wide B-pillars. More than 44,000 were built—far fewer than the Futura—with a $4154 sticker price.

GENERAL
MOTORS CORP.

GM continues its climb toward 60-percent market dominance, edging up to 57.9 percent on record sales of 12.9 million

Intermediates shrink for '78, but prove no less popular

Buick observes its 75th anniversary with a silver "LXXV" Riviera

Newly slimmed Centurys offer wagons and slope-back sedans; turbo V-6 power is offered

Cadillac also turns 75, but makes few changes save for a diesel V-8 option for Seville

Mid-size Chevrolets trade Chevelle name for Malibu badge

Chevy's small Chevette adds a four-door hatchback body style

Corvette turns 25, and gets a glassy fastback roofline and Silver Anniversary package; a 'Vette paces the Indy 500, and Chevy runs off about 7000 replicas

Camaro gets a restyled front with integrated body-color bumper

Vega departs except for the wagon, which is rebadged as a Monza

Among Oldsmobile's new mid-sizers are "aeroback" coupes and sedans, along with a 4-4-2 option

Pontiac axes Astre, though wagon survives with a Sunbird label

Venturas are dropped in favor of Phoenix models from '77

Pontiac's Firebird sees few changes but sets a sales record

LeMans/Grand LeMans offers wagons and notchbacks, and the Grand Am surprisingly returns

1

2

3

4

5

1. Regal was now a separate Buick series, including this Sport Coupe with turbo V-6. 2-4. Century models lost a foot of length and some 600 pounds, but failed to thrill buyers. A new 196-cid V-6 was standard. New "aeroback" coupes and sedans came in three levels: Special, Custom, and Limited. 5. The Century Sport Coupe got body-colored bumpers, a blacked-out grille, and two-tone paint. 6. A 350-cid V-8 was standard in Electra Limited. 7. This Electra Limited cruised U.S. 30 at Colorado Street, in Merrillville, Indiana. 8. Like other full-size models, the Estate Wagon Limited showed little change. 9. LeSabre Sport Coupe held a turbocharged V-6. 10. A 231-cid V-6 was standard in LeSabre Custom sedan. 11-12. Buick dealers sold the Isuzu-built Opels. 13. A Riviera "LXXV" Anniversary Edition coupe marked Buick's 75th birthday. 14. The Skyhawk hatchback came only with a V-6. 15. This Skylark Custom coupe has the Landau roof option.

6

7

8

9

10

11

12

13

14

15

1

2

3

4

Three things you should know before buying any fine car.

1. Total Cadillac value. That's everything you get in a Cadillac. Everything that makes it an American Standard for the World. Cadillac comfort. That superb Cadillac ride. It's all the features that come as standard on a Cadillac—features that often cost extra on other cars... if they're offered at all.

2. Cadillac resale value. It's consistently the highest of any U.S. luxury car make. Which means a Cadillac could cost less in the long run than you anticipated.

3. Cadillac repeat ownership. It consistently tops all U.S. luxury car makes. Cadillac owners tend to come back to Cadillac. Haven't you promised yourself a Cadillac long enough? Whether you buy or lease, see your Cadillac dealer soon.

Cadillac

5

1-2. If a regular $12,842 Cadillac Fleetwood Brougham wasn't quite comfy enough, the d'Elegance decor option added contoured pillow-style seats trimmed in Florentine velour. A bolder grille pattern marked '78 De Villes. **3.** A Coupe de Ville could be equipped with real wire wheels for less than $600. **4.** As usual, the Sedan de Ville did not sell quite as well as the more popular two-door Coupe de Ville. The 425-cid V-8 produced 180 horsepower with a carburetor, or 195 if fuel-injected. **5.** Total value, resale value, brand loyalty—those were some of the factors that attracted shoppers to Cadillac. This fellow might be driving a Chevrolet or Buick, but he aspires to that elegant Coupe de Ville.

1. Custom Biarritz trim gave the Cadillac Eldorado a convertible-like padded vinyl top, opera lamps, and pillow-type leather/vinyl seats. **2.** Starting in midseason, the "international-size" Seville could be equipped with a diesel V-8 engine. **3.** Coach lights joined the Seville's option list. So did chrome wire wheels. **4.** The limited-production Seville Elegante flaunted wire wheels and a choice of two-tone paint treatments: Platinum/Sable Black, or Western Saddle Firemist/Ruidoso Brown.

1

2   3

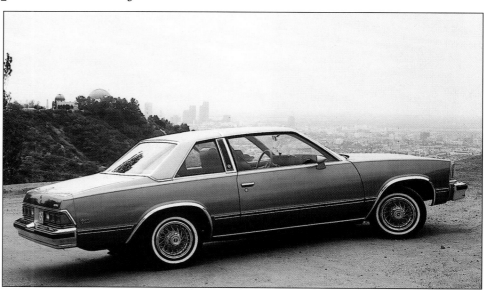

4   5

1. Camaros adopted a soft urethane front end with integrated body-colored bumper. **2.** Enhancing its macho image, the Camaro Z28 added a duct-shaped hood scoop, functional fender louvers, and body-colored rear spoiler. **3.** Rally Sport became a separate Camaro model, shown with newly optional T-top roof. **4.** The Chevelle designation was gone, but the freshly-downsized Malibu drew mid-size buyers. The Malibu Classic sedan stickered for $4561 with the standard V-6 engine. **5.** This Landau coupe was one of four Malibu Classic models. **6.** The Malibu-based El Camino car/pick-up, shown in Conquista trim, shrunk by nearly a foot.

6

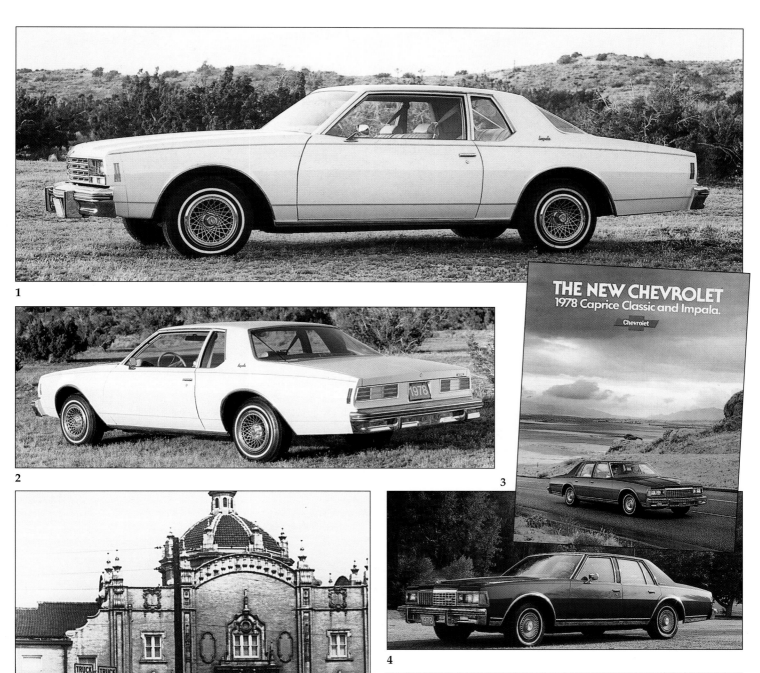

1-2. Chevrolet Impala coupes earned a modest facelift after their '77 downsizing. **3.** Full-size coupes and sedans could have an inline six-cylinder engine, or optional 305- or 350-cid V-8. **4.** Best-selling Chevrolet sedan was the Caprice Classic, starting at $5628. **5.** A four-door hatchback Chevette joined the original two-door subcompact, helping to trigger a sales hike. **6.** A Caprice sedan passes the Gulf, Mobile & Ohio railroad station in Mobile, Alabama.

1

2

SEE WHAT'S
NEW TODAY
IN A
CHEVROLET.

GM

The Third Generation Monte Carlo. A new dimension in affordable luxury.

With immense pride, we present a trim and timely new edition of Chevrolet's popular personal luxury car: The Third Generation Monte Carlo.

Although thoroughly redesigned, today's Monte Carlo retains the unique personality of Monte Carlos past.

Front and rear overhang have been reduced. The turning diameter is over two feet shorter than last year, giving the car added agility in cramped quarters.

The new interior is a virtual "Driver's Suite," with

sumptuous cloths and carpets, tall windows, a totally new instrument panel, and special Monte Carlo "touches" throughout.

Surprisingly, there is more rear-seat leg room, head room and hip-room than last year. More trunk space, too.

There is a new standard powerplant, a 231 Cu. In. V6. A 305 Cu. In. V8 is available. (Monte Carlo is equipped with GM-built engines produced by various divisions. See your dealer for details.)

The Third Generation Monte Carlo. Drive it soon.

Chevrolet

3

1-2. Because a Corvette paced the Indianapolis 500 race, more than 6000 coupes got a Pace Car replica package with special black-over-silver paint, red accent striping, and silver leather on the high-back seats. All 'Vettes gained a "glass-back" roofline. **3-4.** Monte Carlo coupes were downsized, like other mid-size GM models. Base engine was a Buick 231-cid V-6, with a 305 V-8 optional. A twin-hatch sunroof became optional, and the new Landau coupe had a vinyl half-roof.

4

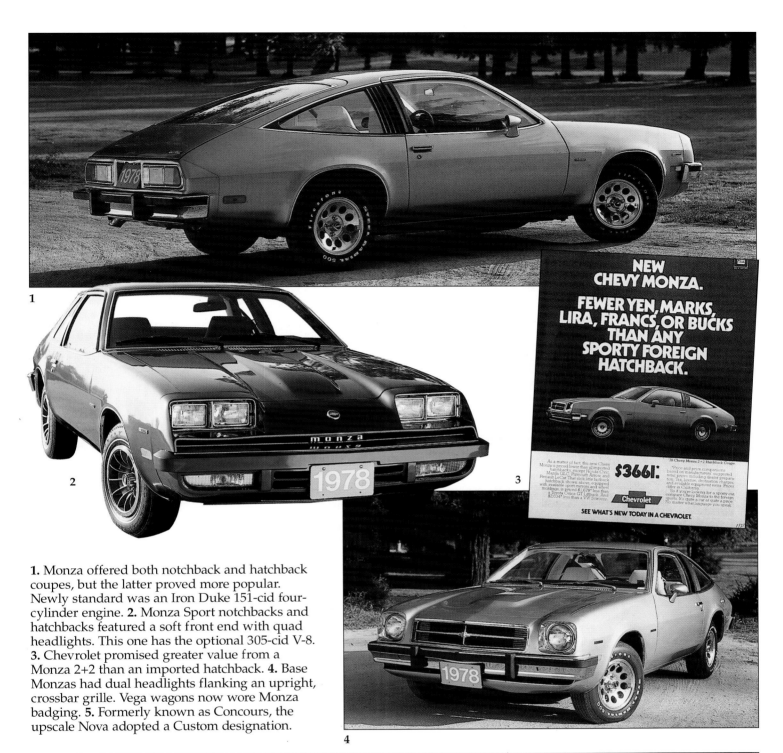

1. Monza offered both notchback and hatchback coupes, but the latter proved more popular. Newly standard was an Iron Duke 151-cid four-cylinder engine. **2.** Monza Sport notchbacks and hatchbacks featured a soft front end with quad headlights. This one has the optional 305-cid V-8. **3.** Chevrolet promised greater value from a Monza 2+2 than an imported hatchback. **4.** Base Monzas had dual headlights flanking an upright, crossbar grille. Vega wagons now wore Monza badging. **5.** Formerly known as Concours, the upscale Nova adopted a Custom designation.

1

2

3

4

5

6

7

1. Oldsmobile's dramatically downsized Cutlass Salon coupe displayed GM's new "aeroback" profile. Conservative-minded buyers did not all praise the look. **2.** Unlike the Cutlass Salon, the Supreme coupe stuck with notchback styling. **3.** Upscale buyers might prefer a Cutlass Calais coupe, which had its own grille and stand-up hood ornament. **4.** A Cutlass Cruiser wagon could have V-6 or V-8 power. **5-6.** Choosing a Brougham added $285 to the price of a Cutlass Salon sedan. **7.** Purists had to be horrified to see "4-4-2" nomenclature on the new "aeroback" Cutlass Salon. The appearance/handling option included a blacked-out grille. **8.** GM's diesel V-8 engine option soon proved troublesome. Basically, it was a modified Oldsmobile 350-cid gasoline V-8.

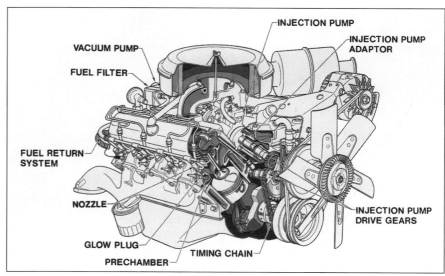

8

1

5

2

3

4

1. Oldsmobile's Custom Cruiser station wagon, still topping the two-ton mark, had its own grille and standard 350-cid V-8 engine. Options included a 403 V-8 or GM's diesel. **2.** Except for a slight grille change, little was new for the Ninety-Eight Regency sedan, priced $375 higher than the Luxury edition. This one has a diesel, but a 350-cid V-8 was standard. **3.** Nearly as big as a Ninety-Eight, the less-costly Delta 88 Royale also had a diesel-engine option. **4.** Base-model Delta 88s drew fewer buyers than their Royale mates. Engine choices included a 231-cid V-6 and 260-cid V-8. **5.** Still flashy after three years, a '75 Cutlass 4-4-2 is parked on Adams Street in Green Bay, Wisconsin, in May 1978.

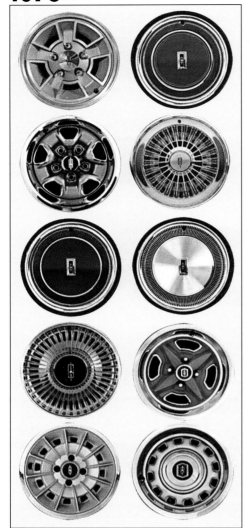

1

2

3

4

5

1. Choices, choices everywhere—especially in the Olds dealer's showroom. Buyers of a Cutlass, Starfire, or Omega needed to consult a wheel chart to decide which style suited them best.
2. Neither truly sporty nor an economy car, the subcompact Starfire hatchback coupe tallied some meager sales totals. Similar to Chevy's Monza, the Starfire was distinguished by a "waterfall" grille. Base and SX editions went on sale, with a standard Iron Duke four-cylinder engine, 231-cid V-6, or 305-cid V-8. Starfires could be dressed up with a GT or Firenza option. **3-4.** Compared to the current Ford/Chrysler compacts, an Olds Omega looked rather old-fashioned. Notchback and hatchback coupes were available, along with a sedan. Priced higher than their Chevrolet and Pontiac kin, Omegas earned only modest sales. The sporty SX option included a Rallye suspension. Base engine was a 231-cid V-6, with 305-cid V-8 optional.
5. Overweight and overblown, best at guzzling gas, the front-wheel-drive Toronado Brougham also was overshadowed in sales—by Cadillac's Eldorado. All Toronados held a 403-cid, four-barrel V-8.

1

2

3

4

5

1. Apart from grille revisions, the big Bonneville Brougham sedan carried on as before, flaunting its recently downsized form. Pontiac's flagship Brougham sedan stickered for $6784, versus $6023 for a plain Bonneville. **2.** A Bonneville coupe could get a Landau roof and alloy wheels. A 301-cid V-8 was standard. **3.** At 4002 pounds, Grand Safari wagons were still heavyweights. **4-5.** Similar in size to Bonneville, Catalina sedans and coupes cost substantially less with a standard 231-cid V-6 engine. Adding a V-8 narrowed the gap. **6.** Offered in coupe or sedan form, the Grand Am was a single series with a soft front end and two-tone paint. Its 301-cid V-8 could have two- or four-barrel carburetion.

6

1

2

3

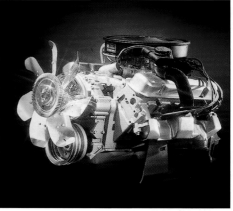

4

5

1. A new two-piece liftgate added to the versatility of a Grand LeMans Safari wagon, downsized like other mid-size models. 2. The Grand LeMans sedan offered luxury in a mid-size package. 3. Shrunken in size, Grand LeMans coupes kept a notchback profile. 4. Pontiac's new 301-cid V-8, available in the Grand Am, Bonneville, Catalina, and Grand Prix SJ, made 140 or 150 horsepower. 5. A padded Landau top could be installed on the sporty Grand Prix SJ. 6. Grand Prix rode a reduced 108-inch wheelbase, losing nearly a foot in length and at least 600 pounds. The coupes retained their traditional profile, including sweeping fenders.

6

1. Actor James Garner, star of *The Rockford Files* on NBC-TV, poses with the Firebird that he drove in his detective pursuits. GMC trucks were used in connection with the show. 2. This stylish Firebird Esprit has Red Bird decor. 3. A Firebird Formula coupe could get the Trans Am's 400-cid V-8 engine. 4. Many people considered the Trans Am as a model all its own. This one has gold Special Edition decor, a $1259 option. 5. Sunbird coupes started at $3590. 6. Sunbirds could sport Formula trim. 7. An LJ option added some extra flair to the compact Phoenix sedan.

IMPORTS

Audi replaces its 100LS with the five-cylinder 5000 and adds a sporty Fox GTI two-door

BMW debuts the 733i, a challenger to the biggest Mercedes

Datsun introduces the distinctive 200SX coupe, plus a new 510 sedan, wagon, and coupe to replace the 710. A 280ZX arrives in two-seat and 2+2 versions

Fiat's 131 gets fresh styling and 2.0-liter power to become the upmarket Brava/Super Brava

Jaguar abandons hardtops and short-wheelbase sedans

Mazda's piston-powered GLC gets four-door hatchback and Sport three-door models; rotary-engine Mazdas remain, but sales are sluggish

Mercedes revises its mid-range sedans and coupes

Porsche's 911 becomes the SC series with an enlarged 3.0-liter six and other changes; the Turbo Carrera goes to 3.2 liters and a fierce 259 horsepower

Renault 5 is renamed Le Car; other models are dropped except for the 17 Gordini coupe

Quick Saab 99 Turbo is first in a long line of "blown" Saabs

Toyota debuts six-cylinder Cressida and restyled Celica

Rabbits start hopping out of Volkswagen's new Pennsylvania plant in April

Volvo adds the sporty 242GT, as well as a luxurious six-cylinder 262C coupe designed with help from Italy's Bertone

1

2

3

4

5

6

1. Power steering was standard in Datsun's 810 luxury wagon, but air conditioning cost extra. 2. *Car and Driver* magazine called the Datsun 810 sedan "a four-door 280Z," alluding to the company's sports car. 3-4. Front-drive Datsun F-10 station wagons and hatchback coupes, smaller than other models, did not sell strongly. 5. Datsun revived the 510, but with a less-sporty image than before. 6. Based on the B-210, Datsun's 200SX coupe got a 1952-cc engine from the departed 710. *Car and Driver* called this one "the poor man's Z-car." 7. Not officially certified for U.S. sale, the Ferrari 400i turned up now and then anyway. Replacing the 365 GT4 2+2, it used a 4823-cc V-12 engine cranking out 340 horsepower.

7

1

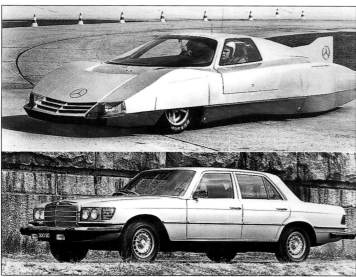

3

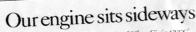

2

1. Fun in an MGB Mark IV now cost $5649. 2. Mercedes-Benz touted its C-111/III turbo-diesel speed record car (top) as well as the 300SD turbo-diesel sedan (bottom). 3. A four-door hatchback joined the Mazda GLC fold. 4-5. Honda Civic CVCC models got a cleaner front end. 6. A CVCC "stratified charge" engine also powered Honda's Accord.

4

5

6

1

2

1. Porsche's new 911SC Targa got a bigger (3.0-liter) "flat" six-cylinder engine, rated at 172 bhp 2. Ferdinand "Ferry" Porsche poses with a 928 coupe, added at midyear with a water-cooled V-8 up front. 3. Subaru's innovative four-wheel-drive BRAT (Bi-Drive Recreational All-terrain Transporter) had seats in its "bed." 4. Restyled in California, Toyota's Celica GT Liftback grew bigger and more modern.

3

4

1

3

2

4

5

6

1-2. Midyear brought a luxurious new six-cylinder Toyota Cressida sedan and wagon to replace the Mark II. It rivaled Datsun's new 810. **3.** New quad headlights made Volkswagen's front-drive Dasher wagon and hatchback sedans look a bit like the new Audi 5000. **4-5.** Production of Volkswagen Rabbit two- and four-door hatchbacks moved to Pennsylvania this year, but diesels came only from Germany. **6.** A vestige of British roadsters past, the Triumph Spitfire 1500 continued to attract sports-car fans.

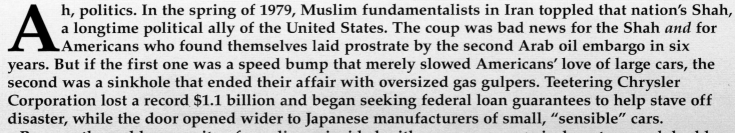

A h, politics. In the spring of 1979, Muslim fundamentalists in Iran toppled that nation's Shah, a longtime political ally of the United States. The coup was bad news for the Shah *and* for Americans who found themselves laid prostrate by the second Arab oil embargo in six years. But if the first one was a speed bump that merely slowed Americans' love of large cars, the second was a sinkhole that ended their affair with oversized gas gulpers. Teetering Chrysler Corporation lost a record $1.1 billion and began seeking federal loan guarantees to help stave off disaster, while the door opened wider to Japanese manufacturers of small, "sensible" cars.

Because the sudden scarcity of gasoline coincided with a severe economic downturn and double-digit inflation, prices of fuel and new cars skyrocketed along with everything else. (A gallon of unleaded gas that had cost 67 cents in 1978 now cost 90 cents.) Loose credit terms stimulated auto sales early in the year—so effectively, in fact, that overselling drove sales into the dumper as the months wore on. Domestic auto sales for 1979 were 8.3 million, a cool million fewer than for '78.

The federal government was beginning to be satisfied because American cars now released 90 percent fewer emissions than at the beginning of the decade, and delivered fuel economy figures that were 35 percent better.

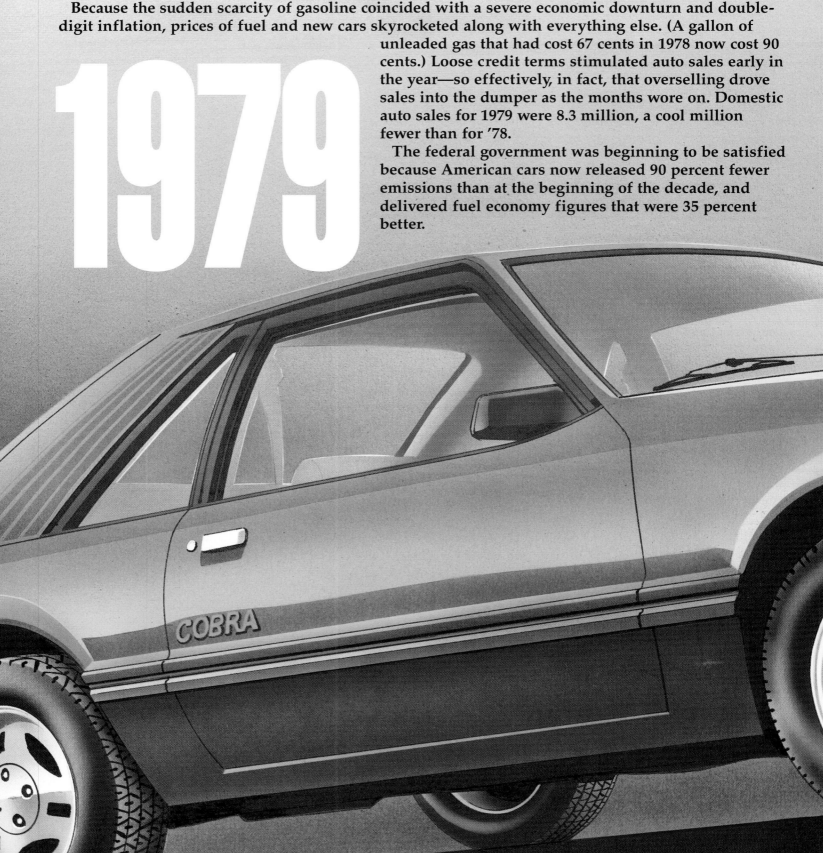

COBRA

The cost of fuel wasn't an issue at Indy, where Rick Mears won the annual 500-mile race in a Gould Penske-Cosworth. Ford's promisingly redesigned Mustang did pace-car duty, with champion driver Jackie Stewart at the wheel. In NASCAR competition, Richard Petty was Winston Cup Champion for the seventh—and final—time in his illustrious career.

The decade's final inductee into the Automotive Hall of Fame was Ernest R. Breech, Ford executive vice president and a key figure in the company's renaissance of 1949.

The troubled American economy was at the forefront of the year's general news. Other important stories: A cooling-system accident at the Three Mile Island, Pennsylvania, nuclear power plant caused the release of dangerous levels of radioactivity into the atmosphere; Cambodia's murderous Khmer Rouge regime was toppled by Cambodian and Vietnamese insurgents. In Britain, Margaret Thatcher was elected prime minister. The year's worst gaffe was committed by the Soviet Army, which stepped into a hornet's nest when it invaded Afghanistan. President Carter and Soviet premier Leonid Brezhnev signed the Salt II nuclear-weapons treaty, but Carter was virtually helpless when Iranian militants seized the U.S. embassy in Tehran and took 52 Americans hostage in November.

At the box office, *The Muppet Movie* tickled audiences of all ages. Other hits included *The Electric Horseman, The Black Stallion, The Amityville Horror, All That Jazz, Kramer vs. Kramer, The Onion Field*, and a real shocker, *Alien*. Couch potatoes blissed themselves out with *Mork & Mindy, The Ropers, Taxi, All in the Family*, and *60 Minutes*, the last still hanging tough after 11 seasons. In a good year for Pittsburgh sports fans, the Pirates topped the Baltimore Orioles in the World Series, four games to three, and the Steelers defeated the Dallas Cowboys, 35-31, to win Super Bowl XIII.

AMC

AMC ends the decade a more distant number-four than ever, as market share dips to 1.77 percent

Even so, sales set a record at more than $3.1 billion, and profits are the second best in company history at nearly $84 million

American Motors becomes more truck than car producer, as Jeep volume edges out AMC car output for the first time

In January, president Gerald Meyers confirms a long-rumored tie-up between AMC and Renault of France; the deal gives AMC an instant $150 million cash infusion

Meantime, AMC returns to its roots as a "small car specialist" by dropping the intermediate Matador

With the Matador's demise, the 360-cid V-8 is dropped, leaving a 125-bhp 304-cube job as the lone V-8 choice—and it is in its last season

The aging Gremlin is dead too, but it lives on in Spirit, offered as a restyled hatchback sedan and a snazzy new "fasthatch" coupe; the latter is also the basis for yet another AMX, this one complete with a Pontiac-style "screaming chicken" hood decal

Concord returns with little change, but a special Silver Anniversary two-door arrives in the spring to mark AMC's 25th birthday; with their 108-inch-wheelbase chassis, compact Concords are now the largest cars the company makes

Pacer model-year production slumps by more than 50 percent to 10,215 units

1

2

3

4

5

1. Virtually unchanged except for a new front-end look with quad headlamps and aluminum bumpers, AMC's Concord two-door sedan now came in top-of-the-line Limited trim, with a larger standard six-cylinder engine of 258 cid. **2.** Instead of the standard six, a Concord DL hatchback coupe could have a four-cylinder engine or AMC's 304-cid V-8. **3.** This Concord Silver Anniversary two-door sedan helped celebrate the 25th birthday of American Motors Corporation. **4.** Even Concord station wagons now came in upscale Limited form. **5.** Available in three trim levels, including this mid-range DL, the Concord was AMC's strongest seller by far.

1

2

3

4

5

1. A 100-bhp 258-cid six became standard in Pacers like this DL station wagon. 2. Leather-covered reclining seats went into the Pacer Limited hatchback. 3. Based on the new Spirit liftback, the sporty AMX wore a hood decal, fender flares, and air dams. "Expect to be noticed," buyers were told. 4. Derived from the late Gremlin, the Spirit sedan had large rear windows. This is a DL. 5. A sloping roof added raciness to the mid-level Spirit DL liftback. A four-cylinder engine was standard, with sixes or a V-8 optional.

377

CHRYSLER
CORPORATION

The year's fuel scare and soaring prices from double-digit inflation take their toll at Chrysler Corporation, where model-year output drops 15 percent

Chrysler's market share dips below 10 percent

Dodge finishes in the seventh spot, Plymouth ninth

Chrysler's financial woes worsen: Sales are down 17.8 percent, and the corporation loses a record $1.1 billion

Chairman John Riccardo seeks advance federal tax credits, but these are denied by the government

Less than a year after coming aboard as Chrylser president, Lee Iacocca is elected chairman, succeeding Riccardo, who resigns in September; J. Paul Bergmoser is president

Omni/Horizon-based Dodge 024 and Plymouth TC3 hatchback coupes debut

The new Dodge St. Regis is kin to the downsized Chrysler Newport/New Yorker; with station wagons and hardtop coupes eliminated, these new full-size cars are available only as four-door sedans

A 360-cid V-8 is the biggest corporate engine

The Dodge Charger is retired, but the related Magnum XE coupe hangs on in Dodge showrooms

Chrysler gives a nod to its high-performance past with a "300" option package for the Cordoba personal-luxury coupe

1

2

3

4   5

1. Big engines were gone, but Chrysler's Cordoba could have a 318- or 360-cid V-8 and optional T-top roof. **2.** Launched at midyear as a reminder of the old "letter-series" cars, the Cordoba-based 300 coupe got a crossbar grille, bucket seats, and 195-bhp V-8. At $8034, it cost $1697 more than Cordoba. **3.** Almost 20,000 LeBaron Town & Country wagons were produced for '79. **4-5.** LeBaron coupes and sedans came in three series, including the top-level Medallion. Sixes and V-8s were sold.

1. Downsizing slashed almost 10 inches and 900 pounds from Chrysler's New Yorker sedan. Rear vent windows were integrated with doors. 2. More than 16,000 New Yorkers got a Fifth Avenue Edition package, with edge-lit quarter windows and a Laredo-grain vinyl landau roof. 3. The Newport was less expensive than the New Yorker, but just as large, qualities that showed up well in police-vehicle tests. 4-5. Exposed headlamps and a checkerboard-style grille quickly separated the Newport from the New Yorker to onlookers. A Slant Six engine was standard.

379

1

2

3

4

5

1. Offered as a single series, the Dodge Aspen could be equipped with a wide variety of option packages to suit the buyer's personality. Quarter-window louvers helped give the coupe a muscular aura. **2.** The last Aspen to get a 195-bhp, 360-cid V-8 was the R/T coupe. Only 75 Aspens had the $651 R/T option, which included strobe-pattern lower-body striping. Far more coupes were sold with the less-expensive "Sunrise" decor. **3.** Dodge decided to promote its compact wagon as a sporty model. The Aspen Sport Wagon option included flared wheel openings, a black grille, air dam, and bucket seats. **4-5.** Even a compact Aspen sedan could be fitted with a police package including a special 360-cid V-8 with dual exhausts.

1-2. One of two '76 Dodge Aspens with a seventh-generation Chrysler turbine engine, this sedan was still undergoing testing by the U.S. Department of Energy in 1979. 3. Mitsubishi-built Colt station wagons were available with woodgrained or plain bodysides. 4. Minimally trimmed, the rear-drive Challenger coupe could have a 1.6- or 2.6-liter engine. 5. The new front-drive Colt hatchback offered a new "Twin-Stick" transmission with eight speeds, for "performance" or "economy" driving. 6. Rear-drive Colts came in three styles, including this two-door sedan.

1. Except for a different grille, Dodge Diplomats carried on as before, in three body styles and three trim levels: base, Salon, and Medallion. Station wagons came only in Salon form, related to the Chrysler LeBaron Town & Country. 2. Diplomat Medallion sedans had a padded vinyl roof. 3. A redesigned landau vinyl roof with rectangular opera windows could be installed on a Diplomat Medallion coupe. 4. Dodge dropped its Charger, leaving only the Magnum XE to draw performance-coupe buyers. Two 360-cid V-8s and a Gran Touring package were available.

1

2

3

4

5

1. Considering they were strong sellers, Dodge Omnis might have turned up anywhere in June '79. This sedan was parked at the Phil Smidt restaurant, a popular eatery on Lake Michigan in Hammond, Indiana. 2. Sleek, sporty Omni 024 hatchback coupes were new. They had the same Volkswagen-derived engine as their sedan cousins, but a unique plastic front end. 3. Though eminently practical, an Omni sedan looked a tad dowdy next to the new 024. 4. No stock pickup on the road looked—or went—like Dodge's "Li'l Red Truck," sprayed in Medium Canyon Red with a towering exhaust stack and 360-cid V-8. 5. The St. Regis four-door sedan was Dodge's version of Chrysler's newly downsized big cars.

1. It took $719 to turn a Plymouth Arrow GT coupe into a boldly trimmed Fire Arrow. **2.** The Arrow hatchback came in base, GS (shown), or GT trim. **3.** An Arrow Jet option cost $256. **4.** Arrows gained rectangular headlamps and a bigger back window. **5.** An optional hatch tent allowed Arrow GT owners to camp out. **6.** Dealers even marketed Arrow pickups.

1

2

3

1. Kin to the newest Dodge Colt, Plymouth's front-drive Champ hatchback sedan had a standard 1.4-liter four-cylinder engine and optional 1.6-liter. Many Champs were equipped with an innovative dual-range "Twin-Stick" transmission, which offered a total of eight forward speeds to suit a variety of driving needs. 2. Longer overall than a Horizon sedan, but on a shorter wheelbase, the new aero-shaped Horizon TC3 hatchback coupe had the same 1.7-liter (104.7-cid) four-cylinder engine, making a modest 70 bhp. 3. With more than 162,000 built, the little-changed front-drive Plymouth Horizon sedan sold better than its Dodge Omni cousin. 4-5. Similar to the Dodge Omni 024, the Horizon TC3 hatchback could be fitted with a Rally package or a Sport Appearance option that included a rear spoiler. Flip-out quarter windows also were available. 6. Detrimmed Sapporo coupes no longer could be had with a vinyl roof. 7. For $7286, the owner of a Trail Duster sport-utility vehicle got full-time four-wheel drive and a 318-cid V-8.

4

5

6

7

385

1. Plymouth Volaré buyers had a choice of seat fabrics and styles, including (top to bottom) all-vinyl bench, all-vinyl buckets, standard cloth/vinyl bench, and Duster plaid cloth/vinyl buckets. **2.** The Volaré Premier option promised "comfort and style" in a sedan, with a Slant Six or choice of two V-8 sizes. **3.** A Volaré Sport Wagon option (left) included a black grille, front air dam, and tape stripes. The Road Runner coupe (right) had "strobe" striping like Dodge's R/T, as well as an available 195-bhp, 360-cid V-8. **4.** Woodgrain trim was among the Volaré Premier's interior features. **5.** A Volaré sedan made the cover of the Chrysler/Plymouth police vehicle catalog now that the Plymouth lineup no longer included larger cars.

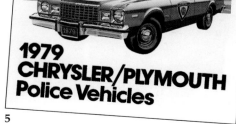

1979 CHRYSLER/PLYMOUTH Police Vehicles

1

5

FORD
MOTOR CO.

Market share dips again, this time to 25.8 percent; total production is up slightly from '78, but profits are down

Dearborn downsizes for real, replacing the old full-sized Ford LTD and Mercury Marquis with smaller, more efficient models on an all-new rear-drive platform dubbed "Panther"

Mustang is reborn as a slightly larger, more attractive ponycar based on the sensible "Fox" platform; V-6 and V-8 engines continue, and there's a new turbocharged four-cylinder for a jazzy Cobra model; more than 11,000 replicas of Mustang's '79 Indy 500 pace car are sold

Mercury revives the Capri as a domestically built kissin' cousin of the new Mustang, but only as a hatchback coupe

Ford Pinto and Mercury Bobcat subcompacts get square headlamps and, allegedly, a bit more interior room

Ford LTD II and Mercury's regular Cougars linger on with little change for the last year of their vintage-'77 design; the same goes for the related Ford Ranchero car/pickup

Ford Thunderbird and Mercury Cougar XR-7 are mostly reruns too; the Diamond Jubilee T-Bird is renamed Heritage

Lincoln hints at big changes to come with specially equipped, limited-edition "Collector Series" versions of the big Continental and Mark V

Still struggling for sales, Lincoln's compact Versailles is reworked with a wide-quarter roofline and longer rear doors

1

100,000,000th U.S. BUILT FORD VEHICLE

2

THE BEST-SELLING NEW CAR EVER INTRODUCED.

THE FORD FAIRMONT.

FORD FAIRMONT

3

4

5

FIESTA. WUNDERCAR!

FORD FIESTA

6

1. Fairmont sedans were newly available with a tilt steering wheel and cruise control, as well as a four-speed overdrive manual transmission. 2. Ford's 100-millionth U.S.-built vehicle was this '79 Fairmont Futura, produced during 1978 as the company celebrated its 75th anniversary. 3. Fairmont had signaled a turnabout in attitude toward design, and record-setting first-year sales reflected the difference. Volume dipped this year, but the cars remained popular. 4. Wide, tapered wrapover B-pillars marked the stylish Futura coupe, one of four Fairmont body styles. Futuras had their own front-end appearance. 5. A Sport option for the Fiesta hatchback sedan included wider wheels, a rear anti-sway bar, and heavy-duty shocks. 6. Ad writers reminded magazine readers of the little Fiesta's German heritage.

1

2

3

4

5

1. Sales of the Ford Granada fell, including this Ghia edition. Optional four-wheel disc brakes were dropped. **2.** The ESS sedan sat atop the Granada line. It featured a blacked-out grille and body trim. **3.** Built on the new, smaller "Panther" platform, the downsized big-car lineup was typified by the LTD Landau coupe and Country Squire wagon. **4.** LTD Landaus, like the four-door sedan, had quad headlamps, versus single lights for base models. **5.** While externally smaller, new full-size Fords yielded more interior room and window area, along with easier handling.

1

2

3

4

5

6

7

1. Priced lower than the newly shrunken LTD, Ford's intermediate LTD II Brougham coupe was almost as large in its final season. Base and "S" editions were also sold. **2.** Distinctive paint marked LTD II coupes with the Sports Touring option. **3.** Ford trucks were among the vehicles of choice for ice fishermen at Duck Creek near Green Bay, Wisconsin, in the winter of 1979-80. **4.** Ford claimed four-cylinder '79 Pintos, Mustangs, and Fairmonts saved owners $514 in scheduled maintenance costs, versus comparable '73 Fords. **5.** Pinto Rallye trim included blacking out the new grille design. **6.** Portholes were part of the $566 Cruising Package for a Pinto wagon. **7.** This was the final year for the LTD II-based Ranchero pickup, sold in GT (shown), 500, and Squire form.

389

1

2

3

1-2. Ford's Mustang Cobra hatchback coupe packed a new 140-bhp, 2.3-liter turbocharged four-cylinder engine. Crisp lines gave the ponycar a more substantial presence than its Mustang II predecessor. **3.** Slightly enlarged in its new form, the Mustang notchback coupe held an unboosted 88-bhp version of the four-cylinder. A V-6 and V-8 were available, and a 200-cid inline six arrived later. **4.** Awaiting downsizing, the Thunderbird earned a bolder grille and revised taillights. A Heritage edition joined the base and Town Landau coupes. **5.** T-tops cost $747 on a T-bird.

4

5

1

2

3

4

5

6

1. Lincoln Continental Owners Club members take time out at a meet in Ohio to ogle a new Continental Collector's Series sedan. 2. Billed as the "pinnacle of Lincoln Continental prestige," the Collector's Series wore special blue or white paint and a gold-toned grille. 3. The Collector's Series treatment was applied to the Mark V coupe and the larger Continental. 4. It took $1527 to turn a Continental into a Town Car. 5-6. Lincoln's luxury compact, the Versailles sedan, gained a fresh roofline and longer back doors for a more formal appearance. A padded vinyl cover now decorated the decklid's simulated spare tire bulge. Versailles was the first U.S. car with standard halogen headlamps.

1

2

3

4

1-2. Replacing the Diamond Jubilee Edition, the Lincoln Mark V Collector's Series coupe wore a gold-color grille, Midnight Blue or white paint, and Midnight Blue upholstery. A 400-cid V-8 was the sole engine. **3.** Mark V coupes came in four Designer Series variants, including this Bill Blass Edition. **4.** A Givenchy Edition Mark V got new crystal blue paint and a matching vinyl roof.

1

2

1. Now made in the U.S., the Mercury Capri retained some vestiges of its European heritage. The RS option (shown) included a handling suspension, black grille, and hood scoop. A turbocharged four-cylinder could be added. **2.** A close relative of the new Ford Mustang, the '79 Capri came only as a hatchback coupe, in base or Ghia form. A 302-cid V-8 was available for the first time to replace the standard four or available V-6. **3.** Cargo space was a greater in the Mustang-based Capri than in its European predecessor.

3

393

1

2

3

4

5

6

7

8

Introducing the all-new 1979 Mercury Marquis.
Science helps create a new Marquis standard of driving comfort.

The most scientifically engineered Marquis in history.
Science contributed extensively to the new Marquis' development. Result: a new Marquis standard of driving comfort. *Read how it compares to the '78*

Not just more beautiful. More aerodynamic.
Lines and proportions evolved for practical as well as aesthetic reasons. They're wind tunnel-tested and refined.

More spacious in almost every dimension.
Computer analysis helped give Marquis more headroom, leg room and shoulder room—even more front seat hip room.

New Command Seating Position for drivers.
The driver's seating position has been re-engineered. New lower hood and redesigned glass areas. New controls within convenient reach.

New maneuverability. More responsive steering.
New maneuverability of a four foot tighter turning diameter, and a 17:1 steering ratio for more responsive steering.

All-new body frame construction.
More computer analysis to determine stress patterns. Body mount tuning evaluated by computer. And entire body and frame assemblies are dipped in a corrosion-resistant electrostatic primer bath.

Ride re-engineered with all-new suspension geometry.
Front suspension: new long-and-short arm coil spring design, stabilizer bar, "Hydro-piercing" precisely aligns suspension and frame elements.

Corners flatter, takes bumps and dips with increased stability.
Rear suspension: new four-bar link design with axle-centered coil springs.

forward mount shock absorbers. All contribute to Marquis' ride and handling characteristics.

Test the 1979 Marquis. Experience the new Marquis standard of driving comfort. Inside, a luxurious driving environment. New front seat cushion with steel flex-o-lator springs for comfort and support. Marquis' trunk has 21.6 cubic feet. Standard 5.0 liter engine accelerates 0 to 50 mph in 10.2 seconds.

Improvements in many minute details.
In many systems, major and small, we have achieved numerous improvements which have created a dramatically outstanding Marquis for 1979.

A new Marquis standard of driving comfort.

MERCURY MARQUIS
LINCOLN-MERCURY DIVISION

9

1. The Capri RS option could be enhanced with a Turbo version that included a 140-bhp four-cylinder engine. 2. This Capri styling mockup wears an RS stripe pattern ultimately rejected. 3. Bobcats gained a sloped grille. 4. Cougar four-door sedan sales were feeble in their final season. 5. The Cougar XR-7, however, proved more popular. 6. Grand Marquis topped the downsized big-car line. 7. Colony Park wagons were longer than Marquis sedans. 8. Grand Marquis owners luxuriated in Twin Comfort Lounge seats. 9. "All-new" wasn't just the usual ad hyperbole for the '79 big Mercs.

1

2

3

4

1. Available with Ghia (shown) or ESS options, Monarch sales lagged behind those of the newer, similar-sized Zephyr. **2.** A near-twin to Ford's Fairmont, the Zephyr came in four body styles. A four-speed overdrive manual transmission became available, along with new convenience options. **3-4.** In addition to its unique wrapover roof pillar, the Zephyr Z-7 coupe wore special striping and large wraparound taillamps. **5.** Zephyr wagons came in plain or woodgrained Villager form.

5

GENERAL
MOTORS CORP.

Despite record import-car sales and another energy crisis, GM's market share hits a new high of 59.2 percent

GM continues its corporate-wide "big shrink" by putting the Oldsmobile Toronado, Buick Riviera, and Cadillac Eldorado on a much trimmer, crisply lined new E-body platform; Riviera becomes a front-drive car for the first time ever

GM's veteran rear-drive compacts—Chevrolet Nova, Pontiac Phoenix, Olds Omega, and Buick Skylark—enjoy a final brief fling before being replaced in April by new 1980-model-year front-wheel-drive "X" cars

GM's full-size and intermediate cars see mostly minor updates; so do Chevy Chevette and the small "H-Special" models like Chevy Monza and Pontiac Sunbird

Chevrolet expands Camaro offerings with a new luxury liner called Berlinetta

Chevy's Corvette sprouts bolt-on front and rear spoilers, plus new seats similar to those of the '78 Indy pace car replica

Oldsmobile extends diesel power to most mid-sized Cutlass models and the new-generation Toronado; signalling a brief resurgence in "muscle cars" is a revived W-30 Hurst/Olds package for the Cutlass Calais coupe

Pontiac keeps Firebird fresh by grafting on a new nose with widely spaced recessed headlamps above a prominent bumper-mount split grille; Trans Am marks its 10th Anniversary with another limited-edition special

1

2

3

4

5

1. Buick's LeSabre Sport Coupe again held a turbocharged V-6 engine. 2. Face-lifted front and rear, a mid-level Electra Limited coupe was loaded with comforts and conveniences. 3. Topping the big-Buick line was the plush Electra Park Avenue sedan, with buttoned-and-tucked velvet upholstery and—count 'em—seven armrests. 4. An Estate Wagon could have Limited features for an extra $1853. 5. A 170-bhp turbocharged V-6 added zest to the Regal Sport Coupe.

1

2

3

4

5

1. Buick had another enthusiast's car up its sleeve in the Turbo Coupe. It packed a 3.8-liter turbo V-6 and displayed bold rear-deck lettering. 2. The top-selling Century model was the Custom wagon. 3. The fastback Century Limited now came only as a four-door sedan. 4. Base Rivieras held a 350-cid V-8, but the new S Type got a special turbo V-6, cranked up to 185 bhp. 5. Aside from their conversion to front-wheel drive, Riviera coupes lost almost a foot of length. 6. A Road Hawk package gave the Skyhawk hatchback sport wheels, a Rallye suspension, and flashy two-tone silver paint. 7. The standard V-6 in subcompact Skyhawks gained 10 bhp.

6

7

The best salesman Cadillac ever had

You're looking at it. It's the car itself that creates a satisfied Cadillac owner. And there are so many of these that Cadillac leads all U.S. luxury car makes in repeat ownership. In fact, it's the best-selling luxury car in the nation. The confidence in knowing that seven out of ten who buy the car stay with the car. That's Cadillac.

1

2

3

Dawn to dusk on a tankful. That's the new diesel-powered Cadillac.

4

5

1. Since its beginning, Cadillac had relied upon the strong loyalty of its owners. Ad writers suggested that owning a Caddy could be an integral part of the "good life." **2.** The crosshatch grille on this Sedan de Ville was a new style feature. The 425-cid V-8 could be carbureted or fuel-injected. A diesel became optional at midseason. **3.** A convertible-like roof covering highlighted the Coupe de Ville Custom Phaeton decor package. Quarter windows were smaller than usual. **4.** Ads extolled the diesel V-8 option available for Fleetwood Broughams and De Villes. **5-6.** The poshest Fleetwood Broughams came with the d'Elegance option. Pillow-style divided seats cosseted the front-seat occupants.

6

1. Downsizing dropped the Eldorado, previously the biggest Cadillac, down to Seville size. More than 20 inches were slashed from the coupe's length. **2.** The Biarritz option gave an Eldorado a brushed stainless roof section, opera lamps, and cast aluminum wheels. **3.** But for a fresh grille texture, the Seville continued mostly unchanged. The $2735 Elegante option featured two-tone paint in black and slate gray, plus wire wheels.

THE 1979 CHEVROLETS
CAPRICE CLASSIC · IMPALA · MONTE CARLO · MALIBU · CAMARO · NOVA · MONZA · CHEVETTE · CORVETTE · WAGONS · RECREATIONAL VEHICLES

Chevrolet

1

2

1979 Camaro Z28: From people who know what performance is all about.

You've seen some of the best drivers in the world driving race-prepped Chevrolet Camaro Z28s in the International Race of Champions. And maybe you imagined yourself behind the wheel.

For when it comes to hugging a road, a Z28 is truly something special.

We start with a special Z28 Sport suspension system. Then we add things like a 4-speed close-ratio manual transmission connected to an 11-inch high-capacity clutch. Front/rear stabilizer bars, special shocks, power steering, power brakes. To top it all off, we pack a 5.7 Litre (350 Cu. In.) 4-barrel V8 under the hood. (Camaro is equipped with GM-built engines produced by various divisions. See your dealer for details.) Because a car of Z28's caliber should

look as good as it moves, we've given special attention to its appearance. It comes with a rear deck spoiler, new front air dam, bold accent striping, simulated air louvers in the front fenders, sport mirrors, distinctive black finished grille, and more.

Inside, you'll find a special large-rim sport steering wheel, full foam bucket seats, tachometer, voltmeter, temperature gage, an electric clock, and more.

Now stop imagining yourself behind the wheel. Grab hold and take it from Chevrolet—people who know what performance is all about. Buy or lease a '79 Camaro Z28. Then go road hunting.

Aluminum wheels shown are available at extra cost. Available white-lettered tires are supplied by various manufacturers.

CAMARO. THE HUGGER. *Chevrolet*

4

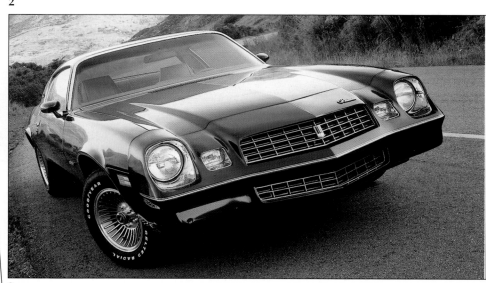

3

5

1. Car shoppers who browsed through the 1979 Chevrolet catalog saw a selection of mostly carry-over models. **2-3.** New to the Camaro line was the upscale Berlinetta. **4.** Ad writers hawking the Z28 Camaro focused on the car's ties to the International Race of Champions series. **5.** Z28s adopted an enlarged front air dam. **6.** Chevrolet trucks had their adherents among ice fishermen on Duck Creek, near Green Bay, Wisconsin, in January '79.

6

1

2

3

5

1. A six-cylinder engine was standard in Caprice Classic sedans, with a 305- or 350-cid V-8 optional. 2. Sales figures revealed why full-size Chevrolets were dubbed "America's pace car." 3. An Impala police car leads the 1979 Independence Day parade in Crown Point, Indiana. 4. Malibus also protected and served with a police package. 5. Caprice Classic wagons only had V-8 power. 6. The Malibu-based El Camino pickup kept on truckin'. A Royal Knight decor option included dragon decals on the hood.

6

1

2

3

4

5

6

1. An Estate equipment group added $258 to the sticker price of Chevrolet's mid-sized Malibu Classic station wagon. Not much changed this year, except for the grille and taillamps. **2.** Stylists developed a tough-looking "Black Sterling" edition of the Malibu Classic coupe in black and silver. Sadly, no such Malibus were produced for sale. **3-4.** Malibu Classics came four ways, versus only three for the less-expensive base Malibu series, which lacked a Landau coupe. A 267-cid V-8 joined the list of available engines. **5.** Despite a whopping $2668 price hike, Corvette sales set a record; production topped 50,000 for the first time. A new low-restriction muffler helped boost horsepower on both 350-cid V-8 engines. All Corvettes now came with high-back seats and bolt-on front and rear spoilers were available. **6.** Two-stage carburetion gave the mild-mannered Chevette welcome power hikes to 70 or 74 bhp, depending on version. The grille was revised, and an F41 sport suspension became available.

1

2

3

4

5

6

1-2. A revised canopy-style roof went on Chevrolet's Monte Carlo Landau coupe. Base and Landau models displayed a restyled grille. Wraparound taillights were new, too. **3.** In addition to plenty of luxury and comfort, Monte Carlos offered a choice of four engines, including 200- or 231-cid V-6s, and 267- or 305-cid V-8s. **4.** The Nova coupe was one of three styles available. A fresh grille and new rectangular headlamps distinguished the venerable compact series in its final year. **5.** A dressier Nova Custom sedan cost $209 more than its basic counterpart. **6.** Estate Wagons and "S" hatchbacks were gone, but the sub-compact Monza rolled on in coupe, 2+2, and wagon form. A Spyder option was available. Engines ranged from a 151-cid "Iron Duke" four-cylinder to a 305-cid V-8, with a pair of V-6s in between.

1

2

4

3

5

1. A 4-4-2 option added wide paint striping and lettering, bucket seats, and a Rallye suspension to an Oldsmobile Cutlass Salon coupe. 2. Painted black and gold or white and gold, a limited-production Hurst/Olds edition was available for the Cutlass Calais coupe. A four-barrel, 350-cid V-8 slipped under the hood, eager to interact with the Hurst sport console shifter for the automatic transmission. 3-4. The Cutlass Cruiser Brougham station wagon shared a grille and other appointments with the Salon Brougham coupe and sedan. Vinyl woodgrain side trim was an available extra, as was a 350-cid diesel V-8. 5. The least-costly Cutlass was the Salon, offered as a coupe or this sedan. There was a corresponding Cruiser wagon, too.

1

2

3

4

5

6

7

8

1. Engine choices for Oldsmobile's full-sized Ninety-Eight four-door sedan, shown in step-up Regency trim, were V-8s of 350-cid (gasoline or diesel) or 403 cubes. **2.** Custom Cruiser wagons could have two or three seats, and plain or woodgrain bodysides. **3.** A V-6 engine was standard in the Delta 88 Royale sedan, which was slightly smaller than a Ninety-Eight. Power options included 260- and 350-cid V-8s, as well as a diesel. **4.** For its final outing in this form, the compact Omega was granted a fresh grille. **5.** Billed as a low-budget sports car, the Starfire hatchback displayed freshened styling. A hard, fiberglass-reinforced front end replaced the previous soft panel. **6.** Introduced during 1978, the Firenza option package for the Starfire included a rear spoiler, flared wheel openings, Rallye suspension, and special paint. **7-8.** Toronado coupes slimmed down dramatically, losing 22 inches of length. A 350-cid gas V-8 was standard, with a diesel optional.

405

1

2

1. Detail changes front and rear marked Pontiac's full-sized Bonneville sedan. A 301-cid V-8 was standard, with Buick- and Oldsmobile-built 350s optional, including one tuned to meet emissions requirements in high-altitude regions. **2.** As usual, Bonneville Broughams flaunted more luxury and convenience touches than basic Bonnevilles. Prices of the two lines were about $800 apart. **3.** A new nose with a bumper-mounted split grille graced the Trans Am, which accounted for more than half of Firebird sales. A " shaker" scoop covered the base 400-cid V-8 or optional 403-cube

3

1

3

2

1. A 10th Anniversary package hailed the birthday of Pontiac's popular Trans Am. 2. A 301-cid V-8 was standard in a Firebird Formula, but big-block power could be specified. 3. Hot-car image meant a lot in a Firebird. The trick "blackout" taillamps installed on Trans Ams and Formulas were trumpeted in this ad. 4. The Grand LeMans group, including this Safari station wagon, topped the mid-size lineup. 5. Safari wagons came two ways: intermediate Grand LeMans and big Bonneville.

4

5

407

1

2

3

1. Introduced a year earlier to ample fanfare, Pontiac's Grand Am coupe again failed to attract substantial numbers of buyers, despite offering European-style handling. 2. The Grand LeMans four-door sedan was the most popular of Pontiac's mid-size cars with 28,577 deliveries. 3. SJ remained the top Grand Prix model. A four-barrel 301-cid V-8 was standard. 4. Base-model Grand Prix coupes sold best, but the LJ also scored well. Prices began at $6555. 5. This styling proposal for the '79 Grand Prix included narrow vertical opera windows not used in production.

4

5

1

2

3

4

1. Though subcompact in size, Pontiac's Sunbird had a choice of four-cylinder, V-6, or V-8 power. This hatchback coupe has the Formula option, with a black grille, front air dam, rear spoiler, striping, and the expected high-visibility decals. 2. The Sunbird notchback coupe came in basic (shown) and dressier Sport Coupe trim. 3. Like other Sunbirds, the weak-selling Safari station wagon seated four. 4. Destined to take on a completely different front-wheel-drive form as an early 1980 model, the compact Phoenix entered 1979 with only slight grille changes. This LJ coupe wears the Landau roof package.

409

IMPORTS

Spurred by the gas scare, import-brand cars claim a record 21.8 percent of the U.S. market, besting every other segment except intermediates (23.9)

Datsun issues the front-drive 310 as a more attractive replacement for the hapless F-10 on which it's based

Fiat's 128s give way to larger new front-drive Strada two- and four-door hatchbacks based on the Euro-market Ritmo

Honda expands Accord's appeal with a four-door sedan marked by a specific grille and nine extra inches in length. Arriving in spring is a Civic-based, Accord-powered sporty coupe called Prelude

Jaguar's Series II XJ sedans are restyled and re-engineered to become Series III models, distinguished by elevated rooflines

Continuing its sales recovery, Mazda adds a wagon version of its "Great Little Car" and confines rotary power to an impressive new two-seat sports car, the RX-7 coupe; replacing previous rotary models at midyear is the conventional 626

Mercedes also has a new wagon, its first factory-built model; for the U.S. it's a 300TD with a 3.0-liter five-cylinder diesel

Porsche goes posh as the V-8-powered 928 makes its U.S. debut with innovative styling, engineering to match, and thrilling thrust

Saab's 99 enters its 10th season with a new upscale companion called 900, a long-nose version with more standard equipment

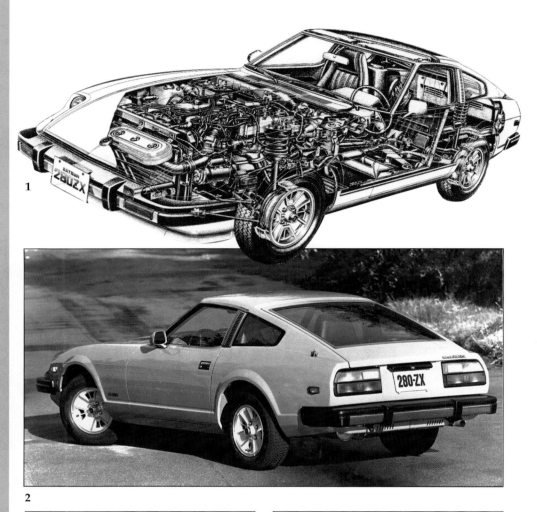

1

2

3

4

5

1-2. Despite similarity to the prior 280Z, Datsun's new 280ZX wore all-new body panels. The 2.8-liter six-cylinder engine made 135 bhp. **3.** A two-door hardtop joined Datsun's restyled 810 lineup. Equipment included a tachometer. **4.** Datsun borrowed the 810's fuel-injected six-cylinder engine from the old 240Z sports car. The 810 station wagon sold for $2815. **5.** Based on the Civic, the new Prelude sport coupe carried an Accord engine. Honda billed the Prelude as "a sports car for grownups." A standard moonroof was part of the $6445 sticker price.

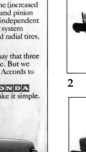

1

2

3

4

5

6

7

1-2. Honda was happy to announce a longer four-door sedan had joined the original two-door Accord. **3.** Accord's engine grew to 1751 cc and 72 bhp. Hatchback coupes came in base and LX (shown) form. **4.** Mazda's new RX-7 sports car was now its only model with the trademark rotary engine. Sports-car fans fell hard for the shapely machine. **5.** Mazda's GLC family included a new four-door wagon, plus a 1415-cc four-cylinder engine that developed 65 bhp. **6.** Packing a 219-bhp V-8, Porsche's 928 coupe hit dealerships for its second season. **7.** Baseball great Mickey Mantle shot a television commercial for Subaru's gas-miserly FE coupe at Yankee Stadium in New York. The EPA rated the FE at 50 mpg on the highway.

411

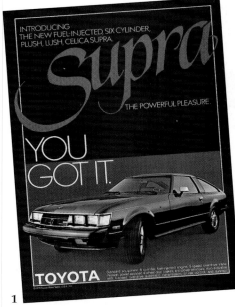

1. Toyota moved into the sporty-car market with its Celica Supra coupe. Essentially a six-cylinder rendition of the Celica, it rode a longer wheelbase. **2.** First seen in the U.S. back in 1960, Toyota Land Cruisers were among the first sport-utility vehicles. The 4.2-liter engine produced 200 horsepower. **3.** Toyota's posh six-cylinder Cressida came in two body styles: sedan and this station wagon. **4.** A long list of models made up Toyota's Corolla line-up, topped by the SR-5 Liftback. Fitted with a five-speed gearbox, it stickered for $5388. **5.** The Volkswagen Scirocco coupe's engine grew in size and power. **6.** Volkswagen Beetle convertibles reached the U.S. for the last time in '79.

412

ETC.

In the up-and-down history of the Avanti II, 1979 goes down as one of the down years: production drops to 142 cars (from 165 the year before); the base price is up, though, to $17,670

A trickle of Checkers for the retail market continues from Kalamazoo; starting prices for Marathons crack the $7000 barrier, while the long-wheelbase Marathon Deluxe begins at more than $8000

Meanwhile, near Milwaukee, David and William Stevens's Excalibur plant turns out the last of its Series III SS "retro" cars at $28,600 a pop (with an even more expensive Series IV waiting in the wings); just 27 of the 367 built—all powered by a 180-bhp 350-cid Chevrolet V-8 —are two-seat roadsters

The first fruits of former GM tyro John DeLorean's DeLorean Motor Company are are awaited in June 1979, as promised, but it will take until 1981 before the Renault-powered gullwing coupes finally emerge from the DMC factory in Northern Ireland

Yet another Duesenberg revival attempt gets under way early in the year when Harlan and Kenneth Duesenberg—nephews of the fabled Fred and Auggie Duesenberg—set up shop in Mundelein, Illinois, with the aid of Robert Peterson (of the Lehmann-Peterson Company); only one Cadillac-powered prototype on a 133-inch wheelbase is built, however

Canadian Andrew Timmis is in the midst of producing a handful of "new old" '34 Ford roadsters—flathead V-8 and all

1

2

3

1. Coach Design Group turned Cadillac Eldorado coupes into San Remo convertibles. A $46,000 San Remo Ultima, based on the Seville, was also sold. 2-3. The Clenet was one of several "neo-classic" makes striving to capture the old-car essence. 4-5. A revived Stutz company made this eye-popping Bearcat convertible.

4

5

Index

Index

416